GLOBAL
BUSINESS ALLIANCES

GLOBAL
BUSINESS ALLIANCES

Theory and Practice

Refik Culpan

Q

QUORUM BOOKS
Westport, Connecticut • London

Library of Congress Cataloging-in-Publication Data

Culpan, Refik.
  Global business alliances : theory and practice / Refik Culpan.
    p. cm.
  Includes bibliographical references and index.
  ISBN 1-56720-313-2 (alk. paper)
    1. Strategic alliances (Business) 2. International business enterprises—Management.
  3. Competition, International. I. Title.
  HD69.S8 C85 2002
  658'.044—dc21   2001048119

British Library Cataloguing in Publication Data is available.

Library of Congress Catalog Card Number: 2001048119
ISBN: 1-56720-313-2

First published in 2002

Quorum Books, 88 Post Road West, Westport, CT 06881
An imprint of Greenwood Publishing Group, Inc.
www.quorumbooks.com

Printed in the United States of America

The paper used in this book complies with the
Permanent Paper Standard issued by the National
Information Standards Organization (Z39.48-1984).

10 9 8 7 6 5 4 3 2 1

In memory of my late brother Nevzat.

Contents

Tables

Figures

Preface

Today's business market can be best described as global, dynamic, and synergistic. Recently, the entire world has become a marketplace; therefore, business competition has increasingly crossed national boundaries. New technological breakthroughs and augmenting global business activities have intensified international business competition. Furthermore, the recent expansion of world markets encompassing the economic transformation in former socialist countries (for example, Russia and other eastern European countries), the economic liberalizations in China, and emerging economies in Asia (for example, South Korea, Taiwan, and Malaysia) and Latin America (for example, Argentina, Brazil, and Chile), has imposed new challenges on businesses. The present state of international business can be attributed to political, economic, social, and technological changes sweeping the world.

In response to all these changes, multinational corporations (MNCs) have increasingly developed global alliances. Concomitantly, in the past decade, publications on strategic alliances augmented. Most of these publications deal with theoretical foundations, motivations of partners, forms, and governance structures, and the performance of strategic collaborations. Yet, they are either purely theoretical explanations or are fragmented—only covering certain facets of the business alliance phenomenon. A systematic and comprehensive study of global interfirm partnerships, demonstrating their theoretical foundations and recent applications in specific industries, is still needed. This urgent need requires new approaches to and explanations of understanding and managing global business alliances. With all these thoughts, I took this challenge two years ago and started gathering information concerning global alliances.

I believe that global alliances deserve closer attention because of the following reasons. First, while strategic alliances increased in number in recent years, they differ from traditional joint ventures and other interfirm partnerships in a significant way. Second, strategic business alliances encompass a variety of forms. In addition to commonly used joint ventures and licensing agreements, they can take forms such as research and development (R&D), marketing, and supplier agreements. Third, strategic alliances affect the competitive posture of participating firms. Thus, some consider strategic alliances as a viable strategic alternative in building or sustaining a competitive advantage, and others view it as an inevitable component of future corporate strategies.

In this book, I tried to outline the essential dimensions of global alliances including conceptual and operational characteristics. The book lays out the theoretical bases of global strategic alliances while demonstrating philosophies and strategies, as well as describing managerial challenges of cooperative ventures.

Additionally, the book elaborates on business strategic alliances in selected industries, including automobile manufacturing, pharmaceuticals, airlines, and telecommunications. Yet, no book provides such an industry-specific analysis of global business alliances. The book also manifests effective approaches to strategic alliances by combining theoretical and practical developments, such as noncompetitor alliances, outsourcing, and alliance networks. This text also demonstrates the strategic importance of alliances for international players. In addition to traditional forms of joint ventures and licensing agreements, it discusses emerging forms of business alignments such as R&D partnerships, supplier agreements, marketing collaborations, and network forms of cooperation.

The principal objective of the book is to provide essential knowledge on global strategic partnerships from various perspectives (economic, organizational, and strategic management) in specific industries and to enhance our understanding of patterns and strategies of partners in given industries. The book elaborates on competitive advantages of firms and links such advantages to better understanding and effective formation and management of such ventures. This text provides insights into multinational partnerships by shedding light on why and under what conditions they emerge and become successful. This book also provides the conceptual tools for both researchers and managers to grasp the dynamics and benefits of global alliances by examining the present trends and characteristics of interfirm cooperation and by analyzing the motives and processes of such enterprises in different industries. As a result of theoretical and practical explanations and analyses, the book reveals patterns and contrasts of global business alliances in selected industries and the underlying factors influencing effective management styles for global cooperation.

Furthermore, the book is a major source of reference in the area of interfirm cooperation in global business. While it manifests common properties in various forms of multinational cooperation, it describes the unique characteristics of each type of collaboration. In this regard, the book reveals the international and inter-industry differences in global partnership. Moreover, it discusses environmental conditions and cross-cultural differences, which have a profound effect on the formation and operation of these ventures.

The growing demand for learning the dynamics of global partnership has been apparent among theoreticians as well as practitioners. Although the book appeals to scholars who are undertaking research or teaching on the subject, it also will respond to the needs of business students both at the undergraduate and graduate levels, corporate managers, and consultants.

Today, many schools around the world are offering undergraduate and graduate programs in business administration with a special emphasis on international management and marketing. The popularity of Master of Business Administration (MBA) programs in the United States as well as other industrialized countries is well documented in recent business publications. Furthermore, some universities and colleges have commenced their specialized undergraduate and graduate degrees in international business. The Association of American Collegiate Schools of Business (AACSB), an international accreditation institution for business schools, has been pressing the member colleges for internationalization of their curricula by adding or increasing international dimensions. Consequently, an increasing number of schools have been incorporating international business courses into their curricula and offering special courses or seminars on strategic alliances. Students of these programs need a comprehensive book capturing the dynamics of and insights into global partnerships among firms. Today, managers of both domestic and international firms are eager to learn more about the means of improving their competitiveness. For an international company, a strategic alliance with another firm is a way of acquiring or sustaining a competitive advantage in today's marketplace. Indeed, major Fortune 500 companies generate a substantial portion of their revenues from overseas markets and have already (or are planning to) engaged in a cooperative venture or agreement with another domestic or overseas firm. Moreover, medium-size and even small-size firms have been expanding their operations beyond domestic markets by linking with overseas partners. Therefore, this book on global partnership will appeal to most managers.

Furthermore, consultants on international business activities would like to learn insights into global alliances so that they can offer better services (or a variety of services) to their clients. This book on global alliances with its systematic treatment of the subject is an excellent source for consultants. Some consultants might differentiate their services by specializing in multinational cooperative practices and by focusing on specific industries, such as automobile manufacturing, telecommunications, airlines, and pharmaceuticals.

During my research, the pace of change of interfirm cooperative arrangements and dynamic competitive forces shaping global alliances overwhelmed me. Before the completion of the book, some of the examples given in the book became outdated. Facing this dynamic alliance phenomenon, I took a different approach from my original plan to provide the general picture with supporting theories and to refer to the cases to illustrate the main points and concepts. Given the rapid changes in the marketplace and the time span for production of a book, no book can claim to be up-to-date with its business examples. The important thing is whether the concepts and practical examples complement each other in order to advance the knowledge of interfirm collaborations. To this end, the book has accomplished its mission.

Despite the practical difficulties, the book—with recent coverage of global strategic alliances and comprehensive analysis—offers significant insights into these increasingly popular business partnerships from a strategic management perspective. I hope that the book meets the needs of students and managers of strategic business alliances.

Introduction

In recent years, businesses' engagements in international alliances has been augmented considerably. While the popularity of such cross-border partnerships has stimulated the formation of a variety of collaborative arrangements between firms, this movement presents a paradox for researchers and managers. On one hand, a traditional view of interfirm competition suggests that businesses are naturally involved in fierce competition with their rivals. On the other hand, today's firms—especially multinational players—recognize the benefits of collaborative ventures. From a strategic point of view, multinational corporations (MNCs) have changed their traditional views of competition and have adopted a variety of new and flexible approaches for achieving sustainable competitive advantages. Such a shift in their business strategies has become more vivid today than ever before. In particular, the frequent use of business alliances as an indispensable tool in their strategic repertoire has manifested itself in the global business. MNCs have started to build business alliances even with their competitors. For example, it is interesting to observe that while two giant automobile manufacturers, General Motors and Toyota, compete intensively, they have built a joint venture called New United Motor Manufacturing Incorporation (NUMMI) in Fremont, California and are manufacturing cars together. This incident is not isolated, however—a number of companies have formed a variety of alliances in telecommunications, pharmaceutical, airline, and steel industries. Similarly, Bell Atlantic/GTE of the United States and Vodafone AirTouch of Britain formed Verizon Wireless, a joint venture to compete in the U.S. market. Also, Hitachi of Japan and TRW of the United States formed a strategic alliance to pursue opportunities in space technologies. McDonnell-Douglas Space Systems and Shimizu, a Japanese architectural and engineering company, announced their collaboration to develop space exploration technologies for the United States lunar/Mars initiative. All of these examples show that global alliances between companies are well underway in different industries.

Consequently, most researchers and managers wish to know the underlying reasons for augmenting global collaborations and the factors leading to their success. They are primarily interested in knowing why alliances occur in the first place and then what contributes to their effective management and success. In searching for a competitive advantage, firms have considered interfirm collaboration as a viable strategic option, and therefore many of them have attempted to exploit this alternative strategy. Nevertheless, there has been a high level of dissatisfaction with their actual outcomes relative to the expectations of partners—and, correspondingly, a high rate of failure of strategic alliances.

From a theoretical perspective, underlying theories and conceptual models alluding to global strategic alliances need to be developed or improved to enhance our understanding of this popular practice. Although some literature has already been developed to address different dimensions of strategic alliances, further refinement is needed to understand and manage strategic alliances between firms in different industries. Most literature has dealt with either general theoretical aspects or a specific form of alliances (for example, joint ventures). The extant literature often makes references to theories such as transaction cost analysis, game theory, and resource-based views in explaining strategic alliances. Basically, each of these theories ultimately addresses the concept of competitive advantage of the firm. Consequently, the basic premise of strategic alliances lies in winning against competitors, but with a different twist that a company can build partnerships even with its competitors to create or sustain a competitive edge. Albeit a traditional view—an industrial organization suggesting that only competition determines the winners in a given industry—firms today have realized the strategic benefits of interfirm partnership, as well.

From a managerial perspective, core capabilities that managers need in order to form and manage successful cross-border alliances should be elaborated upon—what it takes to succeed when crossing borders and forming partnerships. Firms also need to know how to negotiate, build, and manage an alliance. All of these managerial capabilities need to be developed to exploit the benefits of strategic alliances. There will be a demand for those managers who can successfully establish and manage global partnerships to enhance the firm's product breadth, market scope, and profitability worldwide.

So far, most studies of cross-country interfirm cooperation have dealt with theory building or specific cases at global and regional levels, but little attention has been paid to industry-specific situations. While it is important to know the industry forces that shape competition in a given industry, it is equally essential to learn the dynamics of interfirm partnership that are shaping the current global competitive landscape. It is also useful to find out whether interfirm partnership is specific to a given industry where many partnerships are observed most frequently, as is happening in the airline industry right now, or to a strategic requirement for firms in a variety of industries and whether the partnership pattern varies across industries. In this book, we will examine strategic alliances thoroughly to answer all these questions for researchers and managers. The book's coverage ranges from the theory of the firm and the firm's strategic options in general to a variety of forms of alliances.

The suggestion exists that cross-border alliances are one of the most effective ways for firms to access capabilities and new markets without a significant incremental investment risk. They can be complicated to initiate and negotiate, however, and can become messy if implemented carelessly. Beyond general prescriptions, it is also important to find out industry-specific factors that have an impact on the successful formation and management of cross-border alliances.

In contrast to traditional alliances between an MNC from an industrialized country and a local partner in a less-developed country, the modern forms of strategic alliances present a broader scope and variations. Specific industry examples clearly illustrate this point. Four trends are noticeable. First, current strategic alliances embrace both alliances between companies from developed countries (the majority of interfirm partnerships) as well as partnerships between an MNC from a developed country and a local company in a less-developed country. Second, the emphasis is on the creation of new products or technologies, rather than marketing existing products in new markets. Third, the present alliances are also formed across industries to complement the resources and capabilities of firms. Finally, more than ever the recent alliances aim at gaining and building knowledge. Given these trends, we need to approach global alliances with a new perspective and understanding. We must also learn the context in which alliances occur. Hence, an industry perspective provides some insights into global alliance in different industries.

In this book, we will attempt to explore the dynamics of global strategic alliances in four industries—automobile manufacturing, pharmaceuticals, airlines, and telecommunications—to identify strategic factors determining success in their formation and management. Moreover, we will compare and contrast similarities and differences in collaborative ventures in these four industries by taking into consideration industry-specific developments.

The plan of the book includes an overview of global strategic alliances in Chapter 1, "Competition and Cooperation," building alliances versus other strategic business options in Chapter 2, "Theoretical Foundations," global business strategy and alliances in Chapter 3, "International Business Strategy and Alliances," alliances as international business strategy, in Chapter 4, "Equity Alliances," international joint ventures (IJVs), and equity participations in Chapter 5, "Non-Equity Alliances," non-equity agreements including international R&D agreements, supplier agreements, and marketing agreements, and in Chapters 6 through 9, global alliances in automobile manufacturing, pharmaceuticals, airlines, and telecommunications. Moreover, Chapter 10, "Alliance Management," addresses managerial issues and challenges in forming and managing global strategic alliances.

1

Competition and Cooperation

GLOBAL BUSINESS COMPETITION AND ALLIANCES

Globalization of business has been one of the dominant characteristics of the past two decades but will develop even faster in the future. Many companies from both developed and developing countries have become multinational players seeking market opportunities across nations. Globalization has become the cornerstone of firms' overall business strategies. Globalization is no longer only a business option but also a part of effective corporate strategizing. In other words, present business strategy is increasingly global. Today's global scope of business is markedly different from yesterday's business pattern, however. Presently, numerous goods and services are available across borders—even in those countries that were closed markets of command economies. World consumers have been exposed to a variety of products and services that had only been available to affluent consumers in industrialized countries. When customers across nations started demanding products and services for better living, companies strived to meet such demands by competing not only with local firms but also with other multinational firms.

We live in a global village today, where consumers have a chance to see and compare many products and services if not physically but virtually because of the Internet revolution. Consequently, buyers demand quality, variety, convenience, and utility. Needless to say, Internet technology has intensified such consumer demands tremendously. Buyers today can easily search for a product or service around the world. Recent news in *The Wall Street Journal* clearly illustrates the globalization of consumer behavior. An American who lived in Switzerland used Swiss toothpaste and liked it very much. Upon his return to

America, he searched for this particular toothpaste but could not find it anywhere. As he was searching the Web, he found a German store that carried it and then ordered a bulk of these toothpastes through the Internet. Now, in the United States, he uses this favorite Swiss-made toothpaste provided to him by a German retailer. This example illustrates how the information revolution is helping consumers by turning business into a global game.

These developments are not restricted to developed countries and are taking place in many emerging or developing economies. In this vein, a car buyer in Turkey looks for similar features and performance of his or her car to those made in the West. Thus, Toyota and Honda joint ventures in Turkey offer their flagship cars to Turkish customers, as well. These cases demonstrate that worldwide consumer demand for goods and services is pushing firms to engage in global productions and deliveries.

A close examination of such developments shows that a number of factors have contributed to this business globalization.[1] We define these factors as follows.

Liberalization of Economies

With the demise of socialist economies, many former socialist countries such as the Soviet Union (now Russia), Poland, Czechoslovakia (now the Czech and Slovak Republics), Hungary, Romania, and Bulgaria have switched to a market economy from a command economy, which has opened their borders for foreign investment, goods, and services.[2] The times are changing for many economic sectors in Central and Eastern Europe. The primary driver for change in this region is the eagerness of most countries to be accepted into the European Union (EU). While governments strive to meet the EU's economic requirements, the effect on the local industries has intensified because of efforts in privatization, liberalization, and deregulation. The markets in the region fall into three groups according to their likely order of EU accession. The first group of markets is Poland, Hungary, the Czech Republic, Estonia, and Slovenia. The second group includes Bulgaria, Croatia, Romania, Latvia, Lithuania, and Slovakia. The third group consists of the former Soviet states, which lag some distance behind after having suffered from the Asian contagion and a disastrous fall in foreign direct investment.

The unification of East and West Germany is another noteworthy development that expanded the German market considerably. Although the cost of this unification has exceeded its original estimates, it has made Germany the largest market power in Europe.

Even the People's Republic of China, a long-time hard-liner for the communist system, has softened its position on the command economy and enabled private ownership and investment by realizing the practical benefits of a market economy. China, being eager to acquire foreign advanced technology and capital, has welcomed multinational companies and yielded limited private ownership in special trade zones. China's current foreign investment policy encourages foreign firms to form alliances with domestic enterprises, rather than foreigners having full ownership and control of business concerns.

Johnson, a market expert on semiconductors, points out the market potentials in China as follows:

Under the terms of the Chinese WTO (World Trade Organization) accession package, China will become a full participant in the Information Technology Agreement, eliminating tariffs on a wide range of high-tech products, including semiconductors and chip manufacturing equipment. The mandatory requirements that imported goods go through a Chinese agent or middleman will disappear, as foreign vendors will have direct contact with customers. This will permit lower marketing costs, expedient sales, better customer relations and more efficient distribution. China has traditionally imposed conflicting and arbitrary restrictions on direct investment for chipmakers. Access to China's domestic market has been contingent upon a foreign partner's willingness to transfer advanced technologies and Intellectual Property to the Chinese partner.[3]

As in many industries, China's population represents a huge potential marketplace for prescription medicines. The Chinese market is expanding continuously, fueled at least in part by improvements in the standard of living. Greater access to health care and changing disease patterns predicated by improving economic status drive the pharmaceutical market. Many companies play an active role in creating niche markets for their products in China. Yuguan and Jiang, two consultants for the Chinese pharmaceutical industry, make the following observations:

The developing economy and improvement in living standards have made Chinese consumers more aware of their health. Under those circumstances, pharmaceutical companies need to educate patients and introduce new ideas to create demand for products that did not exist previously. SK&F has created a new market for its painkiller Fenbid (ibuprofen). XianJanssen has created a new market for its Motilium (domperidone) by introducing the new concept of stomach motility. Lilly has created a new market for its antidepressant Prozac by educating consumers that depression is a problem of the nervous system. Despite failing to obtain administrative protection from SDA and having lost an appeal with the Beijing High Court for protection against copies of Prozac, Lilly still plans to manufacture the drug in China at its Suzhou joint-venture site.[4]

The U.S. Congress ended its practice of voting annually on the renewal of China's most-favored-nation status and granted China a permanent normal trade relations status. The United States' grant of permanent normal trade relations with China and China's entry (expected soon) into the World Trade Organization (WTO) would be a long-term boon to the business of multinational corporations (MNCs). China, with its 1.2 billion population, has already attracted many MNCs in a variety of industries.

Additionally, privatization of state-owned enterprises in many countries has been a widespread application. Many developed and developing countries including the United Kingdom, France, Italy, Brazil, Argentina, Chile, Malaysia, and Turkey have privatized their inefficient state-owned enterprises for greater economic value. The trend toward privatization of state-owned enterprises gives international firms and international investors an opportunity to enter potentially lucrative markets that were once closed to private enterprise. Privatization also provides international companies an opportunity to capitalize on the comparative advantage of countries that have opened their doors to foreign companies.[5]

Although the success in this transition to a market economy or in the liberalization of economies varies across countries, the movement will accelerate in the next decade. Liberalization of economies worldwide has created many opportunities for newly established domestic firms and MNCs. Many MNCs have established strategic partnerships with national firms in post-socialist countries that transformed their economies (or at least certain industries from command to market economy).

The spread of economic liberalism has been the most important driver of globalization. "The recent and widespread change in ideology—from state socialism to market capitalism—has unleashed much internal deregulation and external liberalization from France to the former Soviet Union."[6] It is true that the deregulation and privatization of industries in developed and developing countries has stimulated economic activity by opening borders for trade and foreign investment—which, in turn, stirred global competition.

Because inefficient state-owned enterprises have contributed to budget deficits in many countries, governments around the world have been privatizing such enterprises at an increasing rate. By doing so, they expect the following benefits: improving enterprise efficiency and performance, developing competitive industry that serves consumers well, assessing the capital, know-how, and markets that permit growth, achieving effective corporate governance, broadening and deepening capital markets, and securing the best price possible for the sale.[7]

A fundamental premise of most economists and management scholars is that state-owned enterprises (SOEs) are less efficient and profitable than private enterprises. Boes states this underlying assumption as follows:

Privatization can be justified because it increases the technological efficiency of operations. Many empirical studies comparing private and public firms confirm that private enterprises are more efficient than public enterprises producing the same goods or very close substitutes, given the same or similar technology, regulatory constraints, and financial capabilities. Therefore there has been little discussion that SOEs in the former socialist countries need to be privatized.[8]

As a result of privatization, market opportunities for domestic and international firms will continue to boom. Hoelscher, a market expert on the telecommunications industry, describes the market opportunities in Central and Eastern European countries as follows: "The Czech Republic, Poland and Hungary have undoubtedly made the most progress of all Eastern European countries in the development of their telecommunications industry during the post-1989 era. Advances include partial privatization of and significant capital investment to the fixed-line and mobile infrastructure, market liberalization moving towards ending monopoly in most market segments and creation of huge demand for communication services of all types among business and residential consumers."[9]

We can extend these same arguments to SOEs in developed countries. Many developed countries around the world, including Britain, Germany, France, and Italy, have privatized numerous state-owned companies.

Privatization in both developed and developing economies has fueled strategic alliances. Privatized enterprises have globally engaged in strategic alliances such as licensing, joint ventures, marketing, and production partnerships to become and stay efficient and competitive. After their privatization in the United Kingdom, British Telecom and British Airlines sought partnerships in Europe and the United States. Likewise, a number of privatized enterprises in former socialist and developing countries have sought strategic partnerships with the belief that such alliances would contribute considerably to the development of Western-like business strategies and structures. The belief exists that the links with Western firms would ensure the successful transfer of capital and technology, which are desperately needed at the time of transformation. In this vein, Russian and Azerbaijani petroleum companies have established a number of links with U.S. and European oil companies. Similarly, telecommunications companies from Mexico to India have established collaborations with Western firms.

Strategic alliances with Western firms have injected new life into privatized firms in developing countries by revitalizing commercial practices and efficient production systems. For many employees of such former state-owned enterprises, customer expectations, cost control, and building core competencies for strategic advantages were strange concepts in the past. They have quickly learned such business planning and practices through their interactions with their Western partners.

Dispersion of Technology

The worldwide dispersion of technology has been one of the determinants of global competition and strategic alliances. As technologies become more sophisticated and are shared by a number of industries, firms find themselves in need of learning and borrowing from and sharing with other firms advanced emerging technologies. Ohmae, an international business consultant, claimed that "today's products rely heavily on many different critical technologies that most companies can no longer maintain cutting-edge sophistication in all of them... The inevitable result is the rapid dispersion of technology. No one company can do it all, simultaneously. No one company can keep all the relevant technologies in-house, as General Motors did during the 1930s and 1940s. And that means no one can truly keep all critical technologies out of the hands of competitors around the globe."[10]

Interspect (United States) and VingMed (Norway), for example, have joined forces to produce the Interspect Cardiac Ultrasound Echocardiography system. This system will use the VingMed Sound continuous and pulsed Doppler in its introduction to color-flow technology. VingMed Sound has been the leader and stands alone in Doppler in Europe and the United States. Although there are numerous Echo/Doppler machines, this system is the first to incorporate the VingMed advanced technology. Standard in this package will be the use of a Panasonic VCR, Mitsubishi black-and-white page printer, and a Hitachi color printer. Indeed, Interspect, in this example, has incorporated the latest technology into one system through interfirm collaboration.

In 1980, General Motors wanted to automate its production line by installing 20,000 robots in its plants. GM approached Fanuc of Japan, a major robot manufacturer. The two companies formed a 50-50 joint venture called GMF Robotics. GM accounted for 80% of sales. In three years, GMF delivered 3,000 robots to the GM plant. In four years, GMF Robotics emerged as the world's largest robot maker with almost one-third of the market. GMF also sold robots to Mercedes-Benz, BMW, Chrysler, and Ford.

The advent of trading blocs such as the European Union (EU) and North American Free Trade Agreement (NAFTA) has also contributed to technology development and sharing. Within the same bloc, governments, research organizations, and businesses tend to cooperate to build their competitive positions against firms out of the bloc. In the EU, the following organizations were developed to promote technological advancements: European Strategic Program for Research and Development in Information Technology (ESPRIT), Basic Research in Industrial Technologies for Europe (BRITE), and Research and Development in Advanced Communication Technology for Europe (RACE). All of these funded alliances seek to develop technology, generally between partners from different EU countries. Similarly, NAFTA has created a new wave of investment and cooperative ventures as a result of opening the Mexican market. General Electric, for example, has invested $200 million in a joint venture to make gas ranges in Mexico.

The explosion of information technology (IT) in particular has substantially changed the way companies conduct business. Phatak, an international business scholar, states that "countries and companies around the world are becoming linked together by networks of computers, wireless services such as cellular phones and the Internet, the worldwide network of computers linked by digital phone lines...high-capacity of fiberoptic cables, digital switches, satellites are making it possible for international companies in Germany, as well as tiny textile mills in Thailand, to conduct business anywhere, anytime, and to work with customers, bankers, and suppliers anywhere in the world."[11] Such use of IT is expanding rapidly and is not limited to a particular region or company. IT is deemed a competitive weapon today. In other words, those companies that fail to incorporate IT in their systems will face the risk of losing in international competition. The rapid pace of technological changes, however, and the limited capabilities of individual companies are forcing them to cooperate in the development, improvement, and use of IT. Many multinational companies moving across borders share their technologies with local partners, which has increased technology dispersion.

Consumer Exposure to Products and Services

As a result of advanced communication technologies, people around the world can hear and watch the high standard of living of others when consuming quality goods and services. This kind of instant exposure to better products and services has stimulated consumer demands that were either nonexistent before or impossible to meet. Consumers worldwide are more informed than ever before; therefore, they demand quality, value, and convenience in products and services. As a result of sophisticated consumer demands, many companies around the world have made customers involved in their manufacturing and/or marketing processes. In other words, customers have become strategic partners of companies that pay careful attention to their customers' needs and demands. Dell Computers and Gateway, for example, effectively use a build-to-order strategy in manufacturing personal computers (PCs) by getting customer specifications and assembling computers rapidly to customer satisfaction. As we will discuss in detail later, automobile manufacturers, after seeing the successful application of build-to-order strategies by PC manufacturers, have undertaken similar projects. The Ford Motor Company, for example, asked for help from Dell Computers to launch a similar build-to-order program in its production system.

In recent years, the Internet has contributed substantially to consumer awareness of availability and quality of products and services. An increasing number of consumers around the world, particularly in industrial countries, can now find most of what they need on the Web as the Internet is becoming easier to use and is expanding worldwide. A rapidly augmenting rate of electronic commerce (e-commerce) has empowered consumers in making informed choices and comparing products and services. The Web's search engines and directories have been useful in helping users easily locate firms and products/services. Some sites even offer comparisons of products and prices for the shoppers, although their benefits might be limited because of their selective or limited databases. Such Web companies with greater sophistication will offer tremendous service to consumers worldwide. As online commerce changes the economics of transactions, it is becoming an unstoppable tidal wave.

In response to the rapid increase of online commerce, while many startup companies have emerged in online business, traditional business firms have started building their own sites on the Internet to compete with new "dotcom" firms. From this changing pattern of competition and doing business online, consumers benefit greatly because they have more choices and can search and compare and ultimately make informed decisions.

Consequently, the competitive landscape of business has been changing rapidly—becoming more Web-based and global. As the new Internet technology evolves, firms new and old are learning from each other and are developing more convenient platforms for shopping. To catch up with GM and Ford's Internet achievements, DaimlerChrysler hired a Silicon Valley expert to map its Web drive and to acquire stakes in Internet startups so that it can get new technologies into its cars faster. Additionally, business-to-business commerce has been moving to the Web to take advantage of economies-of-scale cost advantages.

All this e-commerce movement requires close cooperation between marketers and IT technology firms to provide for huge volumes of traffic, uninterrupted service, and online security. An online company needs to give customers access to all the kinds of information they want or need—everything from order status reports and up-to-the-minute product availability to troubleshooting guides as well as routing their questions directly to the right people in the company. In addition, the online company must analyze customer-purchasing habits so that the company can better target its marketing efforts. Similar, smoother operations are needed for online business to business. Firms such as IBM, Siebel, and Cisco help provide IT services to those online companies. Furthermore, even IT providers have started building alliances among themselves. For example, IBM recently partnered with Siebel, one of the leading suppliers of customer relationship software, to create high-performance solutions for an online company.

Competitive Pressure

Companies operate under increasing competitive pressure in a global business environment that is rapidly changing because of political, social, and technological advances. No company can afford to rely solely on its traditional advantages that it enjoyed for many years in the past. New breakthroughs in technology and product developments, short product cycles, benchmarking, and imitations have increased the level of competition in the global market. A distinction between a multinational and domestic company has become blurred as the customers and competitors have moved across borders. In other words, no domestic company is sheltered from international competition; the opposite is also true for a multinational firm. Given this intense competitive pressure, companies employ a number of innovative strategies to gain and sustain their competitive advantages.

Karnani, a researcher focusing on global competition, argued that companies are under pressure for expansion from three directions: shareholders, employees, and competitors.[12] He asserted that shareholders demand value creation, which is closely related to growth. Employees seek career advancement, financial rewards, job security, and job satisfaction. "Then there is a heat from competitors, particularly in industries such as banking, pharmaceuticals, automotive, defense, airlines, and personal computers which are undergoing consolidation. Here growth is essential if economies of scale in technology development, operations, capacity utilization, marketing, distribution, and network externalities are to be captured. Those companies which fail to expand as fast as competitors will lose competitive advantage and enter a downward spiral."[13]

Under such intense, competitive pressure, companies worldwide search for partnerships to build or strengthen their market power and competitive positions. Such partnerships extend to collaboration between manufacturers and suppliers and even between two rival companies. In 1989, for example, Apple Computer made an arrangement with Sony to manufacture a new notebook Macintosh computer called the PowerBook 100 model. In this partnership, Apple provided the blueprints while Sony—with its great experience in miniaturizing technology—developed Apple's smallest and lightest machine in fewer than 13 months. As we will discuss in Chapter 6, rival companies such as General Motors and Toyota, Ford and Mazda, and DaimlerChrysler and Mitsubishi formed partnerships to build competitive benefits.

CONCLUSION

A global business orientation places emphasis on exploiting business opportunities across nations to synergistically achieve corporate goals. This orientation considers the overall effect of various markets in designing and implementing strategic objectives. With this global mentality, a market is not selected on the basis of its individual potentials but rather on its impact on the overall company interest and its complementary benefits to the existing operations. We must note, however, that despite the existing forces for globalization, there are some countervailing forces for localization that we will elaborate upon in Chapter 3. Nevertheless, we believe that the forces for globalization have been gaining momentum every day and will be more influential in shaping business in the future.

Achieving a synergy among many units of the company across countries is extremely important. Consequently, cross-subsidization across country units often becomes necessary. Although it sounds glorious, accomplishing such a synergy among different units and products is not an easy task given the rapidly changing market conditions, short product life cycles, the fast pace of technological changes, and hypercompetition. No single company, despite its large size and resources (such as GM or IBM) can cope with all these globalization factors and achieve synergy at the same time. As a result, a number of MNCs are seeking collaboration with others either in the same industry or in different industries.

A strong market presence in North America, Europe, and the Pacific Rim is now essential for any company wishing to be a global contender. Nevertheless, such a business strategy would more likely require collaboration among firms. In other words, international collaborative agreements in which each partner's unique assets are shared in return for greater global markets are becoming vital to compete globally. As a result, giants as well as small companies in many industries have been rapidly establishing international links. Strategic alliances are set up to exchange technology, gain market entry, lower production costs, and offset exports. As the biggest partners mate, the global race becomes more difficult for the lone player.

There will be a great need for strategic collaboration in the years ahead. Globalization is mandating alliances and rendering them essential components of strategy. Recent business developments—entering the Chinese market by collaborating with local firms, performing joint R&D between pharmaceutical and biotechnology companies, and code sharing between airlines—reflect global business sentiment and alliances. Old ways of doing business by relying entirely on your own resources and capabilities have been changing rapidly. Global alliances have become common. Now, MNCs often collaborate with other global players or domestic firms from emerging economies.

Similarities in consumer demands and the advancement of IT, combined with competitive pressures, are pushing firms to formulate global business strategies by developing partnerships with various segments in the marketplace, including suppliers, customers, and even their own rivals. Because manufacturer-supplier partnerships have been around for some time, it is not odd any more. Collaborating with customers and competitors had been a strange concept since the establishment of the firm, however. Nonetheless, it is accepted and common practice today. Companies (at least, many of them) have realized that customers are the very reason for their existence. Those firms overlooking this fundamental notion face the risk of becoming dinosaurs. Responsive companies are trying to reach their customers and understand their needs and expectations so that they can offer the right products and services. Two important shifts have occurred in recent years in the marketplace. The first shift is that companies do not have the luxury of selling whatever they produce anymore; rather, the customers are in the driver's seat. Customers demand the type of products and services that the companies should produce. Although some companies, like prospectors, sense and offer products and services that appeal to customers even before customer demand exists for them, it is still based on the needs and implicit expectations of customers. Exploring such expectations and improving the quality of life for consumers is considered an obligation of firms. The second shift is that consumers have become more informed, if not more educated, so that they can suggest some invaluable insights into the design, utility, and quality of products and services that they use. Companies have started to appreciate the inputs of consumers as designers, marketers, and engineers. In this regard, the story of www.music.com is interesting. The company originated in the Philippines selling non-music-related products online. After abbreviating its company name and adopting www.music.com as its online logo, some incidental shoppers suggested that the company carry music cassettes and CDs. The company took their advice, moved to the United States, and is now a significant "player" in the prosperous music industry.

Another phenomenon that was found to be odd is interfirm partnerships among rivals. Classical economics explaining the firm behavior postulates that firms fight each other fiercely in a zero-sum game or win and lose mode, whereas emerging interfirm alliances have proven that even two fierce rivals can benefit from an interfirm collaboration. A well-known example of such an interfirm collaboration is that two global competitors, GM and Toyota, have created the NUMMI joint venture and are manufacturing cars together. Although a lot of firms have not been capable of absorbing this kind of strategic transformation or incorporating inter-rival cooperation into their strategy formulation yet, increasing number of companies have been developing alliances with their competitors to improve their global strategic positions.

NOTES

1. For further discussion, see Refik Culpan (ed.), *Multinational strategic alliances* (New York: International Business Press, 1993).

2. For further information on transforming economies, see R. Culpan and B. N. Kumar (eds.), *Transformation management in postcommunist countries* (Westport, CT: Quorum Books, 1995).

3. G. R. Johnson, Finally! Chipmakers applaud China's WTO acceptance. *Electronic News* (January 10, 2000): 12–14.

4. W. Yuguan, and J. Song, China: A future star for foreign pharma companies, *Pharmaceutical Executive* (August 1999): 78–87.

5. A. V. Phatak, *International management: Concepts and cases* (Cincinnati, OH: South-Western College Publishing, 1997): 36.

6. S. U. Rangan, Seven myths to ponder before going global. "Mastering Strategy, Part Ten," *The Financial Times* (November 29, 1999): 4.

7. International Finance Corporation, *Privatization principles and practice* (Washington, D.C.: IFC, 1995): I.

8. D. Boes, *Privatization: A theoretical treatment* (Oxford, England: Clarendon Press, 1991): 7.

9. G. Hoelscher, Central and Eastern Europe: Changing markets, *Telecommunications* (April 2000): 76.

10. K. Ohmae, The logic of strategic alliances. *Harvard Business Review* (March–April, 1989): 145.

11. A. V. Phatak, *International management: Concepts and cases* (Cincinnati, OH: South Western College Publishing, 1997): 36.

12. A. G. Karnani, Five ways to grow the market and create value. "Mastering Strategy, Part Four," *The Financial Times* (October 18, 1999): 8–10.

13. Ibid.

2

Theoretical Foundations

To understand interfirm business alliances better, you must examine their theoretical foundations and conceptual pillars. Business alliances reflect our concept of the firm; hence, it is first important to appreciate the theory of the firm and then demonstrate its tie to strategic alliances. In linking strategic alliances to firm behavior and market environment, we offer numerous theoretical explanations. We will introduce principal theories on the nature of firms as a foundation of interfirm strategic alliances and then offer our integrated view of strategic alliances in light of extant theories.

Bruce Kogut, one of the pioneering scholars studying strategic alliances, introduced general theoretical foundations of strategic alliances by reviewing three theoretical approaches that are specifically relevant in explaining the motivation and choice of joint ventures.[1] The following explanations are partly based on Kogut's typology, but we will expand the theoretical treatment of alliances to new dimensions and cover all types of strategic alliances, not only joint ventures. Additionally, we will incorporate a value chain perspective in explaining the behaviors of business partners. Basically, the theoretical underpinnings of collaborative firm behavior can be found in the following theories: transaction cost theory, industrial organization model, game theory, resource-based view, organizational learning, and knowledge in the literature.[2] We will discuss each one of them by demonstrating its relevance to strategic alliances.

TRANSACTION COST THEORY

We can summarize the transaction cost economics (TCE) perspective as follows: markets and hierarchies (organizations) are alternative instruments for completing a related set of transactions, and whether a set of transactions should be executed between firms (across markets) or within a firm depends on the relative efficiency of each mode.[3] TCE assumes that firms exchange goods and services in the marketplace by acting in their self-interest while demonstrating an opportunistic behavior. TCE attempts to answer the basic question of how a firm should organize its exchanges and boundary activities with other firms (that is, build or buy decisions). A firm determines how to conduct transactions with other firms with the motive of minimizing the sum of production and transaction costs. While production cost consists of a variety of costs incurred during the transformation of various inputs (materials, components, labor, information, and so on) into products and services, transaction costs refer to the expenses incurred in writing and enforcing contracts, for haggling over terms and contingent claims, for deviating from optimal kinds of investments to increase dependence on a party to stabilize a relationship, and for administering a transaction.[4]

The TCE theory suggests that the ultimate goal of the firm is to choose the most efficient form while opportunistic behaviors exist among parties and bounded rationality hinders decision makers. This theory also specifies that markets are an ideal form of exchange, but when markets fail, organizations are more efficient.[5] Market failure refers to the existence of transactional factors such as uncertainty and small numbers of exchange relations, in which one party's choice of trading partners is restricted. As environments become complex and uncertain, the transaction costs become prohibitive. Contracts become lengthy, number in hundreds, and cannot all be supervised. Consequently, organizations appear as efficient, alternative modes to handle the transaction costs. Then, firms tend to develop asset-specific advantages yielding efficiency in their transactions with others. When internal hierarchy reaches a point where transaction costs become prohibitive, however, the firm looks for alternative arrangements as strategic alliances while still seeking reduced transaction costs.

Oliver Williamson, the prominent scholar of TCE theory, asserted that as investment in asset specificity increases, contracting and monitoring costs also increase to safeguard against opportunistic behavior.[6] In other words, there is a tradeoff between the efficiency of operations and the efficiency of exchange. As we pointed out, while investments in specific assets might increase productivity, it will also increase the transaction costs involved—sometimes offsetting the benefits of specialization.

An extension of transaction cost theory to multinational corporations (MNCs) is called internalization theory, which assumes that an MNC possesses some rent-yielding, firm-specific advantage (primarily some form of know-how).[7] As a result, an MNC often internalizes its operations by engaging in foreign direct investments (FDIs) through its subsidiaries. In other words, it contends that there must be some advantage to "internalizing" foreign activity within the command hierarchy of the firm before FDI occurs. Generally, internalization advantage is thought to arise from the existence of imperfect markets. When the contracting mechanism breaks down, the market cannot correctly value and protect firm-specific advantages that are intangible in nature and calls for alternative modes of doing business by the firm. Between two extreme modes (subsidiary and contractual arrangements), however, an MNC might seek quasi-internalization forms (joint ventures). Joint ownership and/or control and mutual commitment of resources, combined with high uncertainty about specifying and monitoring performances in addition to a high degree of asset specificity and frequency of transactions, encourages a joint venture over a contract. Although TCE primarily emphasizes full ownership mode in explaining the MNC behavior, some researchers extended the theory to interfirm collaborations.[8]

In explaining equity joint ventures by TCE, Hennart claimed that the theory posits that the choice between full ownership (wholly owned subsidiary) and partial ownership (equity joint venture) will depend on the relative costs and benefits of each mode.[9] He asserted that joint ventures are efficient when two conditions simultaneously exist: (1) markets for intermediate goods (know-how, raw materials, parts and components, and so on) held by each party are failing and (2) acquiring or replicating the assets yielding those goods is more expensive than obtaining a right to their use through a joint venture. The author specified four instances where the choice for joint ventures is particularly strong:[10] The first is when the foreign affiliate represents a diversification for the parent. The second is when it is the first-time entry into a given foreign market. The third refers to the intention of foreign firms in obtaining resources controlled by local firms. Finally, the fourth is combining the complementary inputs held by two separate firms when the market for both of these inputs is subject to high transaction costs.

Two situations that particularly justify the choice of joint ventures over the alternatives of replication (greenfield investment) or full acquisitions are (1) building a greenfield plant usually takes more time than effecting a full or partial acquisition, and (2) small firms might find that they do not have the necessary resources to put up the whole capital of greenfield investments or to make full acquisitions of existing firms in industries where the required economies of scale are enormous.

Similarly, Beamish and Banks extended the internalization approach to the theory of MNC to include an expanded role for equity joint ventures.[11] They suggested that joint ventures furnished with certain preconditions and structural arrangements can actually provide a better solution to the problems of opportunism, small number dilemma, and uncertainty in the face of bounded rationality than wholly owned subsidiaries.

Beamish and Banks asserted that "Although there would be costs associated with writing, executing and enforcing pricing agreements and use restrictions regarding the transfer of the MNCs intangible assets these will be more than offset by the enhanced revenue potential of its assets as a result of forming a joint venture. As well, rent can exceed those available through wholly owned subsidiaries due to the potential synergistic effects of combining the MNCs assets with those of a local partner."[12] Nevertheless, they admitted that there are limits to the relative efficiency gains provided by joint ventures. Such limitations include that joint ventures can suffer from the same goal distortions of hierarchies and that there is always the risk of leakage of proprietary knowledge in the joint venture relations.

In assessing TCE with regard to cooperative ventures, we can assert that inter-firm cooperation challenges both the assertions of opportunism and the trade between asset specificity and transaction cost. Cooperative behavior is based on trust between the partners, rather than on opportunistic behavior. Effective communication and information sharing between the partners can curb the opportunistic behavior. Cooperation mode seems an odd phenomenon to TCE, which basically emphasizes either markets or hierarchies. According to TCE, firms have strong incentive to choose wholly owned subsidiaries with full control over joint ventures in which a partner is considered vulnerable for exploitation.

In particular, internalization theory primarily focuses on full ownership. There have been some efforts to extend it to partial ownership (for example, joint ventures), but MNCs engage in a variety of other modes of market entry including franchising, licensing, subcontracting, and consortia. Additionally, MNCs often employ several different modes simultaneously for entering a foreign market (for example, Toyota has both a wholly owned subsidiary and a joint venture in the United States). Moreover, some type of market imperfection is central to the description of internalization advantage, which in turn is based on intangible assets. Defining and empirically testing many possible sources of the elusive internalization advantage is extremely difficult. Therefore, we can conclude that despite its powerful logic, the internalization theory has limitations in explaining all behaviors in organizations. While organizations *do* act to minimize costs, they also seek revenue-enhancing activities. Moreover, many interorganizational activities involve trust and social relations in addition to supervision and control. Another popular theory called industrial organization throws light on the industry structure, the properties of industry structure, and firms competing in an industry or a segment of an industry.

THE INDUSTRIAL ORGANIZATION MODEL

The industrial organization (IO) perspective explains the dominant influence of the external environment on firms' strategic behavior. This perspective specifies that the chosen industry in which the firm is competing has a strong impact on a firm's performance. A host of industry properties, including economies of scale, barriers to entry, diversification, product differentiation, and the degree of integration, determines the firm's performance. In other words, the IO approach is concerned with building competitiveness through a strategic positioning of a firm in a given industry. In this context, Porter offered profound theories of competitive advantage, based on the analysis of five forces in an industry.[13] These five forces include the threat of new entrants, the bargaining power of suppliers, the bargaining power of buyers, the threat of substitute products, and inter-firm rivalry.[14] In Porter's framework, these five forces shape the competitive position of a firm that seeks to position itself in a favorable industry to enjoy superior performance. That is, an industry's potential profitability is a function of interaction among five forces. By using this framework, a firm could figure out an industry's profit potential and the strategy that it should undertake to build a defensible, competitive position given the industry's structural characteristics. Typically, this model suggests that firms can earn above-average returns by manufacturing standardized products at costs below those of competitors (a low-cost leadership strategy) or by offering differentiated products for which customers are willing to pay premium prices (a differentiation strategy).

In extending the IO model to strategic alliances, Porter and Fuller viewed strategic alliances as "coalitions" in the context of a firm's international strategy. They asserted that two key dimensions of international strategy are *configuration* and *coordination* of a firm's activities. The former means where and in how many countries the activities are located while the latter refers to how the activities located in different countries relate. Moreover, they argued that coalitions are a means of performing one or more activities in combination with another firm instead of running them alone. "The choice of coalition implies that it is perceived as a less costly or more effective way to configure than alternatives of, on the one hand, developing the skills to perform the activity in-house or, on the other hand, of merger to gain the capability to perform the activity or by products or skills in arm's length transaction."[15]

Coalitions involving access to knowledge or ability dissolve when the party acquires needed skills through the coalition. On the other hand, coalitions formed to gain the benefits of scale and learning last longer. "The stability of risk-reducing coalitions depends on the source of risk they seek to control. Coalitions hedging against the risk of a single exogenous event will tend to dissolve, while coalitions involving an ongoing risk (e.g., exploration of risk for oil) will be more durable."[16]

Based on its strategic orientation, the involvement of a firm in international markets can take several different forms, including wholly owned subsidiaries or joint ventures. Harrigan argued that different ownership patterns offer varying degrees of strategic flexibility.[17] Full ownership presents inflexibility because of a great amount of resource commitment in uncertain foreign markets, which creates high exit barriers while a joint venture alternative offers strategic flexibility in terms of risk sharing and potential withdrawal from the venture. In other words, despite its high exit barrier and less flexibility, a wholly owned subsidiary is preferred in a more benign environment where there is a greater scope for profit making and demand is less certain, while a joint venture offers greater flexibility and exit opportunity in uncertain markets. Non-equity collaborations with fewer commitments by the partners and lower entry and exit barriers than those of joint ventures present greater flexibility.

Although the IO model provides important insight into the competitive advantage of firms and thereby explains interfirm collaborations, its underlying assumptions are challenged by a resource-based view as we explain next. The IO model makes four major assumptions. First, the external environment is assumed to impose conditions (opportunities as well as limitations) that determine the firm's strategies that would result in satisfactory profits. Second, most firms that compete within a particular industry or within a segment of an industry hold similar resources and pursue similar strategies in light of those resources. Third, necessary resources to implement firm strategies can be moved from one firm to another. Finally, managers make rational decisions and are committed to acting in the best interest of the firm. In fact, managers play an insignificant role in terms of strategy development once they position their companies well within an attractive industry or segments of an industry. Of course, we can easily challenge these assumptions, and it is a well-known fact that the formulation and implementation of a successful business strategy rests upon firm-internal sources as much as externalities (as suggested by the IO model). Moreover, for international engagements it is possible that firms pursue different ownership strategies (wholly owned subsidiary, joint venture, and non-equity collaboration) simultaneously. Another type of theoretical explanation, called game theory, is offered to describe economic gains and payoff in cooperative arrangements. We will discuss the nature and dynamics of game theory next.

GAME THEORY

Game theory suggests that the essence of strategic competition is the interaction among players such that the decisions made by any one player are dependent on actual and anticipated decisions of other players. This concept permits the framing of strategic decisions and offers insight into competition and bargaining. This system can predict the equilibrium outcomes of competitive situations and the consequences of strategic moves by any one player. The continuing tradeoff between cooperation and competition within alliances has led to their conceptualization as repeated games. The most frequently used game scenario is called "prisoner's dilemma," which involves two players who can either cooperate with each other or cheat. Depending on their choice of action, their payoffs will be different. If two players cooperate with each other, they have a much greater payoff than if they both choose to cheat. If one of them cheats while the other one cooperates, however, then the cheating player receives the highest possible payoff while the cooperative player loses. Consequently, two self-interest maximizing players who are aware of their payoff structure will both cheat although they could be better off cooperating. The reason is because no player would knowingly risk cooperating when the chance exists that the other player would cheat.

Robert Axelrod found that in a prisoner's dilemma scenario, a player can perform exceedingly well if he or she adopts a "tit-for-tat" strategy; that is, if he or she starts the game in good faith by cooperating but responds instantly to any opportunism by any other player by beginning to cheat himself or herself in the next period.[18] In this way, players signal that they are going to punish any partner who cheats and revert back to cooperation if the partner chooses to cheat again. Subsequently, some management scholars see a parallel between the prisoner's dilemma game and interfirm alliances and suggest that firms adopt a tit-for-tat strategy in their conduct and governance of alliances.[19] Doz, Hamel, and Prahalad, however, made a different recommendation by considering the benefits of cheating as increasing over time—especially for the firm that learns more quickly from the alliance during the period of cooperation.[20] As a result, they suggested that the participant should try to learn as fast as possible and then quit the alliance at an advantage. All these suggestions based on the prisoner's dilemma game involve short-term gains in joint venture relationships, whereas there are also joint ventures that last a long time (for example, the Shell Oil Company between Dutch and British partners).

On the contrary to a short-term view of prisoner's dilemma, Gulati and Nohria suggested that "the prisoner's dilemma framework is especially unsuited for alliances that involve significant long term commitments on the part of the partners and where partnering firms may indeed obtain their highest payoffs, both in the long and short run, by cooperating."[21] They asserted that by "mutually assured alliances," in which despite the opportunity of parties' short-term benefits in cheating, the parties tend to not do so because cheating will damage their reputation in building new alliances either with the existing parties or with new parties in the future. The researchers claimed that "unlike the prisoner's dilemma game, where the dominant strategy for each player is to cheat, a mutual assurance game has two possible outcomes: either both the partners choose to cooperate or both choose to cheat."[22] In the case of the mutual assurance game, a player's optimal strategy depends upon what he or she expects of the other player. Hence, unlike the prisoner's dilemma game, in the mutual assurance scenario it might be more beneficial for the players to cooperate and convince the other player that it is in the best interest for him or her. To ensure cooperation in alliances that have a mutual assurance payoff structure, Gulati and Nohria recommended the following managerial actions: "Share complete information with your partners: do not conceal anything; constantly update the alliance: don't get stuck on an initial plan; be generous and take the long term view: don't balk at making unilateral commitments; walk through the conflicts: don't jump to conclusions; get incremental small gains: not just big payoffs; and choose your alliances carefully: don't rush into partnerships."[23]

Obviously, Gulati and Nohria's mutual assurance game takes a different view from those in the prisoner's dilemma game by emphasizing cooperation and long-term benefits for the players. Additionally, it encourages a positive reinforcement rather than punitive actions in influencing the choice of the party that might consider cheating. Moreover, a tit-for-tat approach breeds mistrust while a mutual assurance approach is more likely to build trust and commitment.

One of the important implications of the game theory is its capability to view business interactions as compromising both competition and cooperation. Brandenburger and Nalebuff, in their book *Co-opetition*, recognized this duality of competition and cooperation.[24] They identified four types of players: customers, suppliers, competitors, and complementors. They argued that a player can be competitor as well as a complementor. They explained this dynamic as follows: A player is your complementor if customers value your product *more* when they have the other player's product than when they have your product alone. A player is your competitor if customers value your product *less* when they have the other player's product than when they have your product alone. Moreover, customers and suppliers are also players. The same player might have multiple roles, however. According to the authors, the basic model comprises the value net, which represents all players and the interdependencies among them. Along the vertical dimension of value net are the company's customers and suppliers. Traditionally, businesses pay more attention to customers but not enough to suppliers. In recent years, however, firms paying attention to suppliers have made progress in building strategic advantages. Along the horizontal line of a value network are competitors and complementors. The former has been studied extensively, but the latter is a new concept for which the authors coined the term. Complementors refer to people who provide complements to the products and services that the firm produces. The best examples of complementors are computer hardware and software, cars and automobile loans, and television and videocassette recorders. We can see that a natural alliance exists between complementors.

In summary, the game theory recognizes that competition and cooperation are two essential paired components to which firms should pay attention. Players can benefit from cooperation yielding win-win outcomes instead of competition resulting in win-lose results. Contrary to the traditional view of competition, game theory considers the optimal division of the pie between partners for mutual gain. We must also recognize that a player can occupy multiple roles. Unlike traditional views, which offer little insight into firms' choices of whether to compete or to cooperate, game theory identifies the role of cooperation along with competition.

RESOURCE-BASED VIEW

A resource-based view (RBV) of the firm, on the other hand, suggests that the important determinants of competitive advantage are the resources possessed by the firm, deployed by the manager, and used and further developed by the organization. This view holds that there are key assets that give rise to competitive advantage. This view conceives the firm as a unique bundle of heterogeneous resources, capabilities, and competencies.[25] These resources and capabilities are the basis on which a firm's sustainable advantage is built and are the primary determinant of profitability. Establishing a competitive advantage involves formulating and implementing a strategy that recognizes and exploits the unique features of each firm. Firm resources can include tangible resources such as financial and physical resources, intangible resources such as technology, reputation, and culture, and human resources (including specialized skills and knowledge).

The basic premise of RBV is that a sound business strategy should be based on firm resources, competences, and capabilities, which yield a competitive advantage over rivals. Establishing a competitive advantage through the development and deployment of resources and capabilities has become a primary goal for strategy formulation.[26] Prahalad and Hamel called such capabilities "core competences," which are fundamental to a firm's performance and strategy and have to (1) make a disproportionate contribution to ultimate customer value or to the efficiency with which that value is delivered and (2) provide a basis for entering new markets.[27]

Basically, RBV to strategy consists of three key elements: selecting a strategy that exploits a company's principal resources and capabilities, ensuring that the firm's resources are fully employed and that their profit potential is exploited to the limit, and building the company's resource base for the future. For a resource or capability to establish a competitive advantage, however, it should possess the following characteristics: a resource or capability must be heterogeneous, scarce, relevant (helpful in assisting in creating value for customers or in surviving in competition), durable, and inimitable.

An extension of RBV to strategic alliances is that no firm often holds all the necessary resources, capabilities, and competencies for a given business strategy leading to competitive advantage; therefore, firms interested in deploying unique and inimitable resources seek partnerships with others that hold such resources. Resource pooling is considered one of the major factors leading to strategic alliances. This situation refers to the partner's contribution to a collaborative project of resources such as capital, know-how, and personnel.[28] A technological breakthrough often requires technical knowledge beyond a single company's domain. Pooling resources can be accomplished through equity joint ventures and non-equity alliances such as "know-how" licensing, management/marketing service agreements, non-equity cooperative agreements in exploration, research partnerships, and development/co-production.

Firms thrive for competitive advantage, and firms' tangible and intangible resources determine the degree of competitive edge that they hold in relation to their competitors. With rapidly changing technologies and global market conditions, no single firm can afford to ensure all the necessary resources to build or sustain a competitive superiority. As a result, among other options a strategic alliance necessitated by resource requirements has become a viable strategic option. That is, resource needs and complementary qualities are the key to the firm's financial and market performance. Of course, there must be a mutual benefit for partners to exchange resources. Otherwise, no company will give away or share its invaluable resources with another company. A specific version of RBV theory is knowledge-building and development theory, which offers an alternative explanation to "theory of the firm" and subsequently to the establishment of interfirm alliances.

KNOWLEDGE BUILDING AND ORGANIZATIONAL LEARNING

Nonaka, a Japanese organizational scholar, claimed that "knowledge-creating" companies committed to continuous innovation are the successful companies.[29] In other words, the sure source of lasting competitive advantage is knowledge. By giving examples from Japanese companies, he argued that the firm's creation of new knowledge depends upon tapping the tacit and highly subjective insights, intuitions, and hunches of individual employees and making those insights available for testing and use by the company as a whole.

Based on the Polanyi's definition, Nonaka distinguished knowledge as explicit and tacit knowledge.[30] The former refers to formal and systematic knowledge. Therefore, it can be easily communicated and shared in product specifications, in a scientific formula, or in a computer program. The latter means the kind of knowledge that is deeply rooted in action and in an individual's commitment to a specific context—craftsmanship, professional mental models, beliefs, and know-how without written guidelines and procedures. According to Nonaka, this distinction between explicit and tacit knowledge suggests four patterns of creating knowledge in organizations: from tacit to tacit, from explicit to explicit, from tacit to explicit, and from explicit to tacit. At a knowledge-creating company, all four of these patterns exist in a dynamic interaction—a kind of spiral of knowledge. In other words, organizational knowledge creation means a continuous, dynamic process between tacit and explicit knowledge. Such a spiral of knowledge works as follows. New knowledge always begins with the individuals when the individual learns tacit knowledge and then moves up through expanding communities of interaction that cross sectional, departmental, divisional, and organizational boundaries.[31]

Similarly, Kogut and Zander—the two principal proponents of the knowledge perspective—assumed that "organizations are social communities in which individual and social expertise is transformed into economically useful products and services by the application of higher-order organizing principles. Firms exist because they provide a social community of voluntaristic action structured by organizing principles that are not reduceable to individuals."[32] They also pointed out that organizations serve as more than mechanisms by which social knowledge is transferred but also as mechanisms by which new knowledge, or learning, is created.

As a fundamental element in analysis of organizational knowledge, Kogut and Zander distinguished two types of knowledge as information and know-how. The former means knowledge such as facts, axiomatic propositions, and symbols that can be transmitted without loss of integrity once the procedural rules are known. The latter is the accumulated practical skills or expertise that enables one to do something smoothly and efficiently. Moreover, to analyze knowledge, the authors distinguished two dimensions of knowledge as codifiability and complexity. The former means the capability of the firm to structure knowledge into a set of identifiable rules and relationships that can be easily communicated. The latter can be defined as the number of operations required to solve a task. These two dimensions are related, although not identical. These dimensions of noncodifiable and complex knowledge are similar to tacit knowledge as defined by Polanyi and adopted by Nonaka.

The central argument of Kogut and Zander is that knowledge is held by individuals but is also expressed in regularities by which members cooperate in a social community (in other words, a group, organization, or network). Although knowledge is held at an individual level, it is transferred to group and organizational levels. That is, knowledge is embedded in organizational principles by which people cooperate within an organization. In fact, firms learn new skills by recombining their existing capabilities. The authors call it "combinative capabilities," which provides opportunities to expand in new but uncertain markets in the future.

The application of knowledge and learning theory to interfirm alliances signifies the process of learning through collaborations and networks so that they can develop their own capabilities. The basic premise is how knowledge is transferred from one partner to another in an alliance context and why some firms are more successful than others in managing such knowledge transfer in alliances.[33] Knowledge creation through alliances occurs in multiple stages. The first stage is the formation of the alliance and interactions between individuals from two or more partners. The second stage is the internalization process, which means the transfer of individually acquired knowledge to an organization's knowledge database. In this process (both explicit codifiable and tacit), highly context-dependent knowledge is usually transferred. Because tacit knowledge and explicit knowledge are complementary, it is difficult to uncover or understand the tacit knowledge without the help of the knowledge holder, meaning that the collaborators need each other for effective knowledge transfer.

Knowledge creation and learning theory is a derivative of RBV. These concepts basically emphasize the knowledge-building capability of the firm. The firm might develop such a competence and knowledge base by either replication or innovation. Nevertheless, either situation involves a relearning process in which new skills need to be acquired. In the context of alliances, based on the theory of firm competence and resources, the partnering firm will be interested in developing new skills and competences that are available in the other partner. It is sufficient to say here that knowledge and learning theory makes an important contribution to our understanding of the firm's behavior and dynamics and interorganizational relationships in strategic alliances. Establishing competence in forming and managing a strategic alliance will provide a competitive advantage to those firms that learned from such experiences.

NETWORK PERSPECTIVE

Finally, network perspective—based in sociology—expands the level of analysis on interfirm linkages from dyads and triads to networks of relationships (also called constellations or wheels). In essence, network perspective is not a theory but instead a sound analytical tool explaining relationships among actors that could be individuals, groups, or organizations. This tool can define all the primary and secondary relationships between actors in a network or constellation and is grounded in theories of social exchange, power, and resource dependence. Auster pointed out that in a network, "…linkages are formed intentionally in order to manage uncertainty and acquire resources, information, and power. Networks are systems of these resource dependencies that are dynamic as a result of the actions of the actors involved."[34] Basic network properties consist of transactional content (what is exchanged, such as affection, influence or power, information, or goods or services); the nature of links in terms of intensity, reciprocity, clarity of expectations, and multiplexity (multiple types of relationships); structural characteristics referring to the external network, total internal network, and clusters within the network; and members as special nodes (meaning centrality, star, and isolated roles played by members within the network).[35] Network analysis helps us understand the relationships among member organizations. Relationships in a linkage can be one-way (also called asymmetric, or unilateral) or two-way (also called reciprocal, symmetrical, or bilateral), horizontal or vertical.[36] Horizontal linkages refer to exchanges between competing firms while vertical linkages mean exchanges between organizations at different stages of the value chain (for example, supplying, production, and distribution). Typical examples of interorganizational linkages include original equipment manufacturer (OEM) supply relations, licensing, franchising, technology transfers or exchanges, joint R&D, joint production, and joint ventures. As we will see in the following chapter, we consider all these types of relations as forms of strategic alliances. In other words, network perspective provides a conceptual tool to analyze interorganizational linkages to define the intensity, direction, and structure of relationships. Most importantly, network analysis can delineate "resource commitment" by member or partnering organizations; therefore, we can rank the relative resource dependence of different forms of alliances. In general, forms requiring equity participation (such as joint ventures) entail greater resource commitment than those of contractual agreements (for example, OEM supply agreement). Similarly, by using the degree of resource investment, Auster distinguished interorganizational linkages as "low resource investment linkages" and "high resource investment linkages" and made the following argument:

Low resource investment linkages would include relationships such as technological transfers and joint R&D that are more autonomous and severed more easily. High resource investment linkages...would be forms such as joint ventures that require much longer commitment and trust, a great financial investment, the construction or acquisition of a space to house the venture, equipment and technology to produce the output, and more management time and energy to oversee the venture. Given this high resource investment, switching costs and barriers to exist are formidable obstacle to termination.[37]

Network perspective embarks on the concept that the social context influences the economic actions of actors who are embedded in that environment. Gulati argued that

[t]here are two broad approaches for the influence of social networks. The first emphasizes the differential informational advantages bestowed by social networks, while the second highlights the control benefits actors can generate by being advantageously positioned within a social network. These two benefits are analytically distinct but also overlap, since much of the control benefit can arise from the manipulations of information. Networks may provide informational benefits through two mechanisms. Relational embeddedness or cohesion perspectives on networks stress the role of the direct cohesive ties as a mechanism for gaining fine-grain information...Structural embeddedness focuses on the information role of the position an organization occupies in the overall structure of network.[38]

In the case of alliances, firms in a social network can exploit information advantages by three distinct means: access, timing, and referrals.[39] In other words, firms that are heavily involved in alliances will have access to information about many other alliances or alliance potentials and might attract better partners because of their reputation and previous experiences. Additionally, they might obtain good terms of deals because of their possible control advantages that might result from their position within a social network.

In the following chapters, we will distinguish equity alliances from non-equity alliances by presenting their different forms and dynamics. Here, it is sufficient to say that network perspective brings another important dimension to consider the interorganizational relationships in terms of social exchanges, power, and resource dependence. We will use this approach in analyzing strategic alliances in the airline industry in Chapter 8.

A CRITICAL ASSESSMENT AND INTEGRATIVE VIEW

Based on different assumptions, these theories explain different facets of the firm's behavior and alliance phenomenon. Each offers important insights into the behavior and function of the firm and interfirm business alliances vis-à-vis other modes of conducting business, markets, and hierarchies as well as interfirm relationships. Table 2.1 summarizes the basic tenets of those theories and their relevance to strategic alliances. Each theory is a product of its own time and environmental conditions. When cost minimization, for example, is the main concern of firms, it is natural to see a theory emphasizing this particular issue. As we enter the cyber age, knowledge and learning have become important vehicles for a firm gaining and sustaining a competitive advantage. We believe, however, that a new theory of the firm, instead of replacing an older one, usually complements the extant knowledge on the nature of the firm's behavior and dynamics. Essentially, each theory is based on certain facts and practices of the firm. The firm's basic mission and objectives essentially have not changed much since early ages. In a market economy, it is simply an instrument for creating value for its constituents. What has changed over the years, however, is our notion of the firm's constituents. In the past, without questioning we accepted the owners as the only constituent whose interest should be maximized by the firm. Now, however, management scholars and practitioners recognize that the firm's primary stakeholders, in addition to its shareholders, are its customers, employees, and suppliers. This change of perception of stakeholders calls for reinterpretation of the firm's mission, goals, and strategies, because each stakeholder group seeks to obtain different interests from the firm (for example, for shareholders to receive maximum returns on their investments, for customers who value goods and service, and for employees who value good compensation and work life). Another important perceptional change occurring is the notion of competition, which is more global but can exist along with cooperation. Cooperating with your own rivals was unthinkable in the past. Nevertheless, interfirm competition still exists, and the firm thrives to accomplish its strategic and operational goals in the most effective and efficient manner so that it can cope with its competition. Thus, TCE focuses, for example, on minimizing transaction costs for the firm in its business activities with other actors in the marketplace while IO aptly portrays the important role of industry structure and the firm's response to it. On the other hand, the game theory highlights the duality of competition and coop-

eration but reconciles them in its latest interpretations. Moreover, RBV signifies holding a bundle of unique, scarce, immobile, and inimitable resources
and competencies for the company. Furthermore, knowledge theory specifically refers the critical role of knowledge transfer and creation in interfirm
cooperation.

Table 2.1

Major Theories and Their Relevance to Strategic Alliances

Theories	Basic Tenets	Relevance to Alliances
Transaction Cost Economics (internalization theory)	Minimizing transaction cost; choosing the most efficient mode between market or hierarchy; market failure leads to hierarchy in which asset specificities are important	Strategic alliance might be the most efficient mode; joint ventures are quasi-internalization
Industrial Organization	Firm performance is predicted by industry properties. Competitive advantage depends upon the firm's positioning itself in an industry	Coalitions could be advantageous; some dissolve early and some last longer; strategic flexibility is the source of advantage
Game Theory	Decision by one player depends on actual and anticipated decision of other; co-existence of competition and cooperation; opportunity for win-win	Learn fast and quit an alliance; in mutual assurance alliances, cooperation is an option providing long-term benefits; mutual gains
Resource-Based View	Competitive advantage depends upon possession of a bundle of unique, rare, durable, and inimitable resources; exploding such resources fully and building company resource base are important	Strategic alliances can be used to complement resources possessed or to acquire resources that are lacking; resource pooling is important
Knowledge Theory	Knowledge-creation, which leads to innovation which in turn leads to a competitive advantage; learning by combinative capabilities is important	Learning through strategic alliances; knowledge transfer between partners and then internalization of knowledge; building expertise in such knowledge transfers

Table 2.1
Continued.

Theories	Basic Tenets	Relevance to Alliances
Network Perspective	Focusing on networks rather than dyad and triad relationships and on resources, information, and power relations; the degree of exchange and dependence; resource commitment by members	Exchange resources; information and control benefits for members of a network

As demonstrated in Chapter 1, we live in a rapidly changing business environment that has a profound effect on the business practices as well as on the theory of the firm. Lately, the business environment and activities have been changing so fast that many of the theories offered have limitations in explaining the elements and dynamics of such ever-changing business practices. First, the very nature of the marketplace has become a state of flux and obscure. Where is the marketplace today? The distinction between the domestic and foreign market is unrealistic. A location-specific definition of the marketplace is outdated. The marketplace is probably global without geographical boundaries. Classical, nation-bound definitions of markets are no longer valid.

Second, the ways in which transactions are conducted are different from the traditional methods of doing business. Think of electronic commerce where several firms (product or service providers, Web page creators, online connectors, and so on) have to engage in cooperation even in cases that do not use money in transactions, buying clubs, online universities, virtual firms, and alliances between rivals. What theory could predict that firms will compete to offer free services (for example, free e-mail services and free personal Web space)? These are only a few examples of the recent developments in global business that have had a tremendous impact on the firm's strategies and customer behavior.

After all, we do not mean to claim that extant economic and business theories are obsolete. On the contrary, each throws light onto the behavior and dynamics of the firm. They need to be revised, however, or new or integrated theories and models need to be developed in light of the "new economy." Toward this end, we will offer an explanation—an integrative model—based on the premises of the previous theories and articulate it in the context of strategic alliances. Although the thrust of the integrative approach is combinative properties of the earlier theories, it is mostly based on RBV and knowledge management.

It is necessary to note that while cooperative business ventures date back many years, alliances formed in the past two decades show some unique characteristics. The early alliances were typically joint ventures between an MNC and a developing country's firm or state-owned enterprise; therefore, an MNC enters the host country market and bypasses restrictive local laws or simply acquires resources (for example, raw materials and labor). Usually, MNCs had dominated in such alliances, and from the MNC vantage point, the primary and preferred form was FDI. But the less-desirable form was international joint ventures. Therefore, it is not strange for internalization theory to primarily focus on FDI to explain the theory of MNCs. The theory makes sense in the context of such environmental conditions. As elucidated in Chapter 1, however, because of a new economy characterized by the liberalization of markets, formation of regional trading blocks, the advent of new technologies (the Internet, primarily), and the emergence of global competition, strategic alliances have changed significantly. While MNCs from industrialized countries have engaged in a variety of modes of cooperation, MNCs from developing economies have emerged to compete globally.

AN INTEGRATIVE MODEL

In developing their strategies, firms are keenly aware of the importance of the following actions: minimizing production and transaction costs and developing asset specificity but also choosing the most efficient mode; positioning themselves properly in the industry and using industry properties and flexibility for competitive advantage; benefitting from the opportunity of win-win scenarios and cooperating while competing; building the resource and competence base of the firm and transferring and creating knowledge; and exchanging resources and information with other firms. Of course, not all firms perform all these activities successfully. That is why we have successful and unsuccessful firms in the marketplace. Nonetheless, all these activities reflect the important dimensions emphasized by the different theories and models that we discussed. In other words, to be successful, firms should undertake those actions.

We must note, however, that the ultimate goal of the firm is to create value for its stakeholders. Such value creation can only be possible as result of incorporating those appropriate actions into its strategy and selecting a suitable business option or a combination of those options. Figure 2.1 depicts the integrative model incorporating the firm's basic mission, primary stakeholders, its strategy based on the combinative properties of earlier theories and models, and principal business options. The firm's underlying mission is to create value for its primary stakeholders. In doing so, it develops a business strategy that is supposed to be based on the premises of general theories. A firm's accomplishment in achieving all these dimensions will determine its success in generating value for its stakeholders. Because those premises reference each theory, we will not repeat them here. We must re-emphasize, however, that for a firm to meet the expectations of its stakeholders, it should make every effort to realize goals such as cost reductions, competitive advantage through industry analysis and assessment, cooperative and competitive moves for winning, resources development and deployment, organizational learning and knowledge creation, and building links with other organizations in exchanging resources and information. That is, all these vital dimensions should be incorporated into the firm's business strategy.

In accomplishing its business strategy, the firm generally has three strategic options including market transactions, organizational mode (internalization), and strategic alliances. The first two correspond to market and hierarchies in terms of TCE, and the third refers to hybrid structures or quasi-internalization. Nevertheless, these modes of transactions intermingle as firms use a variety of approaches simultaneously and switch from one form to another. Yet, knowing each type of strategic option well would enhance our understanding of business operations and their consequences.

MARKET TRANSACTIONS

Mostly, firms engage in contractual arrangements with other firms to conduct business in the marketplace. Instead of owning a supplier, retailer, or distributor or building a partnership, they might find that it is advantageous to have another party do other necessary activities in the value chain. As explained, the TCE theory makes a distinction between markets and hierarchies. Because contractual agreements involve transaction costs, firms are careful in signing such agreements. Nevertheless, most businesses are conducted on contractual basis because no company is capable of internalizing all the business transactions. The only thing the firm can do is try to control uncertainties and opportunistic behavior. For example, it carefully chooses its counterparts and specifies all the important details to prevent opportunistic behavior. Nonetheless, no matter how carefully the firm acts there is always room for vulnerabilities for a firm that engages in contractual deals. Hence, trustworthiness plays an important role in these kinds of transactions. The issues of control and trust are extremely important in market transactions.

Of course, firms will have many choices when they go to market and select the best deal—for example, the lowest price with the quality—instead of binding themselves to their own subsidiaries, which might produce a higher cost, lower quality, or delivering with long lead time. Back in 1982, Peter Drucker identified the opportunity: "Nowhere in business is there greater potential for benefiting from…interdependence than between customer, firms and their suppliers. This is the largest remaining frontier for gaining competitive advantage—and nowhere has such a frontier been more

Figure 2.1
Integrative model of the firm

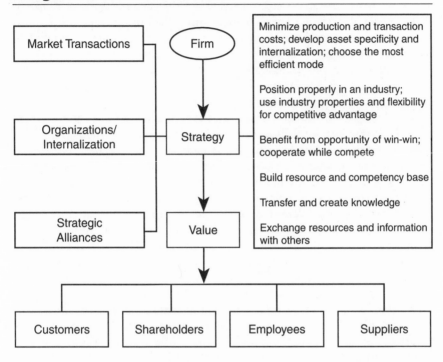

neglected." During the 1990s, this frontier has been discovered, and purchasing and logistics have emerged as a business area worthy of strategic attention. Currently, many producers have built close ties with their suppliers. In fact, the Japanese have often been cited for valuing supplier collaboration in achieving business success. The critical question is building a proper balance between cooperative relationships and developing its own capabilities (in other words, combining cooperative ventures with firm resources and capabilities leading to competitive advantage). Then, a firm has to determine when to cooperate and when to go alone. If it chooses to cooperate, it has to choose an appropriate mode of cooperation.

In this book, some contractual agreements are treated as strategic alliances when those agreements involve a long-term, continual strategic partnership and thereby provide strategic gains for partners. In other words, there might be an overlap between market transactions and strategic alliances. In this regard, one particular contractual agreement needs a special attention that is supplier agreements. A long-term and trust-based agreement between a manufacturer and supplier firm is considered a strategic alliance because it is beyond going to open market and choosing the best deal each time. As we will explain under supplier agreements, whenever manufacturers and suppliers develop a long-lasting, mutually rewarding relationship (for example, cost saving, consistency, and quality improvements for the manufacturer and stable sales and certainty for the suppliers), it is deemed a strategic alliance rather a routine market transaction.

INTERNALIZATION

As discussed, the internalizing advantage is commonly thought to arise from the existence of imperfect markets. When the contracting mechanism breaks down, the market cannot correctly value and protect firm-specific advantages that are intangible in nature. For example, the public nature of information makes it difficult to correctly value and protect intangible assets such as firm-specific R&D, brand reputation, process innovation, or tacit information. Moreover, writing and enforcing these contracts might be further complicated by the uncertainty surrounding future events, the existence of asymmetric information, or by a firm's exposure to opportunistic behavior. All these market conditions lead to the firm's internalization of a business activity within its command of hierarchy.

Additionally, firms tend to increase their assets because they are valued according to the size of their assets. The greater the size of the assets, the more valued the firm. By internalization, firms build both competitive posture and defense mechanisms against their competitors. An increasing number of mergers and acquisitions are indicators of the importance of this mode of business conduct. Another factor encouraging internalization is that it assures control over business operations. Control is one of the fundamental concerns of firms in securing sources, production and marketing operations, and financial activities. Through internalization, firms can exert control effectively.

STRATEGIC ALLIANCES

Although strategic alliances have often been used to refer to a variety of interfirm partnerships, a definition is introduced here with respect to a multinational strategic alliance. They refer to interfirm partnerships involving equity as well as non-equity collaboration among firms from different countries. Of course, this definition is generic and encompasses a variety of interfirm cooperation. Such partnership can range from supplier agreements to international joint ventures.

Although it is easy to differentiate strategic alliances from hierarchies (organizations), it is more complex to distinguish strategic alliances from market transactions. In the case of organizations, a firm expands vertically or horizontally by holding full ownership. A strategic alliance, on the other hand, means forming a long-term collaboration between at least two firms without one firm fully owning the other. Given numerous collaborative forms, the difference between market transactions and alliances is not that clear and might cause confusion or misunderstandings. After all, market transactions also occur between two firms by agreeing upon an exchange. Therefore, it becomes necessary to distinguish the two patterns of business conduct. In fact, strategic alliance and market transaction overlap in some cases while they present distinct differences in other cases. For example, how can a firm's agreement with its supplier be characterized? A strategic alliance should be defined distinctly to distinguish it from a market transaction. A strategic alliance presents two distinct properties: long-term commitment and contribution to strategic performance of the partnering firm(s). A supplier agreement is a strategic alliance when it provides long-term relations that can help build a sustainable competitive edge. For example, it is a typical marketing transaction when a manufacturing firm develops multiple supplier connections and often switches from one to another. On the other hand, a strategic alliance occurs when a manufacturing firm signs a long-term accord with a supplier with the intention of building a just-in-time inventory system and using it for its competitive advantage against its rivals.

From another perspective, because strategic alliances are considered hybrids, it is typical to see them carrying properties of either organizations or market contracts. Borys and Jemison viewed joint ventures, licensing agreements, and supplier arrangements as hybrid forms.[40] They define hybrids as organizational arrangements that use resources and/or governance structures from more than one existing organization. Of course, this definition of hybrid is so broad that it encompasses a range of organizational combinations of various sizes, shapes, and purposes—some of which are formal organizations (for example, a merger) whereas others are formalized relationships that are not properly organizations (for example, license agreements).[41] In this book, only hybrid structures such as equity and non-equity joint ventures are considered.

Strategic alliances can take various forms. They can be classified according to equity involvement in the partnership. Some alliances are equity collaboration while others do not involve any equity input. Equity alliances, in turn, can take two forms: the first is the most well-known form of strategic alliance, international joint venture (IJV). The second is equity participation by which a company owns certain shares of another company for the purpose of control or influence. On the other hand, non-equity alliances include a variety of contractual agreements consisting of technology agreement, R&D partnership, marketing agreements, supplier agreements, franchising, licensing, and production sharing. Here, strategic alliances are introduced as a mode of business conduct versus internalization and market transaction. We will describe each type of strategic alliance in the context of global business in Chapters 4 and 5.

While drawing such distinct modes would help us understand the alliance phenomenon clearly, it would not be realistic. In practice, in developing their strategies, firms often behave under uncertainty and consider multiple, ever-changing conditions. Therefore, a more realistic form would be a contingency approach by which firms, because of internal conditions such as resource and capability reservoirs and constraints and external conditions such as competition and regulations, seek a strategic fit between environmental opportunities and firm capabilities.

NOTES

1. Bruce Kogut, Joint ventures: Theoretical and empirical perspectives, *Strategic Management Journal* 94 (Winter 1988): 319–332.

2. For further discussions on theoretical bases of the firm, see the following. Transaction cost theory: O. E. Williamson, *Markets and hierarchies: Analysis and antitrust implications* (New York: Free Press, 1975). Game theory: Robert Axelrod, *The evolution of cooperation* (New York: Basic Book, 1984). Adam M. Brandenburger and Barry J. Nalebuff, *Co-opetition* (New York: Currency Doubleday, 1996). Resource-based view: Jay B. Barney, Firm resources and sustained competitive advantage, *Journal of Management*, 17 (1991): 99–120. M. A. Peteraf, The cornerstones of competitive advantage: A resource-based vie, *Strategic Management Journal* 24 no. 3 (1993): 179–191. B. Wernerfelt, A resource-based view of the firm, *Strategic Management Journal* 32 (1984): 1223–1230. Knowledge of the firm: B. Kogut and U. Zander, Knowledge of the firm and evolutionary theory of multinational corporation, *Organization Science* 3 (1992): 383–397.

3. Williamson, 24.

4. Kogut, 320.

5. O. E. Williamson, *The economic institutions of capitalism: Firms, markets, relational contracting* (New York: Free Press, 1985).

6. O. E. Williamson, Transaction cost economics, in R. D. W. Schmalensee, editor, *Handbook of Industrial Organization* (Amsterdam: North Holland, 1989).

7. For further elaboration on internalization theory, see Peter J. Buckley and Mark Casson, *The future of multinational enterprise* (London: Macmillan, 1978); and Peter J. Buckley, The limits of explanation: Testing the internalization theory of the multinational enterprise, *Journal of International Business Studies* 19, no. 2 (1988): 181–194.

8. See Paul W. Beamish and John C. Banks, Equity joint ventures and the theory of the multinational enterprise, *Journal of International Business Studies* 18, no. 2 (1987): 1–16. Jean-Francois Hennart, A transaction cost theory of equity joint ventures, *Strategic Management Journal* 9 (1988): 361–374.

9. J-F. Hennart, The transaction cost theory of joint ventures: An empirical study of Japanese subsidiaries in the United States, *Management Science* 37, no. 4 (1991): 483–497.

10. Ibid.

11. Beamish and Banks.

12. Ibid., 3–4.

13. M. E. Porter, *Competitive strategy* (New York: Free Press, 1980). M. E. Porter, *Competitive advantage* (New York: Free Press, 1985). K. R. Harrigan, *Strategic flexibility* (Lexington, MA: Heath, 1985). K. R. Harrigan, Joint ventures and competitive strategy, *Strategic Management Journal*, 9 (1988): 141–158.

14. Porter. 1980 and 1985.

15. M. E. Porter and M. B. Fuller, Coalitions and global strategy. In M. E. Porter (ed), *Competition in global industries* (Boston: Harvard Business School Press, 1986), 321.

16. Porter and Fuller, 329.

17. K. R. Harrigan, *Strategic flexibility* (Lexington, MA: Heath, 1985). K. R. Harrigan, Joint ventures and competitive strategy, *Strategic Management Journal*, 9 (1988): 141–158.

18. Axelrod, 16.

19. R. Johnston, and P. R. Lawrence, Beyond vertical integration—The rise of value added partnership, *Harvard Business Review* 66 (1988): 94–101.

20. Y. Doz, G. Hamel, and C. K. Prahalad, Cooperate with your competitors and win, *Harvard Business Review* 67 (1989): 133–139.

21. R. Gulati, and N. Nohria, "Mutually assured alliances," (working paper, Academy of Management Best papers Proceedings, Las Vegas, NV: August 9–12, 1992): 18.

22. Ibid., 19.

23. Ibid.

24. A. M. Brandenburger, and B. J. Nalebuff, *Co-opetition* (New York: Currency Doubleday, 1996).

25. See J. B. Barney, Firm resources and sustained competitive advantage, *Journal of Management* 17 (1991): 99–120. B. Wernerfelt, A resource-based view of the firm, *Strategic Management Journal* 32 (1984): 1223–1230.

26. Although firm capabilities and competencies are different from firm resources, I consider competency-based view a derivative of resource-based view.

27. C. K. Prahalad, and Gary Hamel, The core comptence of the corporation, *Harvard Business Review* (May–June 1990): 79–91.

28. R. Culpan (ed), *Multinational strategic alliances* (New York: International Business Press, 1993).

29. I. Nonaka, The knowledge-creating company, *Harvard Business Review* (November–December, 1991).

30. M. Polanyi, *The tacit dimension* (New York: Anchor Day Books, 1966). Also I. Nonaka and H. Takeuchi, *The knowledge-creating company* (Oxford, England: The Oxford University Press, 1991).

31. I. Nonaka, and H. Takeuchi, *The knowledge-creating company: How Japanese companies create the dynamics of innovation* (Oxford, England: The Oxford University Press, 1995), 72.

32. B. Kogut, and U. Zander, Knowledge of the firm and evolutionary theory of multinational corporation, *Organization Science* 3 (1992): 384.

33. A. C. Inkpen, A examination of knowledge management in international joint ventures, in P. W. Beamish and J. P. Killing (eds.), *Cooperative strategies: North American perspective* (San Francisco, CA: New Lexington Press, 1977), 337–369.

34. E. R. Auster, The interorganizational environment: Network theory, tools, and applications, in F. Williams and D. Gibson, *Technology transfer: A communication perspective* (Sage Publications, Newbury Park, CA, 1990): 67.

35. N. M. Tichy, M. L. Tushman, and C. Fombrun, Social network analysis for organizations, *Academy of Management Review* 9 no. 4 (1979): 507–519.

36. Auster, 69.

37. Auster, 70.

38. R. Gulati, Alliances and networks, *Strategic Management Journal* 19 (1998): 293–317.

39. R. S. Burt, *Structural holes: The social structure of competition* (Cambridge, MA: Harvard University Press, 1992).

40. B. Borys, and D. B. Jemison, Hybrid arrangements as strategic alliances: Theoretical issues in organizational combinations, in R. Culpan (ed.), *Multinational strategic alliances* (New York: International Business Press, 1993): 33–58.

41. Ibid., 34.

3

International Business Strategy and Alliances

A business strategy reflects managerial choices among different alternatives and signals organizational commitment to particular products, markets, competitive approaches, and ways of operating the enterprise. When firms formulate their business strategies, they define their objectives while considering their resources and capabilities.

Additionally, they respond to the opportunities and constraints in the marketplace. Hence, it is important to understand the driving forces of the competitive environment. In this chapter, we will first define the new competitive dynamics by referring to theoretical and practical considerations with some examples. Second, we will review principal international business strategies. Third, we will introduce a new international business strategy model that embraces the significant characteristics of the previous models in business literature.

THE NEW COMPETITIVE DYNAMICS

The new competitive dynamics refer to forces that shape today's business rivalries. Rapidly changing market conditions (and accordingly, emerging business philosophy) form the new competitive dynamics, which are knowledge-based and global in nature and require continuous improvements in every facet of the value chain and seeking opportunities worldwide. As technology and the globalization of business advance with unprecedented speed and magnitude, firms in almost all industries—traditional and emerging—are engaging in unorthodox competitive modes. This new competitive mode requires product and process innovation, quick responses, and high customer service while maneuvering between competition and cooperation. Some of the similar concepts with the new competitive dynamics are called "the new competitive landscape" and "hypercompetition" in business literature.[1] First, we will briefly delineate these similar concepts and then illustrate the distinct characteristics of the new competitive dynamics.

According to Hitt and his colleagues, the new competitive landscape is shaped by technological changes and the global economy.[2] They noted rapid technological changes and technology diffusion, dramatic changes in information technology, and an increasing importance of knowledge. Additionally, they characterized the global economy with free movement of goods, services, and labor across geographical borders, emerging opportunities in multiple global markets, and internationalization of markets and industries. Although the world economy has not fully reached the free movement of production factors across nations, establishment of regional economic integrations and economic liberation movements worldwide have helped substantially in changing the current global economy. In response to these global economic conditions, firms are in the midst of a revolutionary transformation from industrial-age competition to information-age competition.

Similarly, D'Aveni called the rapidly changing nature of new competition "hypercompetition," which "results from dynamics of strategic maneuvering among global and innovative combatants. It is a condition of rapidly escalating competition based on price-quality positioning, competition to create new know-how and established first-mover advantage, competing to protect or invade established product or geographic markets, and competition based on deep pockets and the creation of even deeper pocketed alliances."[3] As discussed previously, while hypercompetition occurs among rival firms, cooperation happens between or among rival and complementary firms. This competition and cooperation coexistence is one of the dominant elements of the new competitive dynamics as explained in the previous chapters.

After close examination, new competitive dynamics demonstrate several essential characteristics that are interdependent. We can describe them as follows:

a) Rapid changes in competitive base. Today, a competitive edge gained in a given business will not hold long unless the firm continuously innovates it and launches new products and creates market niches. A fast slip of competitive advantage gained over the years is making firms nervous and is forcing them to initiate new alternatives.

A new business undertaking such as a merger, acquisition, or alliance in the competitive landscape can impact the competitive behavior of other players. One move by one or two major players influences the existing competition pattern in that industry. For example, the merger of America Online (AOL) and Time Warner has major reverberations for all online companies.

This merger might lead to possible new acquisitions or partnerships; more mergers between delivery companies such as Yahoo! and content companies such as Walt Disney; more deals to extend broadband service to other platforms beyond cable, such as interactive television; and launching new portals to broadband service.

b) Consolidations. The past decade has witnessed an increasing number of consolidations among firms in various industries. Many firms worldwide have been seeking scale advantages by combining forces. Mergers and acquisitions have become indispensable business strategies of firms. DaimlerChrysler in automobile manufacturing, Glaxo Wellcome and SmithKline Beecham in pharmaceuticals, and Time Warner and EMI in music recording are only few examples of mergers and acquisitions seeking cost savings from consolidations while building market power and competitive advantage.

In general, the reasons for mergers and acquisitions include achieving competitive advantages through market power, overcoming barriers to entry, increasing the speed of market entry, the significant cost involved in developing new products, avoiding the risk of new product development, achieving diversification, and finally avoiding competition.[4] Although small and medium-size firms with product and market niches continue to compete in domestic and global markets, they will have a rough time against mega companies that have plenty of resources. Under the pressure of global competition, the next decade will more likely see the continuation of mergers and acquisitions across nations in a variety of industries.

Increasing consolidations in the business world do not mean that there is no room for medium and small-size companies. But it means that giant companies will make it very hard for medium and small-size companies to compete in the global marketplace unless those companies have their product and market niches or are in alliances with others. This situation has been true for years; however, there would be more pressure on medium and small-size companies even threatening their existence. The incredible expansion of giant retailer Wal-Mart and the mergers of Exxon and Mobile, British Petroleum and Amoco, and Mercedes-Benz and DaimlerChrysler are examples of such developments.

c) Globalization. As described in Chapter 1, a number of factors including the emergence of regional economic integrations such as the European Union (EU) and North American Free Trade Agreement (NAFTA), the economic progress in newly industrialized countries such as Brazil, Taiwan, Turkey, and South Korea, the transformation of economies from a command to a market economy in Russia, Poland, Hungary, the Czech Republics, and Romania, the liberalization of the economy in China, and the privatization of state-owned enterprises in both developed and developing countries have intensified the globalization of business. Many companies today strive for business opportunities not only in a few countries but also worldwide. To achieve strategic competitiveness in the global economy, a firm must view the world as its marketplace. For example, companies such as Procter & Gamble and Toyota believe that they still have the potential to grow internationally, where the demand for their products is not as mature as in developed countries.

Globalization is related to scale economies (discussed previously). Firms are trying to tap market opportunities in huge markets such as China, India, Indonesia, and Russia. For example, Wal-Mart—after its expansion in Latin America and Europe—is now eager to enter the Chinese market. "Others are venturing in China as well ranging from Motorola's $2 billion fabrication plant to joint venture between Enron and Singapore Power."[5] A close look at Fortune 500 companies shows that most of these companies that have operations in numerous countries generate a substantial portion of their revenues from overseas sales. In fact, today it is futile to talk about domestic firms anymore. Even companies that are bounded to only their local markets are subject to foreign competition (that is, if companies are not international but the business competition is). In fact, many firms such as McDonald's, Coca-Cola, Procter & Gamble, Nestle, ABB, Honda, Toyota, and DaimlerChrysler have commitments in so many markets around the world that they should be thought of as global players.

Global competition has improved product quality and customer service while reducing the prices of many products and services. The world consumers have been the final beneficiaries of the global competition. Without global competition, global consumers would not be enjoying Internet services, mobile phones, and broadcasting news—not to mention basic consumer goods that were only available to the consumers of industrial countries. It is interesting to see a porter or a street vendor in a developing country using a mobile phone when having a telephone had been a luxury for a long time. The competition among Ericsson, Nokia, and Motorola has enabled the spread of mobile phone services into markets where (with the wiring connections) it was impossible to provide such a service.

In a more interconnected world, firms not only from developed countries but also from third-world countries have joined international competition. Multinational firms from developing economies have emerged by making investments in even industrialized countries. For example, Petroleos de Venezuela has made major investments in North America, and similarly, Cemetex of Mexico has acquired cement plants in the United States.

   d) Operating in hybrid industries. Because of the advent of new technologies and emerging products and services, boundaries of a single industry have become blurred. The best example of this mix is telephone, cable, and television industries. With the addition of Internet providers, this relationship will become more intermingled. Even the most traditional industries, such as automotive and medical, have been influenced by a number of emerging industries such as computers, robots, and lasers. As a result, it is timely to recognize some industries as "hybrid industries."

In particular, the Internet blurs the boundaries between companies and industries. Information and entertainment industries and companies in such industries illustrate the point well. For example, Yahoo! started as a Web search engine, but now it offers so many diverse functions including a broad-paced online shopping site. Similarly, under what industry can Microsoft or AOL be classified? The giant Microsoft is rapidly diversifying itself into a number of industries, ranging from telecommunications to financial, through acquisitions and alliances.

e) Strategic alliances. As we explained, both academics and managers consider that cooperation is no longer incompatible with competition. In other words, competition and cooperation can coexist. Raymond Noorda, former chief executive of Novell, coined the term "co-opetition" for this emerging development. Barr J. Nalebuff and Adam M. Brandenburger used it for the title of their 1996 book.[6] Currently, the phenomenon seems to be spreading.

In fact, today's cooperation is part of the strategic repertoire of many firms. Firms use cooperation in a variety of ways and situations to build competitive edges. A close look at the relationship between competition and cooperation reveals that cooperative ventures can take various patterns; however, the most common ones are either a firm cooperating with its competitors or with complementary firms (for example, suppliers, distributors, and firms in related industries). In addition, the form of cooperation occurs in a several ways: (a) cooperate first, compete later, (b) cooperate while competing, and (c) cooperating among themselves and competing with outsiders.[7]

Cooperate first, then compete. When companies feel that they need to build their competitive strengths first, before full-fledged competition, they seek the cooperation of others. Partnering firms cooperate to expand the market, and then they can compete to earn their own shares. As Branderburger and Nalebuff recognized, there is a transformation of the economic infrastructure that presents a too-big problem for any company to solve.[8] Hence, firms can cooperate to create value.

Often, a firm finds out that developing a new technology might require acquiring resources and capabilities beyond its own or establishing an industry standard during the technology- or product-development phase. Then, it welcomes the participation of competing firms in a strategic alliance (for example, a technology development consortium). Indeed, many R&D partnerships represent these kinds of collaborations. Resource pooling among pharmaceutical firms enables them to jointly work on formidable new drug discoveries while they reduce the risk of project failure.

Cooperate while competing. Firms can compete and cooperate simultaneously. This simultaneous "competition-cooperation" mode has become common in the automobile manufacturing industry. General Motors and Toyota, for instance, despite their NUMMI joint venture, compete with each other worldwide. Likewise, Ford and Mazda continue to compete while they cooperate in many ways. Such collaborations capitalize on the exchange of know-how and "tacit technology." This mode of cooperation, however, is not unique to the automobile industry.

Facing rising product-development costs, six of the world's largest semiconductor manufacturers joined forces to develop new technology for the most common type of memory chip used inside personal computers. The six companies consist of the Intel Corporation and Micron Technology of the United States, NEC of Japan, Samsung Electronics and Hyundai Electronics of South Korea, and Infenion Technologies AG, a unit of Germany's Siemens. The group—excluding Intel, which mainly makes microprocessors—accounts for about 70 percent of the global market for dynamic random access memory (DRAM). That market reached $21 billion in 1999.

The companies thought this unusually broad alliance should be more cost effective than going alone. The accord refers to a goal of developing high-performance, advanced DRAM technology for the marketplace in 2003. This accord would provide information to facilitate the development of related PC components such as a chipset, which acts as an intermediary between DRAM and the central processing unit (CPU). Consumer interest in high-performance PCs that provide advanced multimedia and graphics is pushing companies to develop higher-speed CPUs that require more powerful yet affordable DRAM chips.

By working on technology that will be in the market in 2003, the alliance is trying to look beyond the current battle lines of industry competition. Each member of the alliance will commit a design team to the project, which will be overseen by a senior technology committee. This situation is an excellent example of how companies attempt to collaborate while they still compete. By pooling their resources, they can come up with advanced technology from which every participant can benefit.

In the same vein, there is a mutual interest of airlines for building an airport or trucking companies for building a highway. Until the facilities are built, they probably worked together to support such investments. But after the facilities are built, they might go their own ways in competing each other. In the early stage of industry development or crises in the industry (for example, the U.S. automobile manufacturers' campaign against Japanese exports to the United States and tobacco companies acting together to fight against anti-smoking litigations), such collaboration often emerges.

Cooperate among them but compete with outsiders. This kind of cooperation is common among companies in Japan, where interlocking among companies is allowed. Japanese *Keiretsu*, postwar corporate networks of interlocking affiliates, plays an important role in achieving synergies within the network while building a strong competitive front against rivals. "Unlike U.S. and European conglomerates, the hundreds of companies in each keitretsu are highly decentralized. While being separate and independent, they are part of an incredible communication network that allows them to cooperate with each other when there is a mutual advantage to do so."[9]

Mitsubishi and Sumitomo are examples of this Japanese form of conglomerates. Mitsubishi Group, for example, holds 28 core members and hundreds of other Mitsubishi-related companies. Within the Mitsubishi family of companies, because its infrastructure is already built, there is an expectation for cooperation among family members, whether drinking Kirin beer, using a Nikon camera, or buying insurance from Meiji Mutual.

Unlike the U.S. conglomerates, which accent financial management, Keiretsu are oriented to cooperate in accord with whatever contribution a family member can make to help the other family member. Business units may be cooperating as suppliers of parts, lenders of capital, contributors of production know-how, or providers of access to markets. All these happen quietly. It takes a lot of digging to find out who is supplying what to whom. Even then, many of the arrangements cannot be uncovered. Most of the agreements will never be known. Keiretsu behavior epitomizes cooperation based on mutual advantage. Keiretsus actively seek out joint ventures with a broad range of partners, all over the world.[10]

Similar to Japanese Keiretsu, South Korean firms have their own conglomerates called Chaebols, which function in the same fashion. Although many conglomerates also exist in the United States and Europe, their structure and operations are different from the Keiretsus in terms of building intense cooperation among family members. Antitrust laws in the United States do not allow such close knitting within the same corporation when it hinders the competition in the marketplace.

We can see another form of building a network of cooperation in the Internet industry. Some of the leading Internet firms are creating Internet "ecosystems." They evolve together, sometimes linked by cross holding, and continually pull more companies into their orbits. For example, Softbank of Japan holds more than 120 Internet investments. Softbank brings a new company, such as Webhire, into the fold and blends it with a more established asset, such as Yahoo!, in which Softbank holds a stake of 23 percent. Softbanks can be deemed today's Internet *zaibatsu*, referring to several powerful companies in prewar Japan that had strong intragroup ties.

This kind of Internet cooperation is sometimes called "Netbatsu" because it combines the words Internet and Zaibatsu. Internet moguls in action today remind us of this powerful model. The American version of Netbatsu is Safeguard Scientific, which operates in Internet-related areas such as software, communications, and services by compromising partner companies and incubating companies.

The second form of interfirm collaboration embraces cooperation between a focal firm and its complementary players. In recent years, the most common ones include agreements between manufacturer-supplier and pharmaceutical and biotechnology companies. To avoid the high inventory cost and to benefit from quality improvements and speedy deliveries of components and raw materials, manufacturers have developed long-range relationships with their suppliers. For example, automotive and PC manufacturers have benefitted greatly from close ties with suppliers. Today, in developing new drugs, more and more pharmaceutical companies rely on biotechnology companies. We will describe this notion of cooperation in more detail when we introduce different forms of alliances in Chapters 4 and 5.

After defining new market dynamics worldwide, we find it useful to focus on major global business strategies proposed in business literature.

GLOBAL BUSINESS STRATEGIES

By realizing the importance of global business, many firms have developed business strategies to respond to market opportunities around the world. There is inflation in terminology describing such business endeavors of firms, however, including terms such as international, multinational, multidomestic, global, and transnational strategy. We will define major categories of business strategies first and then choose appropriate ones for strategic alliances in constructing the "global business model" in the next section.

Company Orientations

Howard V. Perlmutter, in his often-cited article, presented that corporate attitudes determine the strategic orientation of the firm in its international business.[11] He identified three basic strategic predispositions: ethnocentrism, polycentrism, and geocentrism. Although they cannot be viewed as international business strategies per se, they can be accepted as the mindsets or attitudes of management of the firm that influence the type of business strategy that is adopted. Hence, they warrant our attention.

Ethnocentrism refers to an inclination where the parent company steers all strategic decisions while subsidiaries have little to say about strategic directions. The parent company believes that what works domestically works internationally as well; therefore, there is no need to change the business practices that have proven successful for each country's market. The ethnocentric firm is predominantly concerned with its legitimacy only in its home country and with its viability worldwide. From a strategic alliance perspective, these kinds of firms are the least likely to adopt collaborative patterns because they strongly believe in their superiority and do not wish to share it with another firm.

Polycentrism, on the other hand, is a position where the MNC adopts its practices according to the needs of a foreign market. In other words, the MNC customizes its products and operations to suit the market conditions of various countries. In other words, a polycentric multinational is responsive to the local market conditions and is willing to make necessary changes to meet particular needs of the market. Such a firm is primarily concerned with its legitimacy in every country in which it operates. The polycentric firm is open for strategic alliances as a multinational business strategy when the MNC recognizes that local responsiveness is the key to success.

Finally, geocentrism means a situation where the MNC headquarters and subsidiaries across nations are viewed as a single system. Strategic decisions are made at the parent company and its subsidiaries after considering their overall effect on the entire company. Although a geocentric firm focuses on worldwide opportunities and threats, it pays attention to the needs of the host country as well. The incentive system adopted by the MNC encourages the subsidiary managers not only to consider the interest of their own subsidiaries but also to think about the interests of the entire company. The geocentric orientation welcomes strategic alliances more than ethnocentric and polycentric orientations because of its worldwide view and network philosophy.

Although Perlmutter's characterization of the MNC orientations is useful in understanding the attitudes of managers in making decisions in international contexts, it does not specify dynamic elements of international business strategy. Of course, the value orientations of managers and company culture are important determinants of strategy formulation and implementation, but it is necessary to clearly define the bases of international business. A strategy development in competitive context usually rests upon either industry analysis (industry characteristics and forces) or company analysis (firm resources and competencies).

Industry Typology

Based on an industry analysis, Porter introduced an important taxonomy of patterns of international competition by distinguishing industries as *multidomestic* or *global*. In a multidomestic industry, competition in each country is essentially independent of competition in other countries.[12] Multidomestic industries such as retailing, consumer packaged goods, distribution, insurance, consumer finance, and caustic chemicals exist in many countries, but the common and dominant characteristic of these industries is that competition occurs on a country-by-country basis. Competitive advantage of the firms is largely specific to each country. Porter tied the firm's strategy to industry structure and characteristics, corresponding with firms competing internationally, but multidomestic industries follow a multidomestic strategy that requires the firm's transfer of knowledge to its subsidiaries. Then, each subsidiary runs its operations autonomously because each country presents unique market characteristics. In other words, the firm's international strategy is a "country-centered strategy" based on the circumstances in that country. In pursuing multidomestic strategy, a firm can and should manage its international business activities like a portfolio. That is, each country is considered a profit center.

On the other extreme, global industry refers to the industry in which a firm's competitive position in one country is significantly influenced by its position in other countries. "Therefore, the international industry is not merely collection of domestic industries but a series of linked domestic industries in which the rivals compete each other on a truly worldwide basis. Industries exhibiting the global pattern today include commercial aircraft, TV sets, semiconductors, copiers, automobiles, and watches."[13] Firms operating in such global industries are recommended to pursue global business strategy instead of multidomestic strategy. A global strategy can capture competitive advantages for the firm by integrating its activities on a worldwide basis. In global strategy implementation, the headquarters play a dominant and central role to provide standardized policies and coordination. Of course, a global strategy does not totally ignore a country's specific needs, but it tries to establish a balance between worldwide standardization, coordination, and local responsiveness.

According to Porter, a firm's international strategy can be examined in two key dimensions.[14] The first is *configuration* of the firm's activities worldwide—in other words, where to locate the firm's various activities in the value chain (the concentration or dispersion of activities geographically). "Configuration options range from concentrated (performing an activity in one location and serving the world from it—for example, one R&D lab, one large plant) to disperse (performing every activity in each country)."[15] The second is *coordination* of activities performed in different countries. The coordination option ranges from none to high, giving full autonomy to its subsidiaries in each country to tightly coordinating value activities by adopting the same procedures and systems in each operational location. These combinations of configuration and coordination yield different types of international strategies: (1) a geographically disperse configuration and high coordination call for high foreign investment with extensive coordination among subsidiaries; (2) geographically disperse coordination and low coordination request a country-centered strategy by multinationals with a number of domestic firms operating in only one country; (3) geographically concentrated configuration and high coordination need the purest global strategy; and (4) geographically concentrated configuration and low coordination match the export-based strategy with decentralized marketing.

Company Taxonomy

Based on organizational capabilities and strategic mentality, Bartlett and Ghoshal presented four distinct strategic orientations: international, multi-

Figure 3.1
Four strategic mentalities

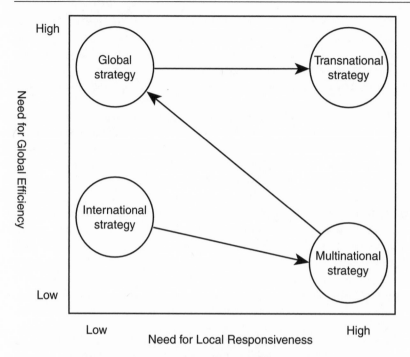

Adapted from C. A. Bartlett and S. Ghoshal, *Transitional Management* (New York: McGraw-Hill, 1992).

national, global, and transnational.[16] They argued that MNCs have different strategic positions, organizational structures, and management processes—not necessarily reflecting dominant industry characteristics. They also asserted that there has been an evolving mentality from international to transnational companies as a result of changes in the international business environment and in MNCs. Their analysis is based on two major dimensions: global efficiency and integration and local responsiveness. Accordingly, Figure 3.1 depicts the four stages of mentalities in these two dimensions.

International mentality reflects the managerial thinking of the company's overseas operations as some kind of extension of its domestic operations, which are to be supported. Hence, overseas operations are designed to contribute the sales of the domestic product lines or supplying raw materials or components to the domestic operations. Products are initially developed for the domestic market, but eventually they are marketed internationally because of foreign demands for the products. For overseas production, technology and know-how are transferred from the parent company to the overseas subsidiaries. Manufacturing abroad is considered a defensive move to protect the domestic market.

Companies that have this kind of mentality view the domestic market as the primary market but perceive overseas markets as appendages. As a result, the parent company dictates the strategic directions by providing the blueprints for policies and operational guidelines and assigning expatriate managers to overseas posts. Strategic decisions concerning foreign operations tend to be made opportunistically or on an ad-hoc basis.

A *multinational company* means that a company recognizes the importance of overseas markets and makes a greater commitment than an international company by considering local market peculiarities. This type of firm leverages foreign market opportunities by responding to the needs of the local market while it faces local competition. Consequently, it adjusts its strategy, products, and even management practices country by country. Its fundamental strategy evolves around having a number of national subsidiaries sensitive and responsive to each national market. As an extension of this strategic approach, each subsidiary is run autonomously by making its own entrepreneurial decisions concerning the new initiatives.

A multinational company is synonymous with Porter's multidomestic company—a firm operating in a multidomestic industry (as defined previously). Therefore, sometimes the terms multinational and multidomestic are used interchangeably.

A *global company*, on the other hand, emphasizes production efficiency rather than responsiveness to the local market. This type of company exploits the scale economy advantages by making and selling products worldwide. While multinational orientation increases the number of product offerings in each country's market, it leads to losses in efficiency in functional areas such as design, production, logistics, and distribution. As a result of viewing the entire world as a single market, some MNCs (for example, Japanese companies) have developed products for the world market and manufacture them on a global scale. To achieve worldwide efficiency, a global company sets up its production facilities in selected countries and distributes its products across countries. The underlying assumption of the global company is that worldwide consumer demand is similar, and therefore there is no need to modify its product country by country.

A *transnational company* refers to a company that combines both the benefits of production efficiency and local responsiveness. This type of company aims at accomplishing production efficiency while making necessary changes in product design, manufacturing, and distribution because of the local market conditions. That is, it combines multinational and global strategic mentalities into a single strategic orientation. Bartlett and Ghoshal professed that a number of factors have contributed to the emergence of transnational patterns: host government demands, consumer behavior, and volatility in international economic and political environments.[17] Many host governments have developed an opposition to export-oriented strategies of global companies and imposed on them increasing constraints. They have often requested MNCs to transfer capital and technology and to create employment in host countries. Additionally, consumers—without giving up on high quality and low cost—have expected homogeneous products for their needs. Finally, volatility in economic and political environments has increased considerably. Particularly rapid changes in exchange rates have had a negative impact on the performance of companies engaged in a centralized global strategy. All these conditions together called for a new approach toward a transnational solution combining the characteristics of multinational and global companies. Although some of the requirements of multinational and global strategies are incompatible, companies such as transnational firms are the ones that can respond effectively to this challenge.

Although Bartlett and Ghoshal's typology of international, multinational, global, and transnational strategic mentalities academically sounds good and grasps the evolution of mindsets of managers in internationalization process and strategy development, as the authors admitted, it is necessarily over-generalized and undoubtedly somewhat arbitrary. In practice, of many companies that have international operations, only a few fall into the purely international, multinational, global, or transnational categories. Attributes of international companies are often so diverse and complex that it becomes difficult to categorize them appropriately.

INTERNATIONAL BUSINESS STRATEGY MODEL

After reviewing major typologies of international business strategies, we would like to offer an integrative model that not only combines fundamental characteristics of some of the earlier approaches but also specifies the role of strategic alliances. Our key premise is that the firm basically offers products and/or services for customers located in different markets by managing a variety of value chain activities through one or a combination of modes: market contracts, internalization, or alliances. In other words, there are three principal modes of operation for the firm: (1) market mode highlighting country-specific or worldwide focus; (2) product mode comprising the firm's product (here, the product is used in a broad sense and covers services as well) and value chain activities; and (3) business conduct mode referring to principal business options. In fact, the firm's strategy reflects how it engages in these three modes (refer to Figure 3.2). Then, international business strategy of the firm can be analyzed in terms of these three modes of market, product and value chain activities, and business conduct—which can involve different emphasis or combinations. Essentially, a domestic or international firm should make decisions on what to produce, how to carry out its value chain activities, for whom to sell, and how to proceed with its transactions in

Figure 3.2

International business strategy model

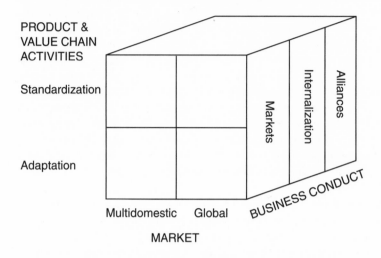

PRODUCT &
VALUE CHAIN
ACTIVITIES

Standardization

Adaptation

Markets   Internalization   Alliances

Multidomestic   Global   BUSINESS CONDUCT

MARKET

the marketplace. They all should be thought of simultaneously, rather than sequentially, and should be synchronized. Hence, there is no priority placed on any of them, but it is accepted that they are interdependent and inter-twined. It is not possible, for example, to isolate a product decision from selections of country markets or the pattern in which business will be con-ducted. Obviously, there are alternatives that exist to choose in each mode, as depicted in Figure 3.2. The following model shows how each mode and its alternative uses shape international business strategy. Because we discussed market dimension and process mode in detail previously, we will place more emphasis on product and value chain functions.

We must note that the choice between global or multidomestic strategy refers to decision making at the corporate level while the decision preference concerning product and value chain activities is made at business unit levels. In business conduct mode, however, the choices could be made both at cor-porate as well as business unit levels.

Market Mode: Global versus Multidomestic

Although we previously defined different forms of international strategies, firms essentially have to choose between two basic patterns—global and multidomestic—when it comes to managing different countries' markets. As we explained earlier, while a multidomestic strategy is based on the notion that each country presents unique characteristics so that the MNC's major responsibility is to respond to those special market needs, global strategy concerns itself with production efficiency worldwide. Managerial implications of each strategy are different: multidomestic strategy requires independently run subsidiaries in each country to determine their own strategies concerning production and marketing, whereas global strategy entails an integration of all subsidiaries across countries so that it can gain scale economies through a network of country units.

Environmental conditions usually influence the formation of a corporate strategy. In other words, there must be a fit between the market environment and corporate strategy, and internationalization strategy is no exception to this general rule. There might be forces for localization or globalization. Forces for localization still include the existence of trade restrictions, cultural differences, nationalistic sentiments, organizational culture, and emerging technologies.

Trade restrictions. Despite the widespread liberalization movements of international trade, a large number of countries still impose some restrictions on the free flow of goods and services across their borders. Although tariff restrictions worldwide have generally been lowered, non-tariff barriers have been hindrances to trade liberalization. Of non-tariff barriers, subsidies are the most commonly used form in distorting the world's free trade. Even the most liberalized economies such as the United States and the EU continue to enjoy some sorts of subsidies. Likewise, developing economies heavily use subsidies to protect their domestic industries, thereby hurting fair competition in the domestic market.

Cultural differences. Cultural differences often lead to special consumer preferences. Tradition, cultural values, and religious beliefs often influence consumer behavior. Typical examples of such religious values can be observed in Judaism and Islam, which prohibit eating pork, and Hinduism, which considers cows sacred (and therefore bans eating beef). Similarly, the buying behaviors of extended families and nuclear families present essential differences. A strict global strategy overlooks such differences in consumer tastes and behaviors in various countries.

Nationalistic sentiments. People might also present differences in terms of their national loyalties to local products. Such nationalistic product loyalties vary from one nation to another. Japanese and Korean consumers, for example, tend to buy domestic products while American consumers pay less attention to the national origin of the product. Especially during the periods of political tensions and crises, nationalistic consumers often boycott the products coming from an unfriendly country. The rise of such nationalistic sentiments can deter globalization.

Organizational culture and behavior. In addition to macroenvironmental factors, organizational culture and behavior might constrain globalization.

As explained earlier, the global strategy requires central control over subsidiary operations whereas some subsidiary managers would not like the headquarters' strict control. Typical American managers tend to enjoy more autonomy in running their units than typical Japanese managers do. From a company's perspective, if a company's heritage entrenched an autonomous management style, it would be difficult to change that culture for a central control.

Emerging technologies. As argued in Chapter 1, new technologies can be instrumental for globalization and at the same time be driving forces for localization. Emerging technologies such as computer-aided design and flexible manufacturing have helped shorten product design time and produce multiple products in the same manufacturing plant. New technologies in some industries with small production runs can be accomplished without incurring high costs. Customization can be achieved more easily in small production runs than through large-batch production.

All these forces call for localization. When such market conditions prevail, globalization might not be feasible. Consequently, it would be better for the MNC to follow a multidomestic strategy that enables the adaptation of products and services to local markets. Then, the company would be better responsive to the needs of local consumers.

Nonetheless, forces also exist for globalization in world markets. Because we discuss them in Chapter 1, it is only sufficient to reiterate them here. Such forces comprise economic liberalizations across nations, the dispersal of technologies worldwide, consumer exposure and reach, and competitive pressure. It is true that many countries have realized the benefits of a liberal economy, and consequently the movement toward a free market economy has accelerated in recent years. Additionally, technological advances (such as e-mail, e-conferences, and other Internet technologies) have enabled companies to communicate with their subsidiaries quickly and easily. Moreover, consumers worldwide have been exposed to similar products and services and can shop online. Finally, both MNCs and domestic companies face stiff competition even in small countries. No country's market is sheltered from an international competition that drives players to reduce the cost of production and marketing and to improve the quality of products and services. Refer to Figure 3.3.

Global strategy is adopted to achieve a number of intermediate goals, such as a global scale in value chain activities, an experience curve effect, and the location of production and distribution facilities in selected countries. The ultimate goal of global strategy, however, is global efficiency—which can be achieved through realizing the intermediate goals and setting up an organizational structure and managing integrated subsidiaries with central coordination and control. Refer to Table 3.1 for a comparison of multidomestic and global strategies.

Figure 3.3
Countervailing forces for globalization and localization

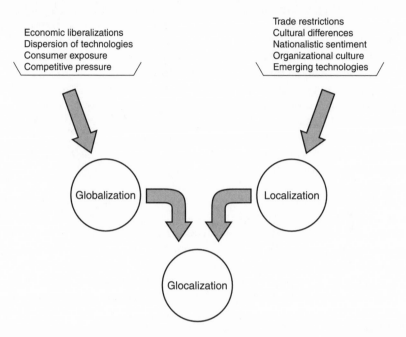

Economic liberalizations
Dispersion of technologies
Consumer exposure
Competitive pressure

Trade restrictions
Cultural differences
Nationalistic sentiment
Organizational culture
Emerging technologies

Globalization

Localization

Glocalization

Table 3.1
A Comparison of Global and Multidomestic Strategies

STRATEGIES	UNDERLYING ASSUMPTIONS	APPROACHES	ORGANI-ZATIONAL STRUCTURE	ULTIMATE GOALS
Globalization	Market focus: The whole world; global consumers have similar demands and preferences	Global scale; experience curve effect; selected production locations	Integrated subsidiaries; central coordi-nation and control	Global efficiency
Multidomestic	Market focus: each country; each national market has its unique features; national markets are different	Modified products and services; effective marketing; flexibility in operations	A cluster of autonomous subsidiaries	Local responsive-ness

According to Porter, one of the implications of globalization is a coalition among firms.[18] A coalition refers to a variety of arrangements that include joint ventures, licenses, supply agreements, and many other kinds of inter-firm relationships. "International coalitions are a way of configuring activities in the value chain on a worldwide basis jointly with a partner...The difficulties of gaining access to foreign markets and surmounting scale and learning thresholds in production, technology development, and other activities have led many firms team up with others."[19]

Having strategic alliances, we believe, is not restricted to only global strategy—but multidomestic strategy as well might justify a partnership with others. Especially, in the case of a partnership between an MNC and a domestic company or between two MNCs, one partner's familiarity with the local market could increase the chances of the alliance's responsiveness to the national market. That is, alliances might occur in either strategy, multidomestic or global.

A close examination of both global and multidomestic strategies reveals that they have both advantages and disadvantages. As demonstrated earlier, while global strategy exploits worldwide efficiency in operations, multido-mestic strategy is suitable for local responsiveness. On the other hand, one's benefit is another's deficiency; that is, the former ignores responsiveness to the local market while the latter overlooks global efficiency considerations. Hence, an integrated strategy of both globalization and multidomestic strategies gives birth to the *glocalization strategy*, which means thinking glob-ally but acting locally. This concept "includes an optimal mix of parental control where it counts, and local initiative at regional and subsidiary lev-els."[20] Glocalization strategy probably corresponds to the *transnational solu-tion* of Bartlett and Ghoshal, as described earlier, which combines the benefits of global and multidomestic companies. International firms employ-ing glocalization mode must be careful that as they strive for worldwide effi-ciencies, they should equally pay attention to local market conditions that might require some adaptations in the products and services that the com-pany offers. Is such a strategic maturity and advancement achievable? Bartlett and Ghoshal thought so. Indeed, numerous companies have imple-mented glocalization. For example, a glocalization of strategic management is evident in the operations of Levi Strauss & Company, Sony, Toshiba, and Matsushita Electric Industrial.

Bartlett and Ghoshal asserted that the fundamental characteristic of a transnational company is simultaneously achieving global efficiency, national responsiveness, and the capability to develop and exploit knowledge on a worldwide basis.[21] Some critics, however, argue that such an integration of three goals is inherently unattainable because of irreconcilable contradictions among the three objectives. As a result, the critics recommended that the company should focus on one at a time. Nevertheless, Bartlett and Ghoshal insisted that the transnational company could overcome this challenge by configuring an integrated network, differentiating organizational roles and responsibilities, and managing multiple organizational processes.[22] In other words, the transnational company can make selective decisions to centralize certain resources and capabilities and decentralize others as market conditions require. These two scholars claimed that balancing different perspectives and capabilities, developing flexible coordinating processes, and unifying the company through vision and co-option can achieve transnational solutions.[23] We believe that the glocalization strategy incorporates transnational features as defined by Bartlett and Ghoshal into strategy formulation and implementation that could be instrumental in forming alliances with a mentality of thinking globally and acting locally.

PRODUCT AND VALUE CHAIN FUNCTION: STANDARDIZATION VERSUS ADAPTATION

International business strategy in general has often been characterized as a choice between worldwide standardization and local adaptation. Such a choice is usually studied in reference to products, however. In this model of international business strategy, they are considered in reference to products as well as to value chain activities. A firm wishing to internationalize basically has to make a decision whether to standardize or customize its product line and value chain activities depending on customer demands and market condition.

Theodore Levitt, in his seminal article, argued that technological force has driven the world toward a converging communality.[24] The result is the emergence of global markets for standardized consumer products on huge economies of scale. "Almost everyone everywhere wants all the things they have heard about, seen, or experienced via the new technologies... (Consequently) the global corporation operates with resolute constancy—at low relative cost—as if the entire world (or major region of it) were a single entity; it sells the same thing in the same way everywhere."[25]

The concept of "global consumer" assumes that consumers worldwide have become similar enough in their tastes and preferences that the same product would satisfy their needs. Based on this concept, MNCs are recommended to produce and market the same product with cosmetic changes worldwide. There is a parallel between global strategy and standardization strategy here. In other words, standardization is a key ingredient of the global strategy. All the intermediate and ultimate benefits expected from a global strategy are true for standardization.

Making and selling standardized products with cosmetic changes in numerous countries yields great economies of scale advantages for a firm. Otherwise, any major changes in product design and manufacturing will increase the unit cost of production, which would have a negative influence on the competitive position of the firm. Beyond the unit cost advantage, product standardization enhances the learning curve and knowledge transfer between the parent company and its subsidiaries (and among its subsidiaries). The firm specializing in particular product lines would master its development, manufacturing, and marketing.

Although product standardization is extremely important, standardization can be achieved in a variety of value chain activities beyond product standardization. Looking at standardization benefits for products only is a limited view. The advantages of standardized products in supplying and manufacturing are obvious and have been studied extensively. Standardization in distribution, promotion, and customer services, however, also provides great advantages for the company. Using the same advertisement, for example, if it were culturally feasible in different countries, would also save significantly on promotion expenses. The major success of MNCs such as Coca-Cola, McDonald's, and Harley Davidson can be attributed to their standardized product and marketing activities worldwide.

On the contrary to standardization, adaptation entails making necessary changes in product and value chain activities as the local market dictates. By doing so, the company responds better to the needs of customers in each country. Some of these changes are compulsory, such as the local legal regulations. When national laws dictate product safety features, MNCs have to meet those requirements in order to sell their products in those national markets. Compulsory adaptations are especially true for service firms such as accounting, law, and insurance companies. Each country has its own legal jurisdiction imposing different practices. As a result, international accounting and insurance companies modify their practices from one country to another. On the other hand, some adaptations are voluntary (not imposed by the local governments), but making such changes improves the marketing of products or services. For example, adaptations such as changing product labels to the local language or changing the product size to meet the consumers' demands would help increase the company's sales in that market. Whether it is compulsory or voluntary, adaptations facilitate the smooth integration of the MNC in the national market and successfully face international and local competition.

Adaptations in product and value chain activities would provide significant economies of scope advantages in marketing and distribution. For example, a firm that specializes in catalog sales should find an alternative distribution channel if the local postal service is inefficient or corrupt. Having experienced such a situation in Mexico, a retail catalog company had to change its product delivery system by using a network of schoolteachers. Similarly, GE had to change product dimensions of home appliances in order to sell successfully in Europe, where the kitchens in apartments are not as spacious as those in the United States. Of course, making changes in products and value chain activities accrues some extra costs, and the benefits of the changes that the company is planning should justify such extra costs that might occur.

BUSINESS CONDUCT: MARKET CONTRACTS, INTERNALIZATION, AND STRATEGIC ALLIANCES

In practice, the firm has three primary options in conducting its business: getting things done through other firms, doing it in-house, or doing things with a partner(s). We called these courses of actions "business conduct mode," which refers to how to conduct the international business even after the decisions on product and value chain activities and market (global versus multinational involvement) are made, as shown in Figure 3.2. From a theoretical perspective, as explained in Chapter 2, they are called markets, internalization (hierarchies), and alliances. The first option is concerned with contractual deals in the marketplace with other firms. The second option means a go-it-alone internalization of activities. The third option refers to interfirm partnerships.Because we discuss them in-depth in Chapter 2, we will recap them here in reference to strategic choice of the firm.

Market Contracts

From a strategic point of view, the firm might find that it is advantageous to conduct its business by contracting with other firms in the marketplace. Especially if the firm does not wish to make substantial investments in several value chain activities, then it uses suppliers and subcontractors to get the products and services it needs. Such an approach provides a great deal of flexibility for the firm as to choosing the party liked best and switching from one to another. In selecting the suppliers and subcontractors, the firms should pay close attention to cost and quality of products and services and the reliability of suppliers and subcontractors. In recent years, there has been an increasing trend in establishing long-term relationships with suppliers and using subcontractors instead of producing in-house.

Establishing long-lasting relationships with suppliers has proven to be beneficial in building a competitive edge for companies. In particular, as proven by Japanese companies, just-in-time management practices as a result of a long-term cooperation between the manufacturing firm and its suppliers yield a competitive edge for the producers. In order for suppliers to get into such relationships with their buyer, however, they want to ensure that the manufacturer has a long-term commitment for sizable orders—because they assume a significant amount of carrying cost of inventories and commit to delivering goods and components whenever needed. A buyer's decision to rely significantly on a single or limited number of suppliers traditionally increases its risk as well as the bargaining power of the supplier(s). The practice has proven that the partnership between the buyer and its supplier has enhanced the competitive positions of the buyer, however. For example, Dell Computer's success, among other things, is attributed to its excellent partnership with its suppliers.

Another worldwide business trend is the frequent use of subcontracting in a variety of primary and supportive value chain activities. It has also been proven that internalization of activities is often not necessarily a less-costly way of doing business than contracting it out another firm. Subcontractors can do the job in a more efficient manner because of their specialization and lower overhead costs than the buyers can. Thus, in cost-saving endeavors, many MNCs have turned to international subcontractors for some of their value chain activities. For example, Levi Strauss and Gap have employed subcontractors to manufacture jeans and shirts in a number of countries. Certainly, in choosing this option the MNC has to watch not only the cost but also the quality of deliveries. Otherwise, the brand name of the company's products could be easily tarnished.

Internalization

When markets are imperfect (and often, they are), to cope with uncertainty and to build control the firm tends to internalize resources needed rather than receiving them through market transactions. Buckley claimed that "in the internalization approach the firm is seen as an internalized bundle of resources that can be allocated (i) between product groups (changes in which are identified as conglomerate diversification) and (ii) between national markets (expansion in this direction is multinational diversification)."[26] Then, the growth of the firm is determined by its internalization decision. Depending upon the concentration in a given industry, the firm makes moves for vertical or horizontal integration. If the industry is not concentrated (a large number of firms in the industry), the MNC might integrate horizontally. On the other hand, if the industry is concentrated, it expands through either backward or forward integration or diversification through horizontal integration.

In the pursuit of internationalization expansion, the firm can engage in a greenfield investment, merger, or acquisition. The underlying reasons for greenfield investments are market expansion or resource acquisition. On the other hand, the reasons for mergers and acquisitions comprise increasing market power, overcoming entry barriers, reducing the risk or the cost of new product development, increasing the speed of market entry, increasing diversification, and avoiding excessive competition. In recent years, there has been a noticeable boost in cross-border mergers and acquisitions. One of the important acquisitions in the automobile manufacturing industry has been Daimler-Benz's acquisition of Chrysler. Similarly, Mexico's Cemex has become a multinational player by acquiring cement plants in the United States, Spain, the Philippines, Central America, South America, and the Caribbean. To compete with multinational companies, numerous European companies wanted to create a critical mass through mergers and acquisitions. For example, Germany's Allianz acquired Assurances Générales de France

(AGF), a French insurance company. Likewise, the British Reed Elsevier, PLC acquired Wolters Kluwer to form one of the world's largest publishing companies. Mergers and acquisitions, however, are closely scrutinized by antitrust agencies in most countries—in particular, the United States and Europe.

While international expansion through greenfield investments, mergers, or acquisitions provides the benefit of full control, it has a built-in inflexibility so that firms cannot get out of their commitments easily. Rapidly changing market environments and technological breakthroughs, however, might require some flexibility in strategic moves and resource acquisitions and deployment. Thus, strategic alliances, an intermediary mode, or a quasi-internalization all present an option between two extremes of market transactions and internalization.

Strategic Alliances

The third alternative strategy is strategic alliances among firms, which is the core topic of this book. With increasing globalization and technological developments, the importance of strategic alliances has augmented. When companies have been faced with dealing with market uncertainties and have deployed diversified resources and capabilities, strategic alliances have emerged as a significant process mode. In an international context, alliances play an even greater role because they frequently might be the only option for entering a foreign market (for example, China) or a preferred market entry mode to wholly owned subsidiaries (for example, India).

Yoshino and Rangan viewed strategic alliances as mechanisms for company entrepreneurship, which depends upon developing a flexible organizational capability. They argued,

The major driver of strategic alliances, the emergence of intense global competition, has rendered less effective the simple generic strategies that have been the staple of many U.S. firms. Today firms must embark on a path of continuous innovation to keep abreast or preferably, forge ahead of equally innovation-conscious rivals. Firms must cultivate organizational flexibility in a number of areas, among them technology, marketing, distribution channels, and plant economics and increasing constraints on resources, both human and physical.[27]

In order to employ interfirm collaboration as a strategy, managers of firms should change their conventional thinking about competition and reorient themselves to collaborative ways of operating in the global economy, because resources and capabilities of firms are so diverse that no single firm has all the necessary ingredients to develop effective global strategies. Firms are realizing that drawing on the competence of others around the world to compete effectively is not only feasible but also often necessary.

Gomes-Casseres, by approaching alliances from a perspective of collective competition, argued that firms—especially high-technology companies—compete in constellations in which they build close ties with partnering firms to strengthen their competitive positions.[28] In other words, the nature of collaboration in a constellation helped determine the group's competitive advantage. Gomes-Casseres claimed that there would be two implications of a strategic alliance. "First, by exploiting barriers to collaboration, firms may interfere with a rival's alliances and so place the rival at a disadvantage. Second, firms that build and manage their constellations more effectively than others may have an edge in the marketplace."[29]

The explanations given earlier confirm that alliances have become an important strategic option in international business. Therefore, the international strategy model introduced previously consists of strategic alliances as an alternative strategy among markets and internalization. Nevertheless, we must clarify again that because strategic alliances are hybrid forms, they compromise some features of market transactions and internalization. For example, an MNC signing a contract with a foreign firm for marketing each other's products (piggy-back marketing) is normally considered a typical market transaction. But if it is a long-term deal with strategic implications, it is deemed in this book as a strategic alliance.

Although managing international strategic alliances is more complex than managing alliances of markets and internalization, firms often have committed to collaborative arrangements in one form or another. Despite reported high failure rates among strategic alliances, firms have increasingly employed alliance mode. Thus, they aptly deserve our attention.

The international business strategy model presented here suggests that firms should think in three principal modes as they develop their strategies: business conduct, markets, and product and value activities modes. All these dimensions are extremely important in strategy development, and therefore they should be embedded in international business strategy formulations and implementations. Indeed, strategic alliances as an intermediate mode (quasi-internalization) between markets and internalization have been receiving increasing attention in recent years. After defining the place of strategic alliances among overall business options and strategies, let us turn to strategic alliances in particular and explain how they are formed and how they work in a conceptual model.

STRATEGIC ALLIANCE MODEL

To explain the phenomenon of strategic alliances, a conceptual model is constructed that integrates earlier discussions on the subject. As I explained, our starting point is that a strategic alliance is an alternative business strategy geared toward ultimately achieving a competitive advantage for the firm. The model of strategic alliances suggests that there are five essential components of building an interfirm collaboration (refer to Figure 3.4). First, partner selection is the central aspect in developing a strategic alliance. Once the firm decides on the strategy of alliance, it looks for partners to engage in collaboration. Such partners could be competitors or non-competitors. Cooperation with a competitor(s) refers to horizontal alliances. As we will describe in Chapters 6 and 8, these kinds of collaborations are common in the automobile manufacturing industry and airline industries. Horizontal strategic alliances occur between partners at the same stage in the value chain. They are often used to improve the strategic competitiveness of the partners involved. "Although horizontal chain alliances usually focus on long-term product and service technology development, many competitors also form joint marketing agreements. Some of these agreements not only reduce costs but increase revenues and market power."[30] On the other hand, cooperation with non-competitors means a vertical alliance, which involves partnerships at the different stages of the value chain. The most common form of such alliances is the collaboration between manufacturer and supplier.

Second, the type of alliance is another important consideration in cooperative ventures. The firm basically has two choices: equity or non-equity alliance. As described previously, equity alliances require equity investment by the partners and can take two principal forms: joint venture or equity participation. In the case of joint ventures, two parent companies create a new company by allocating their assets respectively, while in equity participation one firm buys an equity ownership into

Figure 3.4

Strategic alliance model

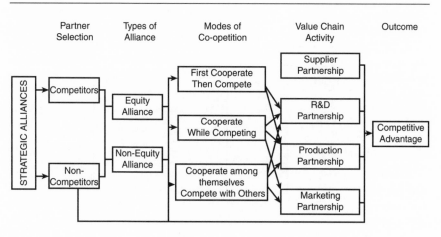

another. On the other hand, non-equity partnerships comprise licensing, franchising, technology partnership, R&D partnership, supplier agreements, marketing agreements, and production sharing (refer to Figure 3.5). We will extensively examine different forms and unique challenges of international strategic alliances in the following chapters.

Third, the mode of co-opetition refers to the notion of cooperating while competing. We described co-opetition earlier in this chapter. Traditionally, firms shied away from collaborating with their competitors, but today their attitudes (at least, most of them) have changed. They are more receptive to cooperation. Basically, this situation happens in three ways: first cooperating then competing, cooperating while competing, and cooperating between themselves and competing with others. Selection of a particular mode depends upon the firm's situation in terms of its resources and competencies and market conditions, such as the intensity of the rivalry, opportunities, threats, and pressing needs for market and product development.

Fourth, the kind of value chain activities needs to be determined as an area of cooperation. In the value chain, collaborations are usually developed in activities such as supply chain, R&D, manufacturing, and marketing. Each type of alliance presents unique characteristics. They also vary from one industry to another, as we will study later. Supply chain agreements, for

Figure 3.5
Forms of strategic alliances

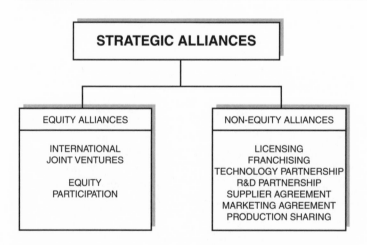

example, have gained popularity between two non-competing parties (manufacturer and supplier) in the automobile industry after their successful
applications in Japan, while R&D collaborations have been common
between pharmaceutical and biotechnology firms.

Fifth and finally, outcome is the ultimate consideration—meaning a competitive advantage for participating companies. There must be an expected
strategic benefit for each collaboration on various projects in numerous
forms. Each collaborator sooner or later will make an assessment of the consequences of the partnership, meaning what it contributes and in return
what it receives. Of course, the partner's expectations and reality might not
always match. Partner expectations and outcome appraisals are the key to
final decisions of the parties. In Chapters 4 and 5, with respect to international joint ventures and non-equity partnerships, we will consider this decision process specifically.

In the following chapters, we will study various alliances and relate them
to the competitive strategy of the firm. After all, they represent the firm's particular mode of business conduct as strategic alliances. We must note, however, that a firm can often use multiple approaches (market transactions,
internalization, and alliances) in the formulation and implementation of
overall corporate and business strategies. For example, McDonald's holds full
ownership of some restaurants and buys potatoes off the market while collaborating through franchising and joint ventures, although its primary
mode is franchising. The business conduct mode simply reflects how the
MNC conducts its business operations. In reality, it can switch from one
mode to another or use a combination of them (for example, GE uses multiple modes—wholly owned subsidiaries and joint ventures) or engage in one
primary mode as a cornerstone of its strategy (for example, Pizza Hut's franchising). The following chapters will address such variations and combinations of international strategic alliances.

NOTES

1. M. A. Hitt, The new competitive landscape, *Strategic Management
   Journal* 16, (1995): 7–19. M. A. Hitt, R. D. Ireland, and R. E.
   Hoskisson, *Strategic management: Competitiveness and globalization*,
   Third Edition (Cincinnati, OH: South-Western College Publishing,
   1999). R. A. D'Aveni, Coping with hypercompetition: Utilizing the
   new 7S's framework. *Academy of Management Executive,* 9, no. 3
   (1995): 46.

2. Hitt, 8.

3. D'Aveni, 46.

4. D. K. Datta, G. E. Pinches, and V. K. Naravyanan, Factors influencing wealth creation from mergers and acquisitions: A metaanalysis, *Strategic Management Journal*, 13 (1992): 67-84.

5. Hitt *et al.*, 13.

6. A. M. Brandenburger, and B. J. Nalebuff, *Co-opetition* (New York: Currency Doubleday, 1996).

7. R. Culpan (ed.) *Multinational strategic alliances* (New York: International Business Press, 1993): 19.

8. A. M. Brandenburger and B. J. Nalebuff, op. cit.

9. M. K. Starr, *Global Corporate alliances and the competitive edge* (Westport: Quorum Books, 1991): 145.

10. Ibid., 145–146.

11. H. V. Perlmutter, The torturous evolution of the multinational company, *Columbia Journal of World Business,* 3, no. 1 (1969): 9–18.

12. M. E. Porter, Changing pattern of international competition, *California Management Review*, 28, no. 2(1986): 9–40.

13. Ibid., 14.

14. Porter, 10.

15. Ibid., 15.

16. C. A. Bartlett, and S. Ghoshal, *Managing across borders: The transnational solution* (Boston, MA: Harvard Business School Press, 1989).

17. Bartlett and Ghoshal, 13.

18. Porter, 21.

19. Ibid., 27.

20. A. V. Phatak, *International management: Concepts and cases* (Cincinnati, OH: South-Western College Publishing, 1997): 303.

21. Bartlett and Ghoshal, 57.

22. Ibid., 59–63.

23. Ibid., 66–71.

24. T. Leavitt, The globalization of markets, *Harvard Business Review* (May–June, 1983): 92–102.

25. Ibid., 92.

26. P. J. Buckley, Problems and developments in the core theory of international business, *Journal of International Business Studies*, 21, no. 4 (1990): 660.

27. M. Y. Yoshino, and U. S. Rangan, *Strategic alliances: An entrepreneurial approach to globalization* (Boston, MA: Harvard Business School Publication, 1995): 51.

28. B. Gomes-Casseres, *The alliance revolution: The new shape of business rivalry* (Cambridge, MA: Harvard University Press, 1996).

29. Ibid., 209.

30. Hitt *et al.*, 321.

4

Equity Alliances

INTERNATIONAL JOINT VENTURES

International joint ventures (IJVs) are the most common form of strategic alliances, which means that two or more firms from different countries create an independent business unit by contributing their share of equities. IJVs are considered independent legal entities from their parents. Because of their significant roles in business, IJVs have been the subject of many studies. Nevertheless, their traditional structures and roles have changed over the years. Harrigan asserted that "firms use ventures differently than they have in the past because they have found that joint ventures offer better ways to cope with the competitive challenges of rapid technological change and increased interdependency in some industries than venturing alone does."[1] Emerging IJVs, which have been mostly formed between multinational firms, present different characteristics from traditional IJVs. Recently, an IJV was established between multinational corporations (MNCs) to gain competitive advantages, whereas a traditional IJV refers to a partnership between an MNC from a developed country and a government agency, state-owned enterprise (SOA), or local firm in a developing country. Therefore, the MNC tries to either acquire needed resources (raw materials or cheap labor) or access the local market while the developing country's government wishes to obtain much-needed technology and capital. Today, in addition to their traditional function, IJVs are used to develop core competencies of MNCs that would lead to a competitive edge against their rivals. Because a great deal of literature exists concerning IJVs, our main purpose here is not to recap the discussion of the subject but to elaborate on the new mission of IJVs as a mechanism for building core competencies in achieving sustainable advantages for partnering firms. Nonetheless, first we will review the traditional role of joint ventures as a point of reference; then we will define their vital strategic function in global business.

IJV Decision-Making Model

The mission and function of joint ventures have been examined from various perspectives. We believe, however, that they can best be studied in a conceptual framework given in Figure 4.1, which is based on the decision-making process by a partner(s). Figure 4.1 depicts that the decisions concerning a joint venture by a partner involve four principal stages: initial, formation, operation, and outcome. This figure also demonstrates that at each stage the following decisions and practices become critical: partner selection, types of venture, and performance and control issues. Finally, the partnering firm makes an assessment of the outcome—whether it is satisfied with the results produced by the joint venture. Accordingly, it decides whether to continue with the venture or exit from it. For the sake of analysis, those stages are presented separately; however, they are in fact interrelated and overlap. We will elaborate upon each stage and its significant elements next.

Considerations of joint ventures are given with a reference to a single partner's motivations and strategic intentions. Of course, a symmetrical decision process takes place with the other partner, as well. To build a joint venture, we do not need to say that the goals of both parties must be compatible. Usually, joint ventures are formed after lengthy negotiations, and sometimes such negotiations extend over a number of years.

Initial Stage

Initially, a firm makes a strategic decision of whether to enter a joint venture with another firm (or firms) for the purposes of achieving economies of scale, reducing risks/costs, accessing markets/resources, developing technology or products, and learning from the partner(s). If the benefits of a joint venture outweigh its costs and risks, the firm decides to engage in a joint venture; otherwise, it might pursue internalization (go-it-alone). Of course, there is always a possibility of not undertaking any actions in pursuing a business opportunity. The assumption here, however, is that the market opportunity is so great that the firm does not wish to bypass it. At the same time, industry and market conditions affect the decisions of firm strategists. The firm's options are between strategic alliance (a joint venture in particular) and internalization, when the business opportunity cannot be exploited by market transactions (or in economists' terms, when markets fail). In particular, the nature and intensity of competition in a given industry and tech-

Figure 4.1
Joint venture decision model

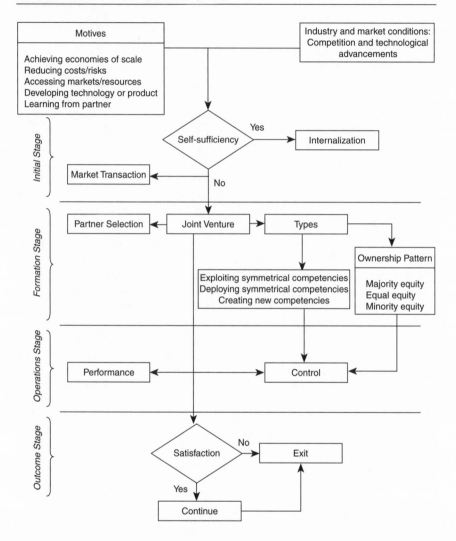

nological advancements influencing product life cycles, production efficiency, and information diffusion would also impinge on the formation of
joint ventures.

Formation Stage

Once the choice is made for a joint venture, the second phase of the process starts. At this point, a number of follow-up decisions need to be made. Such decisions are primarily concerned with whom to choose for a partner and what type of joint venture would be suitable for the purpose defined. With regard to the type of joint venture, the ownership pattern and benefits sought from the partner would be important factors.

Partner selection. Geringer stated that "the specific partner chosen can influence the overall mix of available skills and resources, the operating policies and procedures, and short- and long-term viability of an IJV. Because of this, it is critical for prospective joint ventures to understand the process of partner selection and the variables which influence that process."[2] In partner selection, the key concept is "compatibility." The success of a joint venture largely depends on the compatibility of partners in two areas. The first is "resource compatibility," meaning the degree of fit between the resources of partners. Such resources include tangible and intangible resources and capabilities of partners that allocated or are willing to be allocated to the venture. The second is "cultural compatibility;" that is, a match between organizational cultures of partners. Similarly, Geringer offered two considerations— task- and partner-related dimensions—of partner selection criteria.[3]

The resource compatibility is a significant consideration but often is overlooked in the optimistic atmosphere of new venturing. Partner resourcefulness should be assessed in light of not only their resource inventory but also their fit with the other partner's resources to be allocated to the joint venture. A mismatch between the resources committed by the partners is an early sign of failure. This factor does not necessarily mean the proportional allocation of resources, but rather the allocation of complementary resources. For example, in McDonald's Chinese joint venture, the local government's allocation of a corner store at Tiananmen Square in Beijing can be considered an attractive match to the company's investment of capital and know-how. Thus, in partner selection, special attention should be paid to resourcefulness and the degree of compatibility of partners' resources.

Cultural compatibility is closely associated with the concept of "cultural proximity" between partners, which refers to closeness or sync between organizational cultures of each partner. A more traditional and often-used term, "cultural distance," is an opposite of cultural proximity. With respect to cultural differences, researchers usually examine the differences in core businesses, management practices, decision-making processes, needs, and learning capabilities between partners. Basically, each partner brings its own distinct organizational culture into the venture. If the cultures are not compatible, they often jeopardize the performance of the joint venture. In international joint ventures, there usually exist cross-cultural differences in addition to corporate cultural differences. Partnering firms need to pay attention to such cultural distances that impact the management of the venture. Barkema and his colleagues found that the termination of joint ventures (and acquisitions) was more attributed to cultural distance than wholly owned subsidiaries because the former had to accommodate both national and company cultures.[4]

Types. Traditionally, joint ventures are classified according to ownership pattern. In this fashion, joint ventures are categorized as majority equity ownership: a foreign partner holds a greater than 50 percent equity stake while a local partner owns the rest of the equity in the joint venture. In equal-ownership, both partners own equal shares of equity, and in a minority equity ownership, a foreign company owns fewer than 50 percent of equity in the joint venture. In other words, ownership determines the type of joint venture. The assumptions with such a categorization are as follows: (i) joint ventures are formed between a multinational corporation (MNC) and a local company, and (ii) the relative size of ownership represents the parent's control over the joint venture. Both of these assumptions can easily be challenged.[5] First, joint ventures can be formed between two or more MNCs. Considering the joint venture phenomenon as a partnership only between an MNC from an industrialized country and a local company from a developing country is an outdated view. Second, the relative size of ownership does not necessarily determine the control pattern in the joint venture. As we will discuss in reference to control, the control mechanism also reflects a partner's resource capability besides its equity stake. Also, resource capability is the more important source of influence than ownership pattern. Nevertheless, in practice ownership pattern in a joint venture presents a core issue.

Alternatively, based on nine decision-making areas including pricing decisions, the replacement of a functional manager, setting sales targets, and altering the product design or manufacturing process, Killing classified joint ventures into three categories: *dominant parent joint ventures*, in which one partner dominates the ventures; *shared management ventures*, in which both parents play an active role; and *independent ventures*, in which neither parent plays a strong role.[6] In a dominant parent joint venture, one parent runs the joint venture as if it were a wholly owned subsidiary while the other partner acts like a silent partner. It is easy to manage a dominant parent joint venture because one partner has greater control over the venture. In order to have such joint ventures succeed, the passive partner must have great trust in the dominant partner, which is uncommon. Shared management ventures provide some balance of power between partners in terms of running the venture, but it is difficult to manage the venture when no partner has the upper hand. On the other hand, the success of an independent joint venture also depends on the degree of autonomy given by its parents to the general manager of the venture. It is rare, however, to find parents allowing the venture to be run independently. In practice, usually parent companies tend to interfere with the venture's management.

Although these two categorizations of joint ventures seem similar, Killing's classification is not based on ownership but rather on the dominant perception of joint ventures of general managers and parent company personnel. In seeking another meaningful classification based on organizational resources and capabilities, we will present a new typology of joint ventures. As noted earlier, recent literature recognizes the critical of role of firm resources and capabilities in the strategic success of firms. Thus, we will relate joint ventures to this key concept of firm competencies. Drawing upon the resouce-based view (RBV) of firms, the basic assumption is that joint ventures are formed to acquire, share, and create resources and competencies for parent companies. "Strategically important differences between firms therefore arise from each firm's distinctive mix of competence building and competence-leveraging activities, which in turn are determined by each firm's set of goals, by its strategic logic for achieving its goals, and by the way in which each firm coordinates its deployment of resources in pursuit of its goals."[7] Consequently, in obtaining unique resources and competencies of others and combining it with their own, firms engage in different types of joint ventures. Based on resource and competency maintenance and development objectives, joint ventures can be classified as joint ventures formed with the intention of exploitation of symmetrical resources and competencies, deployment of asymmetrical resources and competencies, and creation of new competencies. Figure 4.2 shows these three types of joint ventures. A firm has some internal resources within the organization that are called "firm-specific resources" or access to (through markets or alliances) some sources of others that are "external resources." Then, competency means the capability of a firm to exploit and explore internal and external resources in achieving its strategic goals. Joint ventures are instrumental in accessing external resources in particular.

Figure 4.2
Joint venture types

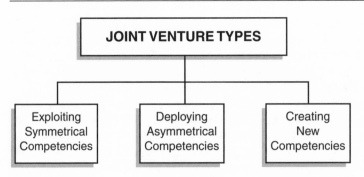

We must note, however, that the departing point in our analysis of joint ventures is that the emphasis is on resource and competence sharing and building for a competitive advantage. In other words, although attaining synergistic dynamics in a joint venture is important, partners are ultimately interested in improving their own value chain activities through inter-partner learning and internalizing core competencies. We seldom see two firms creating another independent firm that would be spun off from the parents. Hence, the level of analysis is at the parent companies rather than at the joint venture itself.

Exploiting symmetrical competencies. These kinds of joint ventures are established between firms to exploit the existing similar competencies that each partner possesses. Although these types of joint ventures are uncommon in comparison to other types, they are formed to leverage combined resources and competencies of partners that would enhance economies of scale or economies of scope of the venture, which in return would eventually add to competency levels of the partners.

Deploying asymmetrical competencies. Firms that have different resources and competencies establish joint ventures that benefit from such diverse capabilities. One partner's resource and competency superiority compensates for the deficiency of the other partner. In order for these types of joint ventures to work, there must be diverse but complementary competencies provided by each partner. The majority of joint ventures fall into this category.

Creating new competencies. This third type refers to joint ventures where partners intend to create new competencies that no partner possesses.Because no partner alone is capable of generating capabilities needed, partners cooperate to build competencies that would provide benefits for each joint venture partner. R&D joint ventures, for example, are often formed to develop new technology or products from which each partner eventually benefits.

Operations Stage

Partners closely watch operations of the joint venture and would like to know how the joint venture is managed and what results are achieved. They are time-by-time directly involved in its management by assigning board directors and other managerial staff. Two of the most important decisions that parents need to make are performance assessment and control.

Performance assessment. Joint venture performance can be determined in different ways, depending on the levels of analysis. The first is at the parent company level, where joint venture performance refers to the extent of satisfaction of parents with the performance of the joint venture, which can be measured by the partners' degree of satisfaction with the international joint venture (IJV) performance and the relationship between partners. Most research on joint ventures employs this type of measurement method. Geringer and Herbert defined this dimension as the extent to which an IJV has achieved the expectations the parent firm had of it when the IJV was formed.[8] This measurement is attitudinal. The second level of analysis is the joint venture level. In this context, business performance of the joint venture can be measured in reference to sales, profitability, and market share. This type of measurement is an objective assessment that involves a comparison of present performance of the joint venture with its past performance with the performance of major competitors or with an industry standard. The third kind of performance analysis combines both parent and joint venture-level analyses. Theoretically, it is possible to have such an assessment, but it is rare to see such studies.

On joint venture performance, Beamish asserted that partner need and commitment are good predictors of performance.[9] MNC executives from the low-performing joint ventures regard their local partners' contributions as unimportant, while those from the high-performing joint ventures consider their partners' contributions important. Also observed was a strong correlation between commitment and joint venture performance. The indicator of commitment included the MNC's willingness to visit and offer assistance, adapt products, employ nationals, voluntarily use the joint venture structure, and hold regular meetings.

A variety of objectives are identified to explain the motives of firms for the formation of IJVs. These objectives include the achievement of economies of scale, reduction of risks, access to markets, and development of new technology or products. But only few researchers have noted organizational learning as a motive for IJVs.[10] According to this learning perspective, IJVs can be instrumental in inter-partner learning. This motive is rather emerging. Based on the concept of core competence building, it is sufficient to say that inter-partner learning plays an important role in assessing the success of joint ventures.

Assessing the performance of joint ventures independently obscures the fact that parent companies have their own objectives, agendas, and interests. If parents feel that the joint venture is not contributing to the objectives of the parents, they tend to dissolve the venture. Therefore, any assessment of performance of joint ventures should taken into consideration of the satisfaction of parents with the objectives that they initially formulated for the venture.

Most often, an MNC forms a joint venture with a local firm to access the host country's market. The competence of the local firm is usually its knowledge of and familiarity with the local market that is lacking with the MNC. Once the MNC learns the local market characteristics and how to operate in that market, it does not need the local partner anymore. In other words, the stability of the IJV depends upon the learning curve of the MNC in the host country's market. If the market access is primary motive and only the locals possess the local market knowledge, the MNC can enter the country through a local partnership. In order for the MNC continue with the joint venture, the local partner must possess some competencies that are unique, inimitable, and immobile.

Performance measurement of joint ventures is usually based on a managerial assessment. Parent managers appraise short-term and long-term as well as actual and potential benefits of the joint venture. It is relatively easier to assess actual short-term benefits but harder to judge potential long-term benefits. Financial measurements such as sales, return on investment (ROI), and stock performance and marketing measures such as market share, product breadth, and segmentation reflect the joint venture's actual performance on an annual basis or in three to five years. Looking beyond actual performance and considering long-term potential is also meaningful from a strategic perspective.

Control. Depending upon the corporate culture (centralized versus decentralized management styles), strategic orientations (ethnocentric, polycentric, or geocentric) of parents, the extent of trustworthiness of other partner(s), and the joint venture protocol, the degree of parent control over the joint venture varies. Nevertheless, parent companies exert some control over the joint venture because of their stake in the venture. The degree of that control ranges from influencing daily operations of the joint venture to outcome-based assessments, leaving a great deal of autonomy to the joint venture. Interfering with the daily operations of the joint venture is not a sound approach and often leads to a break-up partnership with disappointment.

One of the common and effective ways of control by parents is the assignment of expatriate managers from parent companies to the joint venture's critical posts. By doing so, parents try to ensure that their own policies, standards, and interests are safeguarded. While expatriate managers transmit company culture to the joint venture, they act like a watchdog for the company. They represent the interest of their parents because their first loyalty lies with their parent companies. They closely watch operations of the joint venture and report their findings to their respective parents.

Another way to exert control over a joint venture is outcome-based control, by which parents only pay attention to results rather than the processes in which business activities are carried out. This approach provides a great deal of autonomy to the joint venture. Parents appraise the financial and market performance of the joint venture in light of their expectations of the venture. Because each parent's expectation could be different, the assessment of the joint venture outcomes by each partner could result in a disagreement.

Outcome Stage

Finally, based on their overall satisfaction with the joint venture, parent companies decide to either continue to be a partner or to leave the joint venture. Their overall satisfaction could be based on the number factors. Some are related to the poor performance of the joint venture or serious conflict with the other partner. Some others mean, despite the joint venture's success, that there might be unsolvable differences between the partners.

Continuation. A partner who is satisfied with the performance of the joint venture tends to continue with it. There must be a match between the joint venture's performance and the partners' expectations. Sometimes, despite the joint venture's unsuccessful outcomes, a partner still wants to keep its partnership with the joint venture if it sees some potential benefits in the long run. Such decisions depend upon the parents' tolerance level of the venture's failure in the short run and its commitments in the long run. A periodic evaluation of joint venture performance by partners would help with making informed and timely decisions either to continue or to exit the joint venture. Otherwise, an overdue assessment might have costly and time-consuming results.

Exit decision. Another conclusion is to quit the joint venture because of the venture's disappointing results and promising no future benefits. From the beginning, each partner should have an exit strategy in mind if the joint venture does not function to its satisfaction. Often, however, an exit strategy is overlooked in happy times of marriage formation. When a serious conflict arises between partners, developing an exit strategy might take time and be costly. "After a rocky relationship spanning eight years, Daewoo and GM ended their 50-50 joint venture in Inchon, South Korea...The actual termination took several months as lawyers and executives from both sides worked out the details of divorce."[11] As a result of their empirical investigation, Serapio and Cascio found that "alliances typically end for one or more of six reasons: (1) alliance is not successful; (2) differences between partners (e.g., people incompatibilities, different management styles, disagreement over the objectives); (3) breach of agreement; (4) the alliance no longer fits goals/strategies of a partner; (5) a partner needs to exit the alliance because of financial difficulties or to take advantage of financial opportunities; and (6) the alliance met its goal."[12]

Termination of a joint venture occurs with or without a planned exit strategy. Then, the termination outcome could be an acquisition of the venture by one of the partners, dissolution of the venture, or reorganization and restructuring of the venture.[13] An agreement between partners on the termination of the venture or the way to do it would help produce a painless ending. Nevertheless, partnering firms should deem legal and business ramifications of a termination of the joint venture by considering legal implications such as conditions of termination, disposition of assets and liabilities, and dispute resolution methods and business implications such as time to exit, employee-related issues (for example, compensations and severance payments), and relations with the host government.

Equity Participation

Equity participation, like IJVs, is not as common as IJVs. In equity participation one partner owns a certain percentage of equity stakes in another
firm. Sometimes it could be a cross holding, by which the partners hold
some percentages of equities of each other. It is believed that an ownership of
substantial equity in a company provides insights into and some control over
that company's strategies and operations. Firms that have equity relationships feel closer to each other than companies that do not have such ties. By
using their ownership leverage, the investors can get information from and
influence the new initiatives of the target companies. GM, for example, has
effectively used its equity participation on Isuzu and Suzuki to penetrate the
Japanese automobile market by co-production and co-marketing. GM also
used its Japanese partners in venturing with other Japanese automobile manufacturers. Similarly, DaimlerChrysler took a controlling 34 percent stake in
Japan's Mitsubishi Motors and is in the early stages of planning a "world car"
jointly with its Japanese partner and South Korea's Hyundai Motors, in
which DaimlerChrysler holds 10 percent equity stake. As we will present in
Chapters 6, 8, and 9, this kind of equity participation alliances are common
in the automobile manufacturing, airline, and telecommunications industries.

Equity partnerships enable hierarchical control over the target firm,
whereas non-equity alliances do not enable this control between two partners. When the investing company does not hold the majority equity shares
of the target company, however, it should find a way in which it can exert
control. It could use its clout in terms of financial or technological advantages in shaping the strategy and operations of the target firm. Otherwise,
the investing company accepts being a silent partner, but often it is not the
intention of the investor.

In some cases, an equity stake in a target firm makes it easier to acquire it
by the investor firm in a later stage than outsider firms can. The equity tie
helps the investing firm be a better candidate to take over the target firm if
the partners have good relationships. Usually, in case of the target firm's
divestiture, the investing firm could make the first takeover offer or be
approached to make an offer.

We will offer a conceptual model in Figure 4.3 that will help our understanding of equity participation alliances. In a typical equity participation
alliance, the investing firm buys an influencing equity stake in the target
firm, which welcomes such an investment. Generally, principal strategic
goals of both parties can be characterized as market expansion and potential
synergies. In particular, when the target firm is experiencing a financial crisis, it seeks resource leverage and/or company revitalization. Because both

firms agree on the terms of the transaction, it can be considered a strategic alliance. In such dealings, the target firm is either vulnerable as being in financial trouble (which might make it attractive for the investing firm) or ambitious to expand into new markets (although it has solid production capabilities but needs additional resources and competencies). The investing firm can choose equity participation vis-à-vis a greenfield investment because the former provides better market entry (for example, entering a controlled foreign market) and/or more flexibility in terms of switching strategies later. The firm might prefer equity participation against a joint venture because it does not wish to create additional capacity but wants to exploit the relative easiness in governance of equity participation over a joint venture.

Figure 4.3

Equity participation model

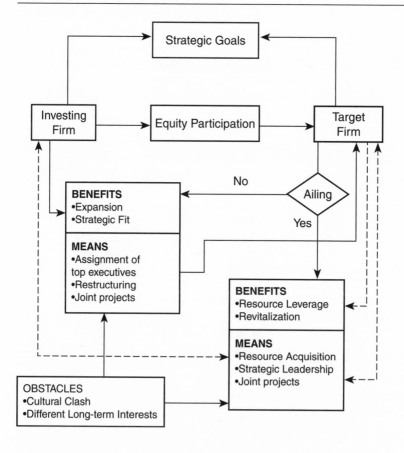

Once the investor holds an influencing stake in the target firm, it exerts its power on the target firm by assigning top executives (for example, a chief executive officer and board directors), launching a restructuring plan, or developing joint projects to exploit the synergistic benefits of the two firms. In the case of a troubled target firm, the investing firm first intends to turn its partner around while the target firm seeks recovery from its deteriorating operations. If the investor's turnaround strategy fails, it might seek other options such as divesting its stake or inviting other partners.

On the other hand, the target firm might view this relationship as a long-term collaboration and look for mutual prosperity with the investor. Alternatively, it might consider this relationship temporary and wish to get out of the deal once it recovers from its crisis. In achieving its strategic goals, it tries to obtain resources that are desperately needed (for example, pressing loan payments, modernizing production technology, and expanding product line), effective leadership and direction (such as changing the current culture and practices), and joint projects (for example, co-design and co-production of new products). In the case of a healthy target firm, both the investing and target firms jointly try to expand their competitive advantages by exploding their combined resources and competencies without anxiety over one rescuing the other.

Nevertheless, such collaboration is not problem-free. A number of issues arise in implementing an equity participation strategy. The most common obstacles include cultural clashes between the investor and target firms. The companies evolved in different management styles, and leadership might present an important barrier to carry out the intended turnaround strategy. Additionally, long-term interests of the two parties might be different—one seeking a long-term partnership while other one is looking at the alliance as a temporary measure.

With this conceptual background, we will examine some specific cases in the global automobile manufacturing industry in Chapter 6.

NOTES

1. K. R. Harrigan, *Managing for joint venture success* (Lexington, MA: D.C. Heath and Company, 1986).
2. M. J. Geringer, Strategic determinants of partner selection criteria in international joint ventures, *Journal of International Business Studies* (Fall Quarter, 1991): 54–56.
3. Ibid.
4. H. G. Berkama, J. H. Ball, and J. M. Pennings, Foreign entry, cultural barriers, and learning, *Strategic Management Journal*, 17, no. 2 (1996): 151–166.

5. S. Makino, and P. W. Baemish, Performance and survival of joint ventures with non-conventional ownership structures, *Journal of International Business Studies,* 29, no. 4 (1998): 797–818.

6. J. P. Killing, *Strategies for joint venture success* (New York: Praeger Publishers, 1983): 16.

7. R. Sanchez, and A. Heene, Competence-based strategic management: Concepts and issues for theory, research, and practice, in A. Heene and R. Sanchez (eds.), *Competence-based strategic management* (Chichester, West Sussex, England: John Wiley & Sons, 1997): 8.

8. M. J. Geringer, and L. Herbert, Measuring joint venture performance, *Journal of International Business Studies* 22, no. 2 (1991): 249–263.

9. P. W. Beamish, *Multinational joint ventures in developing countries* (London: Routledge, 1988): 56.

10. For a detailed discussion of learning aspects see Andrew Inkpen, *The management of international joint ventures: An organizational learning perspective* (London: Routledge, 1995) and Gary Hamil, Competition for competence and inter-partner learning within international strategic alliances, *Strategic Management Journal,* 12 (1991): 83–104.

11. M. G. Serapio, Jr., and W. F. Cascio, End-games in international alliances, *The Academy of Management Executive*s, 10, no. 1 (1996): 62.

12. Ibid., 64.

13. Ibid.

5

Non-Equity Alliances

Besides international equity joint ventures or equity investments in another firm, firms might still form alliances without any equity ownership. This type of collaboration is called a non-equity alliance. The major forms include licensing, franchising, management contracts, turn-key operations, subcontracting, buyer coalitions, supplier partnership, R&D partnership, marketing agreements, technology partnership, and joint production. This list, however, is not all-inclusive. There might be some other types given increasingly changing market conditions, technological advancements, and creative new arrangements by firms. The common characteristic of these kinds of ventures is that they do not require any equity ownership differently from equity-based alliances discussed in the previous chapter.

Although non-equity alliances are contractual agreements (market transactions) between firms, as we pointed out earlier they are different from typical contractual agreements in the way they are constructed and managed. In other words, to be considered a strategic alliance, a contractual venture should be a long-term agreement affecting the value chain activity of the firm and providing benefits for the firm's sustainable competitive advantage. Therefore, for example, while a long-term supply-chain agreement is deemed a non-equity agreement, an interim procurement agreement is not considered a strategic alliance. This general category of non-equity alliances is called international contractual ventures (ICVs).[1]

INTERNATIONAL CONTRACTUAL VENTURES

Although the motives behind ICVs are slightly different from those behind international joint ventures (IJVs), the framework used for international joint ventures (equity joint ventures) in Chapter 4, with some modifications, can be used for international non-equity alliances. We must note that each type of ICV is formed with different purposes. They all, however, essentially present similar characteristics from the standpoint of partners. Again, in explaining their formation, operations, and performance outcomes, we use a managerial decision-making model. Figure 5.1 depicts this decision model for ICVs. Because ownership is not an issue in ICVs, the model for ICVs does not include the ownership aspect; instead, it consists of a variety of contractual engagements, each presenting distinguishing characteristics and dynamics. Obviously, embracing different contractual ventures into a single category such as non-equity alliances is a major challenge. Nevertheless, they all present two distinct, common characteristics: none involves equity commitment, but all require strategic commitment for mutual benefits through a partnership. Hence, the non-equity involvement feature of ICVs separates them from IJVs and equity participation while strategic commitment for mutual benefits and often competence building motives distinguishes them from other market transactions. We must also note that types of ICVs might take a variety of new forms. Therefore, it is not possible to present an inclusive list of all ICVs. Probably, for this reason they have not been studied as a whole but rather individually.

As we can see in Figure 5.1, the decision to engage in an ICV is a multistage process, including decisions concerning initial choice, formation, operations, and outcome assessments. Nonetheless, we must note that in any given case, the actual decision-making might be sequential as well as a simultaneous process. For example, when a firm decides to go for an ICV, it might have been already targeting a particular partner.

In the context of global strategic alliances, this book's primary interest is international non-equity alliances; however, the general theoretical underpinnings of both domestic and ICVs are the same. In general, conducting international business presents some unique characteristics in comparison to conducting domestic business. Some of the most distinguished features of international business are handling different currencies and managing in different legal and cultural environments. This situation is also true for ICVs. Thus, currency fluctuations, host country regulations, and cross-cultural differences present a greater challenge for ICVs in comparison to domestic contractual ventures.

THE ICV DECISION-MAKING MODEL

The ICV model consists of the motives of partners, industry and market conditions, influencing factors, and the decision-making process for alliance building. This model suggests that motives of the parties are important

Figure 5.1
International contractual ventures decision model

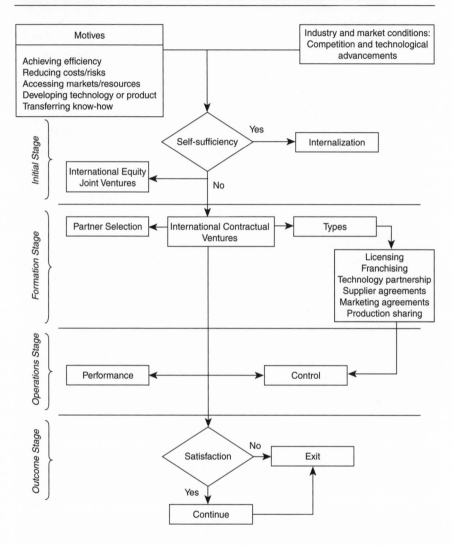

determinants of ICVs. As defined in reference to the IJV decision-making model, such incentives present diversity because of a variety of non-equity alliances and relative positions of partners in the partnership. For example, the motives of parties in a supply-chain agreement might be quite different from those of a franchising agreement or R&D agreement. Nonetheless, in general the following motives play a role in forming ICVs: achieving efficiency (such as outsourcing), reducing costs/risks (for example, a joint R&D accord), accessing markets/resources (for example, franchising), securing a supply source (such as a supply-chain agreement), developing technology and products (for example, joint R&D and co-production), and transferring know-how (through licensing and franchising). In addition, industry and market conditions comprising competitive dynamics, hypercompetition, technological advancements, and innovation influence firm strategists in the consideration and formation of ICVs.

Moreover, similar to the IJV decision-making model (Figure 4.1), the ICV model consists of stages such as initial, formation, operations, and outcome. For analytical purposes, we will examine each stage separately—although in reality, they might intermingle. Managers of firms make critical choices at each stage concerning ICVs; therefore, each stage will be highlighted to demonstrate its significance to ICVs.

Initial Stage

Firm strategists initially make a decision as to whether they have the necessary resources and capabilities to go alone or to seek cooperation from others. In other words, they decide whether the firm is self-sufficient in pursuing a given strategy or whether it needs the resources and capabilities of either a complementary or competing firm(s). They compare and contrast the benefits and cost of internalization against collaboration. Once they choose the cooperation alternative, they might accomplish it by equity investment (a joint venture or equity holding in another firm) or non-equity investment. Equity investments are covered in the previous chapter; therefore, here I will focus on ICVs.

Formation Stage

At this stage, two important decisions play a significant role: the selection of a partner and a decision as to the type of ICV. In practice, one choice affects the other. If a firm decides to subcontract, it usually has an idea of the potential companies that offer such services. Or, a certain ICV type (such as franchising) could be the firm's built-in strategy (for example, McDonald's and Pizza Hut); therefore, the firm more likely might have been already developed some guidelines for selecting its franchisees. Partner selection very much depends on the type of partnership and availability of candidates that are suitable for a given partnership. Experienced companies such as McDonald's and Toyota have already developed certain standards and guidelines in their selection of partners (franchisees or suppliers, respectively). Partner resourcefulness, experience, and competence are important factors to consider. Once an MNC builds a reputation, numerous candidates will apply for partnership so that the MNC will have a chance to screen them in accordance with its own standards and local intelligence. For example, when entering a developing country, McDonald's had picked a local energetic entrepreneur with restaurant experience over a domestic conglomerate company with a deep pocket. In other words, the choice depends on the situation; the partners consider different parameters. The potential partner's resources and competencies are the key to selection, however.

Type of ICV. Although there might be many forms of ICVs, two types that we will mention here are traditionally popular ones and emerging cooperative ventures due to technological advancement and globalization. The former includes ICVs such as licensing and franchising, whereas the latter refers to cooperation such as technology partnerships, joint marketing, joint production, supply-chain agreements, and subcontracting. We will briefly discuss some types of ICVs.

Licensing. In an international licensing agreement, a firm, the licensor, grants the rights of using its patents and trademarks, technology, or know-how to another company abroad, which is the licensee. In return, the licensee agrees to pay a royalty or other form of payment, usually based on either production volume or sales, as agreed upon by the two parties. In a broader sense, contractor-defined licensing as a transfer of technology, which is the transfer of a capability in production, management, or marketing.[2] "It includes (a) rights to the use of patented information and trademarks in certain territories abdicated by agreement in favor of the licensee; (b) information that is proprietory but not patented, commonly called know-how...; and (c) services such as equipment installations, startups, testing, recruitment, management development, etc."[3] If a licensing agreement is not broad (as defined earlier) and is just a one-shot deal, it should not be considered a strategic alliance. On the other hand, in this book, a licensing agreement lasting over an extended period of time requiring continuous collaboration of both licensor and licensee is considered a strategic alliance.

As a form of market entry, international licensing is deemed as more risky than exporting but less risky than direct investment in a foreign country. The licensor exports its know-how instead of products but does not invest any equities. There might be a number of reasons for a company to use licensing as a vehicle of tapping foreign markets. As Phatak pointed out, by licensing their products, know-how, patents, or trademarks, companies attempt to achieve the following goals: generating extra income from existing technologies and services that they developed, spreading out the costs of their R&D projects, accessing markets that have been closed or protected, testing new markets before making capital investments, and minimizing risks in entering and expanding foreign markets.[4]

This list is not exhaustive, however. It also reflects the motives from mostly the standpoint of the licensor. Some of the same motives can stimulate the licensee. When a licensor at the same time becomes a licensee, it is called cross-licensing (where two companies exchange know-how with each other).

Although a simple licensing agreement is limited to a patent, trademark, or know-how, "more complex licensing agreements include the delivery by the licensor to the licensee one or more of the following: a patented product or process, a trade name, manufacturing techniques and other proprietary rights generally referred to as company or industry know-how, supply by the licensor to the licensee of components, materials, or equipment essential to a manufacturing process, technical advice and services of various sorts, market advice and assistance of various sorts, capital and/or managerial personnel."[5] Sometimes a licensing agreement is a part of another collaboration. Two firms establish a joint venture, then one of the partners grants its proprietary rights to the joint venture. For example, McDonald's used this kind of collaboration on a number of occasions when expanding its foreign markets.

Although licensing offers advantages such as entering into a foreign market without capital investment, testing a foreign market, and receiving know-how without large capital investments, it is not free of some risks. The licensee might become a competitor, fail to pay royalties, imitate the technology or trademark licensed, and sell the patent or trademark without consent of the licensor. The experience of many MNCs that licensed their patents or trademarks to a firm in a developing country shows that it is very difficult for the licensor to exert full control over the licensee's manufacturing and marketing operations. On the other hand, we can observe a more professional conduct in licensing agreements between two MNCs from industrialized countries. Nevertheless, it is my observation that emerging MNCs from developing countries demonstrate more and more of the same organizational behavior as those of MNCs from developed countries. MNCs from developing countries have realized the importance of the company's reputation in conducting international business.

For a licensing agreement, first the licensor or licensee should clearly define the objectives (for example, market development or know-how acquisition) and make an assessment of how this objective fits into the overall business strategy. The licensor or licensee should also pay attention to the kinds of advantages that will be gained through such partnership in comparison to the potential risks. Next, the firm should carefully choose its partner by considering the partner's reputation, capabilities, and previous experience. Moreover, special attention should be paid to exclusiveness and sub-licensing issues, because most of conflict arises on these two matters. The licensor can grant the exclusive right to the licensee to manufacture or distribute goods or services in a specified country or region or can grant non-exclusive manufacturing and distribution rights. The latter means that the licensor can grant its manufacturing and/or distribution rights to another firm as well in the same area. Of course, from the licensee's point of view, an exclusive licensing agreement is preferred. Also, it must be clear in the licensing agreement whether the licensee has a right to license the patent or trademark to another party. In rare occasions, subcontracting is allowed. Overall, like other partnership patterns, having mutual trust and a control mechanism for exploitive behavior is extremely important for licensing agreements to work to the satisfaction of both licensors and licensees.

Franchising. Franchising is a special form of licensing in which the franchisor grants the use of a brand name, trademark, business system, and other property rights to a franchisee that agrees, in return, to pay a fee based on the volume of sales. In recent years, there has been an explosion of franchising throughout the world due to the expansion of major franchising companies such as Coca-Cola, Pepsico, McDonald's, Burger King, Kentucky Fried Chicken (KFC), Hilton Hotels, and Holiday Inns. Franchising works similarly to licensing except that franchising is considered a more continuous type of relationship between franchisor and franchisee. Also, the franchisor usually exerts more control over the franchisee to assure product or service quality. Moreover, it is common to see the franchisor mandating that the franchisee must buy the equipment and some key ingredients from the franchisor. For example, McDonald's and Burger King dictate in their franchising agreements that the franchisees should buy from them the cooking equipment, patties for burgers, and other company-specified products.

It turns out that the hottest U.S. export might not be a singular product or service in the traditional sense but plain American "know-how." In particular, a variety of U.S. firms have embraced international franchising as a way to get their products into foreign markets. When combined with the phenomenal growth of emerging markets, international franchising as a business-development strategy has proven to be incredibly successful for many companies.

International franchising opportunities are enjoyed by not only big MNCs but also by medium and small-size companies. Kott Koatings, for example, a pioneer in the porcelain reglazing industry, fell into international franchising serendipitously. The company had already opened 350 franchises in the United States over 20 years and had not thought about going overseas until 1991, when a Hong Kong inquiry came in during a franchising trade show. Since then, most of the company's franchise growth has come from overseas. They now have franchises throughout Asia, the Middle East, Europe, and Latin America.

Other companies, however, have pursued international franchising for sheer business survival; for example, to expand beyond a saturated domestic market or to establish a presence in the international market before the competition arrives. International franchising also helps companies spread out costs and risks across the entire network. For example, the overseas expansion of Kott Koatings helped the company survive the downturn in the domestic economy during 1993 and 1994. Companies that were less diversified were hit hard at the time, and some were forced out of business.

www.ZLand.com can attest that overseas franchising can be very lucrative. The company, a software developer and application service provider of Web-based business solutions for small- and mid-size companies worldwide, is also the first to offer franchise opportunities in the field of Internet business software solutions. ZLand.com's first international presence began in Germany during the second quarter of 1999. After studying the market, ZLand.com found that there were three times as many small and mid-size companies in the Europe compared to the United States. As a result, the company gave franchising opportunities to European countries. Additionally, the company has expanded to Vancouver and Toronto as well as to Melbourne and Sydney, Australia.

Choosing the best countries for franchising historically has been based on, besides the qualities of franchise, geographical proximity to the home market and perceptions of cultural similarity. Other factors can be equally important, though, such as preferential trade pacts and existing business relationships. Today, however, franchisors from fast food restaurants to hotel chains have aggressively expanded their markets worldwide. California-based New Horizons Computer Learning Centers chose to open its first international franchise in Mexico City. New Horizons is the world's largest independent information technology training network. Among other things, students have access to instructor-led classes, Web-based training, and computer-based training on CD-ROM. The information technology industry is hot worldwide, and the company's profits reflect this situation. International gross revenues of the company grew at a rate of 54 percent in 1999. Product consistency is vital. Multinational clients want to be assured that the training offered in one country will be of the same high quality offered in other countries. At the same time, cultural, competitive, and legal differences sometimes require customizing the product and the sales and marketing materials.

China is a good example of growing a franchising business internationally. China's fast-food industry reported huge growth in 1999—more than 20 percent. Indigenous franchisors are beginning to emerge in China. The franchising movement will be affected by a huge surge of Chinese between the ages of 25–37—more than the entire population of the United States. When U.S. franchisors go to China today and in the years to come, they are thus likely to find a pool of candidates (for franchisees, employees, and joint venture partners) that is far larger, more sophisticated, and certainly more ambitious than could have been imagined only a few years ago. In gravitating toward franchising as the embodiment of western lifestyles, a vivid manifestation of globalism, young Chinese welcome franchising as a way of modern living. The Chinese government itself might well be warily approaching recognition that franchising is an activity with benefits for the society as a whole.

Subcontracting. The best manufacturers take advantage of two global trends: outsourcing and supply-chain cooperation. We will discuss outsourcing here as subcontracting and then discuss the supply-chain cooperation under supply-chain partnership. Outsourcing has become a popular practice among many competitive manufacturers. In other words, outsourcing has been considered one of the major factors contributing to a company's competitive advantage. The chief vehicle to accomplish outsourcing is subtracting agreements.

Hilsenrath pointed out how global competitors such as Nike and Timberland utilize outsourcing in their operations. "Nike discovered years ago that it can pay to let somebody else do your manufacturing. Its skills were in research, marketing, and distribution. Others are increasingly making the same calculation. Five years ago, Timberland produced 80% of its shoes in its own plants. Today, it produces just 18% by itself."[6]

Also, Motorola unveiled plans to outsource more than $30 billion of consumer-electronics production over the next five years with Flextronics International Ltd. and take a small stake in the contract manufacturer. The deal is the largest outsourcing agreement between a name-brand electronics company and a contract manufacturer. By 2005, the companies expect Flextronics to make more than $10 billion of cellular phones, two-way pagers, set-top boxes, and wireless communications gear and components for Motorola. That would be nearly twice Flextronics' total revenue of $5.7 billion in the fiscal year 2000.

Although Motorola will continue to do most of its manufacturing itself, it will assign an increasing share of its growth to contract manufacturers. Internal manufacturing will continue to grow, but it seems that the outsourcing piece will grow faster. The company wants to reduce its complement of roughly 25 contract manufacturers and will consolidate much of the work with Flextronics, based in Singapore but operated from San Jose, California.

The deal is the latest and most recent example of the broad outsourcing trend by electronics makers who rely on little-known companies such as Flextronics, Solectron, and SCI Systems to make the guts, and increasingly the entirety, of their machines.

The Motorola-Flextronics deal will not involve transferring any factories. To accommodate Motorola's business, Flextronics will be building non-stop. Flextronics already builds parts and products for Motorola in three U.S. plants as well as in factories in Mexico, Malaysia, Hungary, China, and Brazil. As part of the deal, Motorola will pay $100 million for an equity instrument convertible to 11 million shares of Flextronics, which would represent roughly a 5 percent stake in Flextronics. Motorola and Flextronics hope to use Internet technology to tie themselves more closely together and to streamline Motorola's supply chain.

Supply-chain partnership. It has been proven that manufacturers building effective links with suppliers pay off. After observing the successful procurement management of Japanese companies, many Western multinational companies have adopted similar practices. Instead of searching for the cheapest suppliers in the market by accepting bids from many potential suppliers, a number of MNCs have established a long-lasting relationship with a select, limited number of suppliers. In return, they assured the timely delivery of quality parts and components. The underlying reason for such a close tie between manufacturers and suppliers is the benefits that are expected from a just-in-time (JIT) inventory system.

The idea behind the JIT system is that large companies such as GM, Toyota, and GE have billions of dollars tied up in inventories. Even for small companies, it is possible to see that a significant amount of their cash resources is tied to their inventories. Then, any savings in inventory cost improves the firm's productivity. Firms engaged in JIT systems with their suppliers can make significant saving by switching most of their inventory costs to their suppliers because they do not need to carry a large amount of inventories anymore; instead, they obtain those inventories whenever needed from their suppliers. In other words, inventory items arrive when they are needed in the production process instead of being stored in stock. The JIT system implies a complete change in the technology of handling inventories.

The JIT system originated in Japan and is effectively utilized by many Japanese companies, including Toyota, Nissan, Honda, Sony, and Matsushita. In Japan, JIT systems are called *kanban*, a word that gets to the essence of just-in-time concept. *Kanban* is Japanese for "card" or "sign." Japanese suppliers ship parts in containers. Each container has a card, or kanban, slipped into a side pocket. When a production worker at the manufacturing plant opens a container, he or she takes out the card sends it back to the supplier. Receipt of the card initiates the shipping of a second container of parts that, ideally, reaches the production worker just as the last part in the first container is being used up. The ultimate goal of a JIT inventory system is to eliminate raw material inventories by coordinating production and supply deliveries precisely. When the system is designed properly, it results in a number of positive benefits for a manufacturer: "reduced inventories, reduced setup time, better work flow, shorter manufacturing time, less space consumption, and even higher quality. Of course, suppliers who can be depended on to deliver quality materials on time must be found. Because there are no inventories, there is no slack in the system so compensate for defective materials or delays in shipping."[7]

Consequently, an increasing number of firms ranging from automobile manufacturers to PC manufacturers have used supplier partnerships to improve their productivity—and thereby their comparative advantages. In building such partnerships, price is not the only consideration. "If price were the only criterion when top brands shop for suppliers, Asia's manufacturers might indeed be in struck in uninspiring business. But branded companies also need supplier deliver products at a breakneck pace, help hold inventories to razor-thin margins and search out cheap but reliable raw materials. So rather than shop for cheaper suppliers, many big multinationals have been consolidating their supply bases and building closer relationships with the very best."[8]

Flextronics, mentioned earlier, has established close ties with Cisco Systems. Cisco orders show up automatically on Flextronics' computers, and Flextronics frequently ships finished products directly to Cisco's customers. Similarly, Canadian telecommunications equipment maker Nortel Networks agreed to sell four factories to Solectron and agreed to buy roughly $10 billion of products from Solectron over four years.

Joint marketing. Often, two firms from different countries or two MNCs operating in many different countries reach a marketing accord by which each company helps each other in marketing others' products or services. When one company established in a country markets the products and services of another company, which does the same and vice-versa, we call it "piggy-back marketing." In such situations, partners feel that it is advantageous to penetrate a country's market without making direct investments, where the volume of sales probably does not justify the direct market entry. Additionally, coupled companies might extend their cooperation into new country markets. For example, based on their previous marketing alliance between Wal-Mart and America Online (AOL), Wal-Mart and AOL U.K. had signed a four-year strategic marketing deal. Under the agreement, Wal-Mart's 240 Asda stores in the United Kingdom will distribute disks with AOL U.K.'s PC-based interactive service, and Asda will be integrated into the AOL U.K. shopping, interests, and lifestyle channels as a preferred food and drink retailer.[9]

Furthermore, Wal-Mart and AOL U.K. units are taking a combined 22.5 percent stake in ShopSmart, the United Kingdom online price-comparison service. No cash is likely to change hands, but AOL and Wal-Mart will try to promote ShopSmart, and Wal-Mart will inject its rival price-comparison portal, Valuemad, into ShopSmart.[10] In return, ShopSmart will receive permanent exposure in Wal-Mart's Asda stores in the United Kingdom and in Wal-Mart shops in Germany. ShopSmart enables consumers to search through its online directory to find the best deal on a wide range of goods and services. About 75 percent of its 800,000 customers are in the United Kingdom, but the group also caters to the German and Swedish markets.

Another example is from a medical field between Carl Zeiss of France and Linvatec of the United States. Zeiss, the recognized world leader in surgical microscopes and image-guided surgical systems, announced a worldwide strategic alliance with Linvatec Corporation of Largo, Florida. Linvatec, a leading manufacturer of power surgical instruments and equipment in the United States, is at the forefront of developing technology and equipment for a growing range of least-invasive surgical procedures for use in otolaryngology, orthopedics, and neurosurgery.

Under the terms of the agreement, Zeiss and Linvatec will jointly market an integrated solution that combines Linvatec's E9000 Hall Surgical high-speed drill and blade system with the Zeiss STN image-guided surgery system. The STN is Zeiss' latest image-guided surgical system. It incorporates the Windows NT-based, industry standard SNN software platform adopted by all member companies of the SNN. This versatile and user-friendly platform provides effortless, hands-free instrument and microscope-based navigation and integration with a variety of applications, such as intra-operative radiation therapy supplied by other SNN member companies. The E9000 system features integrated irrigation and advanced software that maintains constant speeds and torque, even under load conditions. The system's high attainable speed enables surgeons to work faster and more efficiently. Integrating the E9000 system with STN image-guidance capabilities will also enable greater precision, increasing the surgeons' confidence and reducing invasiveness for the patient.[11]

Michael Kaschke, general manager of the Surgical Products Division of Carl Zeiss, commented, "The agreement we have entered into with Linvatec is an excellent example of the opportunities presented by membership in the SNN. The collaborative relationships of the SNN helps us broaden our product platform and deliver workflow enhancing solutions that combine the best of our core expertise with that of the other SNN member companies. We are very excited about working with Linvatec, a leader in powered surgical instruments."[12] On the other hand, Joe Gross, president of Linvatec, asserted, "The endoscopic sinus image guided surgery system is an excellent example of the company's focus on and concern for cost-effective measures that can be passed on to patients all over the world. We are also pleased to augment our sales and marketing resources by joining forces with a leader like Carl Zeiss."[13]

Although the nature of marketing collaboration varies from one industry to another, the collaborators aim at promoting each other's products or services to customers in respective countries. Through such agreements, customers in different countries have access to products or services of partnering firms that do not have to commit extensive resources. On the negative side, collaborating firms are heavily dependent on each other and do not have full control over operations in the other's country.

R&D partnerships. An increasing number of firms across nations have been collaborating to research and develop new products or technologies. Firms pool their resources by sharing the costs of a huge capital outlay of a project or combine their human and technological resources and capabilities to introduce an innovation. It is more visible that multidisciplinary research crossing the boundaries of specific applied sciences has yielded incredible successful outcomes in material development and solutions for disease treatments and information technologies. Kaounides emphasized such developments particularly in three areas:

"Three science-based technological revolutions are currently under way: one is in materials science and engineering, another is in biosciences and biotechnology, and the third is in information technologies and the convergence of computers, communications, and multimedia content. These advances are multidisciplinary, largely interdependent and are proceeding at a rapid pace from local networks and research centers of excellence located within different national systems of innovation around the world."[14] All of these developments would lead to further cooperation of firms across nations to come up with innovative materials and solutions.

IBM, Infineon Technologies Inc. (formerly Siemens), and United Microelectronics Corp. (UMC) have unveiled their R&D partnership for making integrated circuits (ICs) based on 0.13- and 0.10-micron copper-wired Complementary Metal-Oxide Semiconductors (CMOS) processes. The combined experience of the three partners will enable faster technology development at a lower cost per company. Production of the chips will beat the Semiconductor Industry Association's roadmap by several months. They hope that the combined efforts of IBM, Infineon, and UMC will result in the availability of the world's most advanced processes. Design and production of the 0.13-micron chip is expected around the second quarter and fourth quarter. Pilot production for the 0.10 micron is slated for 2002. The chips, under the brand name Worldlogic, will be marketed in Asia, Europe, and the United States.

According to the alliance's plan, the production capacity of the 0.13-micron ICs will augment through the year 2001 and should reach large volumes in late 2002, making the chip a mainstream-marketed product. The scope of the project includes logic, mixed signals, embedded DRAM, and copper wiring. Research will be conducted by engineers and scientists staffed by all three companies at the IBM Semiconductor Research and Development Center in the United States. This endeavor is IBM's second partnership with Infineon since their mid-'80s 16Mbits development project, which also involved Toshiba. This time, IBM and Infineon are adding UMC's manufacturing expertise, which might help the group come up with more cost-effective processes.

This situation basically means that in today's complex technological production systems and overlying industries, not many companies might have the entire technical competency to generate new products and services. Such situations require technological collaboration between companies. For example, Genome Therapeutics Corp. is one of the leaders in the field of genomics—the identification and functional characterization of genes. Genome Therapeutics and bioMerieux, a France-based company that specializes in infectious disease diagnostics and industrial microbiology control, agreed on a strategic alliance to develop, manufacture, and sell in vitro diagnostic products for human, clinical, and industrial applications. As part of the alliance, bioMerieux has purchased a subscription to Genome Therapeutics' proprietary microbial database PathoGenome™ and made an equity investment in Genome Therapeutics. The firm also guaranteed first-year funding to Genome Therapeutics, including the equity investment of approximately $6.2 million. In this case, equity and non-equity partnerships exist simultaneously.

bioMerieux has initiated an R&D program called Anais™, which will be significantly supported by this agreement. This program's aim is to develop a next-generation, fully automated molecular diagnostic system that will enable a more rapid identification of the causes of human infections, especially those caused by drug-resistant organisms. Anais will introduce innovative technologies originating in molecular biology combined with advanced bioinformatics technologies into in vitro diagnostics, providing hospitals and reference laboratories (and industrial companies for controlling the safety of products for human consumption) with solutions based on direct methods that are at once fully automated, rapid, highly sensitive, and cost-effective. In the field of clinical diagnostics, these new-generation products are designed to enable rapid intervention and a better-targeted treatment as well as reduced treatment and hospitalization time. At a time when the global health care environment is undergoing profound changes and is facing new challenges—the emergence of new infectious diseases, increasing drug resistance, and the worldwide circulation of pathogenic agents—Anais will bring a new approach to infectious disease diagnosis.

Alain Merieux, chairman and CEO of bioMerieux, claimed that "this alliance moves bioMerieux closer to our goal of a real-time, accurate diagnostic system to address in particular the problem of drug resistance and allow physicians to make better treatment recommendations. This alliance with Genome Therapeutics, a pioneer and the established leader in the field of pathogen genomics, enables us to stay at the cutting edge of genomics-based product development, strongly complements our product development efforts in the sphere of human clinical diagnostics, and enhances our programs in industrial areas including water, food, pharmaceuticals and cosmetic testing."[15]

As part of the alliance, the parties will utilize genomic sequence information contained within Genome Therapeutics' PathoGenome database to identify genetic markers that can be employed in diagnostic product development. Additional high-quality sequence information and molecular biology analyses will further define the genetic signature of various organisms as well as different strains of the same organism in order to rapidly identify organisms, determine their virulence, expose resistance potential, and determine sensitivity to specific antibiotics. bioMerieux will incorporate this genetic information into its Anais system by using the GeneChip® Array technology from Affymetrix. The PathoGenome database provides genome sequence information for nearly 30 microbial organisms assembled through Genome Therapeutics' pathogen genomics research in combination with public domain sources. The database utilizes proprietary bioinformatics software and enables researchers to search for novel target genes among multiple pathogens and to cross-reference genomic information.

Robert J. Hennessey, chairman, president, and CEO of Genome Therapeutics, noted the benefits of the alliance as follows: "Three aspects of this alliance are especially favorable for Genome Therapeutics. First, it enables us to expand our scientific leadership and our successful database product PathoGenome from drug discovery into diagnostics, thereby positioning us along the continuum of infectious disease management. Second, it strengthens our commercial potential by aligning us with the most rapidly growing player in the in vitro diagnostics field. With bioMerieux's world leadership in infectious disease diagnostics and a distribution network in 110 countries, we have gained a pathway to more near-term product revenues. Third, it positions our technology even beyond human health care into the industrial arena, where the potential markets are extremely large."[16]

Under the terms of the alliance, Genome Therapeutics granted bioMerieux all rights not previously granted to others in the area of pathogen genetics for the development of diagnostic products. In return, bioMerieux paid an upfront technology access fee and made a $3.75 million equity investment in Genome Therapeutics' common stock. In addition, bioMerieux will fund a research program for at least four years, subscribe to the PathoGenome database, and pay royalties on future products. Guaranteed first-year funding, including the equity investment, is approximately $6.2 million to Genome Therapeutics.

Joint production. Joint production is also called co-production or production sharing, where two or more companies contribute to the manufacturing of a final product. If each participating firm mastered in manufacturing certain parts of the product or at processes through cost minimization or differentiation (for example, a quality leader), they would complement each other in coming up with a superior final product. This kind of partnership can be carried out as part of another collaboration (for example, equity participation) or as an entirely new collaboration. As an example of the former, GM and Fuji Heavy Industries agreed upon manufacturing cars together. GM will benefit from Fuji's strengths in all-wheel drive and continuously variable transmissions, while Fuji will benefit from GM's research on alternative power plants and other environmental orientations. The alliance will focus initially on the design and manufacture of small and mid-size sport-utilities and crossover vehicles. In reference to an entirely new cooperation, GM and Honda decided to collaborate on the production of hybrid and diesel engines.

Some U.S. manufacturers have some parts of their products made in Taiwan, the Caribbean, or Mexico to take advantage of cheap labor in those countries. In doing so, they ship components from the United States, have the labor-intensive parts assembled in those countries, and finish the final assembly in the United States. So, production sharing is the way to reduce the total manufacturing cost to stay competitive.

As these different types illustrate, a firm could engage in a variety of ICVs or a combination of them.

Operations and *outcomes* stages of ICVs present very similar characteristics as those of IJVs. The control of such ventures is more difficult than with IJVs because there is no equity stake in the venture by parties to support their influence. Instead, they rely on only contractual norms. Of course, trust between partners plays an important role in complying with the agreement and achieving desired results. Because we discussed operations and outcomes stages in the previous chapter in reference to IJVs, we will not repeat them here.

In conclusion, companies use ICVs in one form or another as efficient means of achieving their corporate and business objectives. They are risky, but they present a fundamental necessity of strategic ends. ICVs offer flexibility to the partners in comparison with equity partnerships. The most important characteristic that distinguishes an ICV from a typical contractual one is the emphasis on long-term goals and strategic benefits for both partners. Lanser, by giving examples from the health care industry, described the ways of turning "contractual agreements" into "partnership agreements," which includes emphasizing the long term, putting trust before price, and revisiting the agreement periodically.[17] In recent years, ICVs have become increasingly popular instruments in achieving strategic purposes of companies.

NOTES

1. S. B. Tallman, and O. Shenkar, Managerial decision model of international cooperative venture formation, *Journal of International Business Studies*, 25, no. 1 (1994): 91–113.

2. F. J. Contractor, *Licensing in international strategy: A guide for planning and negotiations* (Westport, CT: Quorum Books, 1985).

3. Ibid., 6.

4. A. V. Phatak, *International management: Concepts and cases* (Cincinnati, OH: South-Western College Publishing, 1997): 254–255.

5. Ibid., 255–256.

6. Jon H. Hilsenrath, Overseas suppliers to U.S. brands thrive, *The Wall Street Journal* (March 10, 2000): p. A18.

7. Stephen P. Robbins, and David A. De Cenzo, *Fundamentals of management*, Second edition (Upper Saddle River, N.J.: Prentice Hall, Inc., 1998): 168.

8. Hilsenrath, A18.

9. Wall Street Journal, Wal-Mart, AOL Europe take a 22.5% stake in ShopSmart (August 9, 2000): A16.

10. Ibid.

11. PR Newswire Association (October 6, 1999).

12. Ibid.

13. Ibid.

14. L. C. Kaounides, Science, technology, and global competitive advantage, *International Studies of Management & Organization*, 29, no. 1 (Spring 1999): 53–79.

15. PR Newswire Association (October 6, 1999): 1.

16. Ibid.

17. E. G. Lanser, Building partnership agreements, *Healthcare Executive*, 16, no. 1 (Chicago, January–February 2001): 54–55.

6

Global Alliances in the Automobile Manufacturing Industry

The principal objective of this chapter is to enhance our understanding of patterns of strategic partnerships in the automobile manufacturing industry from economic, organizational, and strategic management perspectives. This chapter describes the strategic links of automobile manufacturers by providing insight into their international partnerships and critical issues they experience during such endeavors. This chapter highlights the advantages of global alliances between automobile manufacturers as well as non-manufacturers by describing the present trends and dynamics of interfirm cooperation and by analyzing the motives and processes of such ventures. To fully understand interfirm partnerships in automobile manufacturing, we must first grasp the industry's dynamics and then describe the alliance patterns and processes.

INDUSTRY DYNAMICS

Market Size

The global market represents about 44 million vehicles per year in sales.[1] This number is expected to grow to about 64 million by 2002. The biggest growth is expected in China, India, the Pacific Rim, South Africa, and South America. The global market in the automotive industry is well more than $1 trillion and involves more than 10 million employees, meaning that it is the world's largest manufacturing business.[2] The major producing countries are the United States with 23 percent, Japan with 20 percent, and Germany with 10 percent. The largest single market is the United States with annual sales of about 15 million units.

Demand is projected to reach 60 million units by 2002, and capacity is expected to be 80 million units for the same period.³ The slow growth can be attributed to recent price increases, outpaced income growth, and the increase in the age of registered automobiles (the average car is eight years old). Presently, it takes 24.5 weeks of family earnings to purchase an automobile compared to 17.5 weeks of income in 1994.⁴

Scope of Competitive Rivalry

The automotive industry has become globally competitive and has undergone significant restructuring and consolidation. All of the major industry participants are continuing to increase their focus on efficiency and cost improvements while announced capacity increases for the North American market and excess capacity in the European market have led to continuing price pressures.

General Motors (GM), Ford, and Chrysler (now DaimlerChrysler), known as the Big Three, accounted for 69.4 percent of the U.S. market in 1999, down from 1998's 71.0 percent and 1997's 71.7 percent. Their 1999 market shares (cars and trucks combined) are as follows: GM with 29.5 percent, Ford with 24.1 percent, and Chrysler with 16.8 percent.⁵ Japan accounts for 31 percent of the market with Honda at 10 percent, Toyota at 9.9 percent, Nissan at 5.7 percent, Mazda at 2 percent, and Subaru at 1.4 percent.⁶ Other foreign manufacturers sustain a 10.2 percent market share.

In the mature European market, Volkswagen stands as the market leader with GM in second position. In Japan, foreign automakers are experiencing sluggish sales growth, with U.S. manufacturers only gaining 3.1 percent.⁷ In the Asian market, Japanese automakers are dominating while the U.S. manufacturers are pursuing strategies such as local production and distribution.⁸ By 2005, some are projecting that total industry sales in the South American and Asian regions will double more than 35 percent of the worldwide market.⁹ There are three global developments that put U.S. automakers in a shifting competitive position: The fastest-growing auto markets are in countries that are struggling to develop their own industries; new technologies must address environmental and safety concerns; and manufacturers depend increasingly on the important players in a long and complex supply chain.¹⁰

There are basically four categories in the motor vehicle market. The U.S. manufacturers dominate the truck and *sport* utility vehicle (SUV) market; the Japanese dominate in family sedans (such as Toyota Camry and Honda Accord); the Europeans lead in luxury sedans (Mercedes and BMW); and the economy market is highly fragmented. The major manufacturers have ranges of products that play to all the major market segments. Only a few manufacturers have chosen to focus on niches, such as Isuzu (trucks) and Subaru (all-wheel drive passenger cars). The primary battle is now in light trucks, which include minivans and SUVs. These vehicles yield the greatest unit profits. In addition to the big three, virtually all of the major importers have SUVs.

For GM, competing on a global basis is a priority that is driving the largest international production capacity expansion in the company's history. GM has five new manufacturing facilities either under development or up and running in Argentina, China, Brazil, Poland, and Thailand. These facilities are the cornerstone of GM's expansion into new markets. GM derives 20 percent to 25 percent of its revenues from international vehicle sales and only six percent from the Asia/Pacific region. Ford, which garners about 20 percent of its profits from outside North America, has been losing money in Latin America. But profits have been increasing in the bigger European market.

Market Growth and Stage in Product Life Cycle

While the market in the United States and Europe is mature, in developing countries there is room for growth. A worldwide growth is expected to be significant, with approximately 10 million units added in the next 10 years.[11]

Over the past few years, American automakers have seen a steady 2 percent to 3 percent growth.[12] This growth has been fueled by increases in light truck sales. Passenger car sales have remained at or below 9 million units since 1992. The peak was reached in 1986 at 11.5 million units.[13] Growth will have to come from developing countries as the developed nations represent mature auto markets. Barriers to growth in these markets, however, are that they are developing their own automotive industries and/or preventing access to foreign automakers. On the other hand, auto parts manufacturers' long-term prospects are promising, despite the fierce competition. Growth arises from several sources: the rush to add more high-tech features to vehicles, the United States-Japan trade accord, global expansion, and the standardization of parts. In addition, growth in the United States has also been observed in the sales of light trucks and SUVs over the past several years.

Although the automobile industry is mature, cyclical, and saturated, manufacturers can still rev up the demand for vehicles by making them more affordable.[14]

Number of Rivals and Their Relative Sizes

The automobile industry worldwide is concentrated. The big three are now the big six, as Toyota, Nissan, and Honda continue to expand their assembly and powertrain (engines and transmission) operations in North America. Over the past several years, many foreign manufacturers, such as Honda and BMW, have seen great opportunities for growth in the U.S. market. Building plants in the United States and producing vehicles that are sold in the United States and Canada have produced this growth. Not only can they promote their vehicles by claiming "Built in the USA," but they can also nearly eliminate tariffs, take advantage of currency fluctuations, reduce logistic costs, and operate close to the customer. Many non-U.S. automakers are targeting for more growth, because part of the corporate strategy is focusing on future products for the light truck market.

The automobile industry is global, given the fact that all players are competing in each other's markets. The principal players in the vehicle manufacturing industry include GM, Ford, and DaimlerChrysler (an American-German company) in the United States, and other major players include Toyota, Nissan, and Honda from Japan; Volkswagen and BMW from Germany; Renault and Peugeot-Citroen from France; Fiat from Italy; Saab (owned by GM now) and Volvo (owned by Ford) from Sweden; and Hyundai and Kia from South Korea. The U.S. auto market is the only truly open market. All other markets are protected to some extent. The bulk of the import nameplate vehicles are actually assembled in North America. Although GM, the number one manufacturer, is continually losing market share to foreign competitors, it is aggressively trying to regain market share with rebates and discount financing.

Number of Buyers and Their Relative Sizes

The majority of buyers are consumers at large. According to the U.S. Industry Survey, the average family owns 1.5 cars, and in fact this average number might rise by two or three.[15] Other major buyers are industrial and business organizations. Government and car-rental companies (some are vertically integrated with automobile makers) are also important customers. Overcapacity ensures competition for sales, and this situation has taken pricing power away from the automobile makers.

The Degree of Vertical Integration

The automobile industry has been very competitive. Although, in the U.S. market, which is the largest market, the big three have been dominant in controlling a large portion of market share, foreign competition has eroded their strong position.

Increasing competition and weaknesses in some world markets are causing some horizontal integration among manufacturers and increasing consolidations. The most recent merger was Chrysler and Daimler-Benz. Automobile manufacturers with cost containment and safety reasons assert a high degree of influence over supply and distribution channels. Most manufacturers have full control over their dealers. It is common to observe strategic alliances between automobile manufacturers and their suppliers. The suppliers are rewarded with long-term contracts as they incur most of the program costs. GM is the most vertically integrated manufacturer, buying only 30 percent of its components. The part industry consists of more than 10,000 U.S. suppliers, 2,300 European suppliers, and 2,100 Japanese suppliers and does more than $50 million in business.[16] More than 2,500 worldwide original equipment manufacturers (OEMs) exist that help produce the 15,000 components that automakers need to build a new vehicle. Companies such as Johnson Controls, Goodyear, Dana, and Tenneco are among the largest independent OEMs. Some suppliers are OEM subsidiaries within large, diversified companies such as GE, 3M, Allied Signal, and Eaton. Generally speaking, vehicle manufacturers are mainly concerned with assembly but are not extremely vertically integrated, meaning that they outsource a good share of their components. For example, Ford and Chrysler purchase more than 55 percent and 70 percent, respectively, from OEMs. Furthermore, Japanese manufacturers are not highly integrated either, often purchasing around 65 percent of their components from American or Japanese OEMs.

Besides manufacturing, all firms are highly integrated. Most have rental car subsidiaries to ensure sales, some have their own part manufacturing subsidiaries, and most have their own financial arms to provide consumer loans. In addition, the big three are running their own dealerships (and service departments) to further integrate. Currently, 22,000 car dealerships exist in the United States, many of which have common ownership (in other words, an individual or corporation has multiple ownership).[17]

Ease of Entry or Exit

Capital requirements, the need for a distribution network, and regulatory issues make entering the automobile manufacturing market extremely difficult. Large capital commitments are needed to keep up with new product development and model changeovers. For instance, for 1985 and 1986, GM's capital investments reached $22.2 billion while capital expenditures of Ford and Chrysler (now part of DaimlerChrysler) were about $8 billion and $4 billion, respectively.[18] Almost all existing automotive manufacturers have been in existence since the early part of the century. Today, even existing companies are seeking consolidations. In other words, the industry has a high barrier to entry. Entry barriers are extensive because high infrastructure costs deter new competition. International markets present a challenge because some markets are closed or limited to foreign competition.

Because of the huge capital outlays in large plants and equipment, it is also difficult to exit the market. As a result, several manufacturers have continued in business through several years of losing large amounts of money. Exiting from the industry appears to occur through a takeover or a merger with another manufacturer. For example, Ford acquired Jaguar of Britain and Volvo of Sweden; GM acquired Saab of Sweden; two French carmakers,

Peugeot and Citroen, merged; Volkswagen acquired SEAT of Spain and Skoda of the Czech Republic; and Hyundai bought 51 percent shares of Kia (another Korean manufacturer).

Technology and Innovation

Currently, motor vehicle manufacturers use a significant amount of advanced technology in manufacturing their products. These technological advances include anti-lock braking systems, electronic problem sensors, memory systems, automated emissions equipment, on-board navigation systems, and night vision imaging systems. The design of new vehicles is an innovative process that takes into account fuel economy, safety, reliability, performance, and aesthetics. The consumer can easily observe that each vehicle model is more advanced than its predecessor.

A recent industry publication by Chrysler and Ford indicates that depending on "platform," today's automobiles have anywhere between 10,000–12,000 individual parts. Development time varies based on the complexity of the vehicle, options, and the reuse of components from other platforms. Technology plays a key role in depressing design time. In addition, international competition is characterized by an increasing dynamism of innovation. The gradually increasing time of product marketing—in some situations, even shorter than the time of product development—demands that a corporation accomplish a growing number of new product developments and rapid prototype developments in order to compete in the global market successfully. The new technology and innovation issues, such as lean/agile manufacturing and faster prototyping, total quality management, mechatronics, robotics, motion and machine vision, and logistics management, will be major concerns in the automobile manufacturing industry.

Over the past several years, many motor vehicle makers have been making great strides in rebuilding their internal structures. Automakers such as the big three have slashed costs, restored their financial health, accumulated cash buffers, improved quality and design, and improved efficiency. Companies such as GM are seeking to reduce costs and improve efficiencies by utilizing common global designs, platforms, parts, and processes. Furthermore, many automakers are trying to cut the number of components in their vehicles. By accomplishing this goal, cycle times will be reduced; production costs will lower; and assembly errors will likely be reduced. For example, GM's newest vehicle designs incorporate 20 percent to 30 percent fewer parts and require about 25 percent less assembly time than did their predecessors. Another example is that of Ford's 2000 Plan. Ford intends to realize cost efficiencies by consolidating worldwide design and engineering. The manufacturers are also responding to environmental concerns and lowering costs by minimizing industrial waste and pollution. Several automakers are divesting their non-core units to help raise cash for cyclical downturns.

Additionally, information technology is affecting the automotive industry at all levels—from the manufacturer down to the dealers. The Automotive Network Exchange (ANX), originated by Chrysler and then adopted by GM and Ford, will enable automakers and suppliers to save $76 per car or $1.1 billion annually. The ANX uses many different data communications technologies for various applications such as billing, just-in-time (JIT) delivery, electronic data interchange (EDI), and computer-aided design and computer-aided manufacturing (CAD/CAM). This system will replace those multiple, costly, and redundant network connections with a single extranet that eventually will support many of the specialized enterprise resource planning applications that the automobile industry demands. The system will enable OEMs and large suppliers to substantially reduce the cost associated with proprietary communication technologies that were previously too expensive.

Digital dealers, the most technologically advanced automotive retailers, are emerging as a leading force in deploying information technology to fulfill their customers' needs and to communicate with them throughout the vehicle-ownership cycle. Dealers are becoming digital in response to digital consumers who research vehicle content, prices, and availability on the Internet. Some of the Internet-based automotive services are now available to consumers to simplify the information-gathering and pre-purchase stages.

In the United States, the Environmental Protection Agency's Clean Air Act is also forcing innovation in the automobile industry. Automakers have developed the technology needed to manufacture the low-emission vehicle required by the act. They estimate this technology will cost the industry more than $1 billion, or about $95 per car.[19]

Product Characteristics

For the motor vehicle industry, products are both standardized and differentiated. Across the industry, products are differentiated—ranging from SUVs and heavy trucks to automobiles and light trucks.Over the past 20 years, however, it has become more difficult for manufacturers to distinguish their products. In response, automakers have product development strategies that focus on areas that stand out to consumers: exterior sheet metal, windows, dashboard design, engines, wheels, and passenger seating. This differentiation enables consumers to choose their vehicle model based on their preferences, expectations, and tastes. Vehicles of the same model are standardized except for the options, color, and transmission type.

Over the past several years, vehicles have included more features as a standard part of the package, but they have also added features to differentiate themselves from the competition. For example, air conditioning, power locks, and power windows are becoming more standard in vehicles along with safety features (airbags, side-impact bars, and anti-lock braking systems, or ABS). Features such as computerized dashboards, remote keyless entry, and built-in child seats, however, help further differentiate the product from similar models and from the competition. The modern automobile industry, especially, consists of differentiated products. Products are primarily differentiated by price and body style, and differentiation is the key to sale success. Technological innovations and improved production methods have increased the variability and frequency of new model vehicles. Competitive advantages, however, usually occur through a shift in market preferences to models of vehicles that only one or two companies dominate. For example, to compete in the European market, U.S. automakers are hanging their hopes on growth in the minivan and SUV markets.

At the same time, there is a move for a standard car for the global market. Cars traditionally were complex and highly differentiated, but with the advent of "global" cars, this differentiation is decreasing. Ford has instituted its "Ford 2000" plan to improve quality and to lower total costs. The initiative's goal is to eliminate duplication in the design and production of cars and car parts around the world. The Ford 2000 plan stripped authority away from the company's strong and parallel organizations in Dearborn, Michigan and in Europe. In their places are five "vehicle centers," each of which is charged with developing cars and trucks for the entire world.

Scale Economies

Automobile production requires a very large investment in the plant and equipment. While improvements in technology and production methods have reduced some of the traditional economies of scale, the initial and ongoing investment in the plant and equipment presents a formidable barrier to any new entrant into the industry. To realize innovation, which is essential for becoming and staying competitive, a large amount of R&D spending is required.

The Ford 2000 program and copycat programs at other multinational automobile manufacturers will enable firms to realize tremendous cost savings from scale economies. With the homogenization of products, costs associated with line retooling and other product-diversification costs will also decrease. In the past several years, there has been a great degree of consolidation as companies seek to create alliances to share infrastructure costs.

The need for economies of scale is driving the urge to merge in the automobile industry. Specific operational strategies include reducing the labor costs and overcapacity through closing plants, consolidating operations, merging, and forming joint ventures. A large production volume is needed for a new model. Badge engineering enables GM and DaimlerChrysler to market multiple vehicles that share basic platforms and components.

Experience Curve

The automobile industry has a history of major production innovation breakthroughs based on a firm's experience. Henry Ford's ability to produce consistent interchangeable parts and simple assembly production provided the basis for automobile mass production and produced a significant competitive advantage. Similarly, today's lean production techniques, resulting from years of continuous improvement experience, have provided a sustainable competitive advantage for the Japanese. The automobile industry's high experience curve poses a significant barrier to new entrants.

The experience curve battle in the automotive industry is primarily concerned with the time it takes to bring a vehicle to the market. The Japanese are the best at new model development, with model changeovers occurring at roughly four-year intervals. Model runs for U.S. automakers are typically in the five- to seven-year ranges. Honda is the champion at model launches with model-year changes. On the other hand, GM has had problematic launches of all its new vehicles over the past few years.

Dove suggested that manufacturing knowledge is one of the core competencies in the automotive industry and that management of knowledge provides a competitive advantage.[20] The other area where experience plays a significant role is in new product design, or the period from conception to production.

Overall, experience curves play a vital role in helping to lower costs, improve efficiencies, and improve quality. The more experienced the company in the automobile industry, the more familiar and knowledgeable its employees are with design, process, manufacturing, sales, and marketing of the vehicle. Reaching efficient and profitable levels does not occur overnight, however. This goal requires many years to reach sustainable, productive, and profitable levels. Companies that have sustained themselves in this industry have a big advantage over newcomers. These advantages are observed in the areas of capital, manufacturing efficiencies, skilled labor, and capacities.

Capacity Utilization

The world automobile industry has an excessive capacity of uncompetitive mass-production and an under-capacity of lean production manufacturing plants as automobile manufacturing capacity is increasing in developing countries. The automobile industry in Korea, Brazil, China, and India is going through impressive growth. Governments have played a key role in the evolution of the industry in all these developing countries. The Korean industry, despite its recent setback, has made the most significant progress and is now exporting cars to developed markets. It is the only country that invested in R&D for product development, retained management control in joint ventures with multinational companies, and had ambitious export targets. The industry in Brazil is controlled entirely by multinational corporations (MNCs). Although this situation has led to growth and the adoption of lean production, indigenous product development is lacking. Tariff barriers have come down, forcing domestic production to become more market responsive. Fluctuating tariffs and taxes and cyclical demand have characterized the industry. The Indian automotive industry is experiencing a revolution with rapid growth and the entry of nine MNCs, and another three plan to enter in the next two years. The Chinese industry is also growing very rapidly, although it is still highly fragmented. Passenger cars are only 15 percent of total vehicle production in China. Demand in Brazil, India, and China is highly price sensitive, and growth is led by the demand for a small car. Higher taxes on mid- and large-size cars give the small car a big price advantage. Import duties for components imply that the supplier base in these countries needs to develop fast. The supplier industry in the merging economies could become a bottleneck for growth.

A major implication is that the future in China and India, the two biggest potential markets with the highest growth rates, is uncertain (although bright). Governments seem to appreciate the necessity for stable policies and progressive deregulation and regard the automotive industry as one of the pillars of economic growth. Uncertainty exists about the extent of growth, the degree to which suppliers can meet demand, and the number of players that will be able to survive in the long run, however. The automotive MNCs have kept introducing their models that succeeded in the West to emerging markets. It remains to be seen whether this strategy will succeed. The Brazilian industry, which is much older than that of China or India, will probably continue to experience significant growth. Capacity is expected to increase in the next couple of years. Korean carmakers are also entering India and could enter other emerging markets, as well. Korea is a lucrative market for the automotive MNCs but is emerging as a trade partner rather than as a major net importer of cars. Daewoo, one of the Korean manufacturers, is a takeover subject by a Western multinational. With stagnation in developed markets and huge additions of capacity in emerging markets, market power of MNCs over car production could erode, although they will continue to dominate product development.

Nevertheless, with companies rushing to capture new markets in Asia and Latin America, analysts predict that the industry will have the capacity to produce about 22 million more vehicles than the world wants.[21] Current global production of automobiles by major vehicle manufacturers is given in Table 6.1.

Table 6.1

Production Profile in the Global Automobile Industry— 1999

Companies	Annual Production (in Thousands)
General Motors (GM, Opel, Vaxhaull, Saab)	7.497
Ford (Ford, Jaguar, Volvo)	7.100
Toyota (Toyota, Lexus, Duihatsu, Hino)	5.314
Renault-Nissan (Renault, Nissan, Mack)	4.820
Volkswagen (VW, Audi, Seat, Skoda, Lamborghini, Rolls-Royce)	4.818
DaimlerChrysler (combined for 2000)	4.749
Fiat (Fiat, Iveco, Alfa Romeo, Lancia, Ferrari, Maserati)	2.663
Honda	2.593
PSA Peugeot Citroen	2.270
Mitsubishi	1.542
Suzuki	1.253

Industry Profitability

The big three manufacturers are benefiting from restructuring efforts and efficiency gains. Their earnings were up to $16.9 billion in 1997 from $13.9 billion in 1994. Their revenues have suffered in recent years, however. In particular, Chrysler has been losing money in the past two years. The gross margins of companies fluctuate greatly with production volume. After the breakeven point, the automaker can earn substantial profits on each additional unit of production because fixed costs are spread over more units. Even so, it is rare for an automaker's gross margin to exceed 25 percent of its revenues.

"The automobile manufacturing company is often trying to earn a return on sales averaging 5% over the full course of the automotive cycle, which may run more than four years. For much of the past 20 years, U.S. automakers haven't even reached this meager target of a 5% return on sales, because of the strenuous competition they have faced."[22]

We should point out that most of the growth in the U.S. market has been at the high end and for SUVs. Long-term trend demand is growing at less than 1 percent per year through 2002, and normal trend demand for 2000 was approximately 15.3 million vehicles.[23]

External Factors

There are also several external factors affecting the profitability in the motor vehicle industry. First of all, the value of local currency can either stimulate or slow down sales internationally. For example, currency fluctuations have encouraged the production of foreign models in North America and reduced the flow of imports. Presently, most moderately priced vehicles sold in the United States are also made domestically. The transfer process is just beginning for luxury cars. Another aspect of the economy influencing demand is the level of interest rates. Interest rate increases cramp consumer confidence and cause people to postpone replacing their aging vehicles. Finally, government regulations can constrain technological capabilities and have an impact on many features of the vehicle. The features of the vehicle that concern safety and emissions are the areas that are most subject to government standards and regulations.

In recent years, one of the most important events in automobile industry is the merger of Chrysler and Daimler-Benz. One of the largest industrial marriages in history occurred between the world's No. 6 car company, Chrysler, and No. 15 Daimler-Benz, to produce the world's fifth-biggest automobile company. The new combination, valued at $40 billion, will generate $130 billion in sales and employ more than 400,000 people. The merger is notable not only because of its size and complexity but also because of its symbolism. The creation of DaimlerChrysler AG represents a triumph of the global economy and the end of car companies as national emblems of industrial might. The car business is too capital and customer-hungry to care about flags.

Nevertheless, a close look at the DaimlerChrysler merger shows some potential problem areas with which the company's management should deal. Those problems include structural issues of the combined company, differences in management styles and cultures, and financial improvement.

The overall picture of the world auto industry presents a great deal of consolidation and interfirm links. Big auto manufacturers including GM, Ford, DaimlerChrysler, Toyota, and Renault have engaged in either acquisitions or strategic alliances with other car makers.

Despite their shortcomings, American automakers are doing better than most of their competitors. The Japanese automakers were in a very good position just a few years ago, but today, foreigners control many of them. Renault runs Nissan. DaimlerChrysler bought a one-third interest in Mitsubishi Motors (the Mitsubishi scandal over defective cars did not break the deal). Ford manages Mazda. GM bought a 20 percent stake in Fuji Heavy Industries, the maker of Subaru, while owning 49 percent of Isuzu and 10 percent of Suzuki. In other words, foreigners control three Japanese automakers, have a major interest in another, and have important interests in two more. Only two companies, Toyota and Honda, are pure Japanese.

Worldwide auto manufacturing companies present a complex picture. In Korea just a few years ago, there were five independent car makers boasting about selling six million units a year, up from two million. But Hyundai bought a 51 percent stake in Kia and Daewoo, which is now number two but in financial trouble on the market. Renault has bought Samsung. China has made deals with numerous car makers but is dominated by Volkswagen and General Motors. India is dominated by Suzuki of Japan, in which GM has a 10 percent interest. In Great Britain, sales are dominated by foreigners— Ford, General Motors (Ford and GM manufacture in Britain, as do Toyota, Nissan, and Honda), Peugeot, and BMW. The old British names, such as Jaguar, Land Rover, Rolls-Royce, and Mini are all foreign-owned with one exception: Land Rover. Land Rover did belong to BMW but was doing so badly that the Germans promised some Brits hundreds of millions just to take it off their hands. They did, but Rover is not likely to survive independently. In Sweden, Ford owns Volvo and GM owns Saab. In Italy, there is really only one producer—Fiat—in which General Motors has a 20 percent stake. In France, two are independent companies—Renault and Peugeot-Citroen—after the merger of those two. Apart from Renault's move into the Far East, its global extension is limited. In Germany, other great powers in the auto world are Daimler, which owns Chrysler, and Volkswagen, which owns Skoda of the Czech Republic and Seat of Spain. BMW and Porsche remain strong and independent. Ford, GM, and the Chrysler half of DaimlerChrysler make more profit, roughly $16 billion, than the remainder of the world's car industry put together (although Fiat owns 5 percent of GM, but that is not a controlling interest).

Despite all these consolidations and alliances, the global auto industry experiences some problems that can be attributed to a number of factors: losing market share to foreign competition in the United States, increasing costs in Germany, over-expanding in Korea, never preparing for a rainy day in Japan, and sheer incompetence in Britain. The economic slowdown in the United States follows the record years of profits of the past two years.

ALLIANCES IN GLOBAL AUTO MANUFACTURING

Since the early 1980s, many strategic alliances have been formed in the motor vehicle industry as car and truck manufacturers and automotive parts suppliers moved aggressively to compete globally. Not only have there been alliances between automakers that are strong in one region of the world and automakers that are strong in another region, but there have also been strategic alliances between vehicle makers and key manufacturers of parts and suppliers (especially those that have high-quality parts and strong technological capabilities).[24] Moreover, major automobile manufacturers have recently been forming strategic alliances with companies in different industries to complement their resources. For example, Ford has set up a joint venture with Qualcomm to deliver wireless services to automobiles, including a mobile phone service. Such telematics services include bringing phone, Internet, entertainment, navigation, and safety services to vehicles. Similarly, GM offers some of those services now through its Onstar unit. Automakers believe that telematics and mobile commerce will be a lucrative source of revenue, assuming that government concerns about the safety of on-board communications devices do not limit consumers' abilities to use the new services. To illustrate alliances better in the auto manufacturing industry, we will examine several distinct cases specifically in reference to the typology of strategic alliances given in Chapter 3.

International Joint Ventures in the Auto Industry

Forging joint ventures between major automakers is not uncommon anymore. Even big players such as GM, Ford, Toyota, and Volkswagen have formed joint ventures to enhance their production capability or market power. They have realized that pooling resources would be mutually beneficial, so combining their traditional competition with collaboration would strengthen their competitive position in the long run. We would like to review some of these major international joint ventures (IJVs) that have made an impact on the industry by explaining their functionalities and structures. Table 6.2 summarizes some of the major IJVs established among the principal players in the automobile industry.

Table 6.2

Joint Ventures in the Global Automobile Manufacturing Industry

GM	Toyota	NUMMI	50-50 joint venture auto production in Fremont, California
GM	American Isuzu Motors	Joint Venture (JV)	Consolidated medium-duty commercial vehicle sales, services, and marketing in the United States
GM	Isuzu	CAMI, Canada	50-50 JV to develop a sub-B car for production in Europe
GM	ELZA, Tatarstan	EZLAZ-GM	Builds Chevrolet Blazers; GM holds 25 shares

Table 6.2
Continued.

GM	Delta Motors Corp., South Africa	JV	GM owns 49% of the JV to produce cars and trucks
GM	Isuzu (Japan) and local company, Egypt	GM Egypt	Manufacture commercial vehicles in Egypt GM and Isuzu owns 31% and 20% shares, respectively
GM	Isuzu and local company of Tunisia	IMM	Assembles Isuzu light trucks in Tunisia; GM and Isuzu own 11% and 4% shares, respectively, of the JV
GM	Isuzu	Isuzu-GM Australia	Builds trucks at a Holden plant in Australia
GM	Kenyan government and Itochu (Japan)	GM Kenya	Assembles Isuzu trucks. Owned 57.5% by GM, 38.5% by the Kenyan government, and 4.5% by Itochu
GM	Jinbei Automobile Co., China	Jinbei GM	GM holds 30% equity in the JV in Shenyang, China; assembles pickup trucks
GM	Shanghai Automotive Industry Corp., China	JV	50-50 JV to build Buick Regal engines and transmissions
GM	UAC, Nigeria	GM of Nigeria	Assembles Isuzu pickups and medium-duty trucks in Lagos; GM holds 30%, UAC 60%, and employees 10%.
Ford	Mazda	Auto Alliance International, Inc., Ford Union	U.S.-based JV
Ford	Republic of Belarus and Lada-OMC		Produces Escort cars and Transit vans in Belarus
Ford	Koc Holding, Turkey	JV	Produces Ford cars in Turkey
Ford	Lio Ho, Taiwan	Ford Lio Ho	Ford owns 70% of the JV
Ford	Mahindra & Mahindra, Ltd., India	Mahindra Ford India	Assembly JV in India; Ford also owns 5.8% of Mahindra & Mahindra

Table 6.2

Continued.

Ford	PSA Peugeot Citroen	JV	Produces diesel engines in France
Ford	Yuejin Automotive Group, China	JV	50-50 JV to produce engines in Najing, Jiangsu, China
Ford	Song Diesel, Vietnam	JV	Ford owns 75% of the JV to produce cars and trucks
Daimler-Chrysler	Beijing Automotive Works	Beijing Jeep	DaimlerChrysler owns 42% of the JV
Daimler-Chrysler	Tata Engineering Locomotive, Ltd.	Mercedes-Benz, India Ltd.	Daimler-Benz owns 76% of the JV
BMW	DaimlerChrysler	JV	Builds 1.4L and 3.6L cylinder gasoline engines in Brazil
BMW	Grupo Bavaria SA de CV, Mexico	JV	Assembles and sells cars in Mexico; BMW holds the majority stake in the JV
Daewoo (South Korea)	FLS, Poland	JV	Daewoo owns 61% of the joint venture to build vans
Daewoo	Star Surya Group Indonesia	JV	50-50 joint venture to export and sell 11,000 Daewoo cars annually
Daewoo	Local partner, The Philippines	JV	Produces the LeMans Racer and Espero compact; Daewoo owns 90% of the JV
Daewoo	Oltcit, Romania	Rodea Autombile SA	Daewoo owns 51% of the JV.
Daewoo	State enterprise, Vietnam	JV	Daewoo owns 65% of the JV.
Daewoo	Government of Uzbekistan	JV	50-50 joint venture with a yearly capacity of 200,000 vehicles
Daihatsu (Japan)	Malaysian government	Perodua	Daihatsu owns 20% of the JV
Fiat	Ford	Iveco-Ford Truck, U.K.	Manufacturing trucks in the United Kingdom

Table 6.2

Continued.

Fiat	Local partner, Ukraine	Iveco-Kraz	Fiat's Iveco has a JV to build Iveco commercial vehicles in Kramenchuk, Ukraine.
Fiat	Motor Sich, Ukraine	JV	Produces diesel engines and gear boxes for Iveco-Kraz
Fiat	Nanjing Motors Corp., China	JV	Fiat Iveco has a 50-50 JV with the Chinese truck maker to produce commercial vehicles and engines
Fiat	Yuejin Motor, China	Naveco	Fiat Iveco has a 50-50 JV to produce Iveco commercial vehicles (CVs) and diesel engines
Fiat	Nizhegorod Motors GAZ	JV	Produces 150,000 cars in Russia
Fiat Italy	Peugeot	JV	Builds minivans in France and CVs in
Fiat	Premier Automobiles, India	Fiat Auto India, Ltd	JV to produce 100,000 Fiat Palios annually
Fiat	Government concern, Algeria	Fatia	Fiat holds 36% of the JV to build Fiat Unos
Fiat	Local company, Turkey	TOFAS	Fiat holds 41.5% of the JV
Mitsubishi	Volvo	Netherlands, Car BV	Assembling cars for both companies; Mitsubishi, Volvo, and Dutch government own stakes in Nedcar
Mitsubishi	Proton (Malaysia) and Vietnamese government	JV	Equally owned JV to build minibuses
Nissan	Siam Motors, Thailand	SNA	Nissan owns 25% of the JV
PSA Peugeot	Cukurova Holding, Turkey	JV	Peugeot holds 63% of the JV to produce cars in Turkey
PSA Peugeot	Dongfeng Motors, China	Aelous-Citroen China	JV to build small cars

Table 6.2
Continued.

PSA Peugeot	Proton, Malaysia	USPD	JV to build cars
Renault	Sanjiang Space Group China	Sanjiang Renualt Automotive	JV to produce vans
Renault	City of Moscow	OAO Avtoframos	50-50 JV to produce Renault Megane cars in Russia
Renault	Volvo, Swedish Motors	Thai-Swedish Assembly JV	Renault, Volvo, and Swedish Motors own 20%, 56%, and 24%, respectively, to make Volvo and Renault
Renault	Toyota, Mitsui, and Colombian local company	SOFAS, Colombia	Renault, Toyota, Mitsui, and a local company own 23.7%, 17.5%, 7.5%, and 11.3% of the JV
Renault	OYAK, Turkey	Renault-OYAK	Renault holds 57% of the JV to assemble cars in Turkey
Suzuki	Chang'an Automobile	Chang'an Automobile	Suzuki owns 35%, Nisho Iwai owns 15%, and Chang'an Auto owns 50% in Chengguing, Szechuan, China
Suzuki	Indian Government	Mariti Udyog	50-50 JV
Toyota	Sabanci Holding, Turkey	ToyotaSA	50-50 JV to produce Corolla cars in Turkey
Toyota	Kriloscar Group, India	Toyota Kriloscar Motor	Produce passenger vans in India
Volkswagen	Shanghai Tractor and Auto Co., China	Shanghai Volkswagen Automotive Co., Ltd.	50-50 joint venture auto production in Shanghai, China
Volkswagen	First Auto Works China	FAW-Volkswagen	VW holds 30% and Audi holds 10 of the JV to build in Changchung, China; Golfs, Jettas, and engines
Volkswagen	Eicher Group, India	JV	Builds VW cars in India
Volkswagen	Chinfon, Taiwan	Chinchun Motor Co.	VW holds 33.3% of the JV to assemble T4 Transporter and Caravelle vans in Taiwan

Table 6.2
Continued.

Volkswagen	TAS, Yugoslavia	JV	50-50 JV to build cars in Yugoslavia
Volkswagen	UNIS Holding, Bosnia	JV	VW and UNIS Holding own 58% and 42%, respectively
Volkswagen	Tarpan, Poland	VW Poznan	VW owns 51% of the JV to build Transporter vans and Skoda Felicia cars in Poland.

Source: Compiled from Standard & Poor's Industry Survey: Automotive Industry—
Global Joint Ventures & Affiliations for 2000.

A review of Table 6.2 reveals that GM and Fiat are heavily used IJVs while VW, Ford, Daewoo, and Renault formed IJVs moderately. Still others have the following number of joint ventures: Toyota 4, PSA Peugeot 3, all DaimlerChrysler, BMW, Honda, Suzuki, and Daewoo 2, and Daihatsu 1. In terms of ownership structure, the majority of IJVs (28) are equally owned ventures while minority ownership by a Western company (22) are the second preference, and minority ownership by a Western company is a less-common form of IJVs. In addition, in terms of motives of the Western partners, the majority of IJVs (56) are formed to enter a foreign market and a fewer number of IJVs (12) is established for learning and technology exchange purposes. In reference to the general strategic alliance model, Figure 3.4, they all represent partnerships between competing firms that involve mostly production and technology development partnerships but fewer marketing agreements. Later in this chapter, we will analyze selected alliances in detail.

GM-Toyota NUMMI joint venture. In 1984, General Motors and Toyota formed a 50-50 partnership called New United Motor Manufacturing Inc. (NUMMI) to produce cars for both companies at an old GM plant in Fremont, California. The strategic value of the GM-Toyota alliance was that Toyota would learn how to deal with suppliers and workers in the United States (as a prelude to building its own plants in the United States) while GM would learn about Toyota's lean manufacturing methods. In fact, as a result of the NUMMI partnership, GM had transferred some of those methods to its Saturn plant in Tennessee.

At the outset, GM, then in the midst of one of its worst slumps in history, looked at NUMMI as a way of adding a badly needed small car to its lineup. GM also hoped to gain firsthand knowledge of Toyota's enormously productive manufacturing system and halt the widening efficiency gap between Japanese and U.S. makers. GM's efforts to learn from Toyota were coined "NUMMInization." Experts claim that NUMMInization can produce few results unless GM managers and engineers become less dominating and encourage worker initiatives.[25]

In light of the IJV model (Figure 4.1), we can claim that GM entered this venture to acquire the knowledge that would enable them to efficiently manufacture high-quality small cars. Toyota had condensed much of this knowledge base into a set of management principles and assumptions that were known as the Toyota Production System (TPS), which included its well-known practice of JIT production. GM got the opportunity to observe this production closely. For Toyota, dealing with the federal, state, and local governments was a new experience. This situation meant that both companies made an assessment of their resources and capabilities and then determined that they needed each other.

The use of quality circles to accomplish continuous quality improvement and team-based manufacturing were among the approaches that Toyota brought to the table. Although the specific practices associated with the Toyota system were well-known and openly practiced, the transfer of these programs to a GM operating environment was difficult because they required a new philosophy and set of beliefs regarding the appropriate relationship between shop-floor employees and management. The Toyota practices assume long-term relationships between employees and the company and regard the shop-floor employee as an important source of added value. Toyota employees, working in decentralized groups, are expected to take the initiative in solving problems and to apply their creativity to improve all aspects of the production system.[26] In contrast, at GM the shop-floor employee has been viewed primarily as a variable cost to be controlled through layoffs as the demand for product varies. Historically, the relationship between management and manufacturing employees at GM has been antagonistic, and management as well as labor has jealously guarded what they consider to be their domain of responsibilities and activities. As a result, work practices at most GM plants are narrowly defined by union contract, and there is little room for added responsibility.

The successful introduction of TPS to the NUMMI venture required much more than just learning the procedures comprising various practices. This introduction required the creation of entirely new performance standards for shop-floor employees and plant management as well as a fundamental change in how the employee-management relationship should be regarded. GM had been successful in transferring some of Toyota's practices learned through the NUMMI experience into its Saturn plant, which was established with a new philosophy of teamwork and continuous quality consciousness, although it is difficult to claim that GM demonstrated the same success of NUMMInization in its traditional production facilities, where long-standing beliefs and assumptions block the learning of new practices. GM's attempt to change its human resource philosophy and practice is still questionable, but it had the opportunity to see an alternative approach to human resource management.

GM had been inflexible to be effective in a highly competitive market characterized by increasingly high product cycles and rapidly shifting consumer tastes.[27] The Fremont plant is a stark commentary on GM's failure to make a clear and decisive departure from its anticipated production system. The claim was made that the problems rested on the NUMMI assembly line group and team leaders—akin to supervisors and foremen—who did not let the workers do their jobs according to Toyota-prescribed formulas. These leaders allegedly had little faith in the ability and potential of the workers and were strongly preoccupied with maintaining the status quo (and also showed disrespect for methods and improvements enhanced by the Japanese.) On the other hand, GM claimed that in reality there were only 16 employees at the plant sent directly by the company. Many salaried, management-installed group leaders, hourly union workers who were previously trained by GM, found it difficult to shake off old habits.[28]

The experience of NUMMI was making Toyota wonder whether the exposure of workers to the ways of GM would ultimately threaten the plant's failure. Still, Japanese executives believed much, if not all, of the blame for NUMMI's trouble should be fixed not by the rank-and-file laborers but by group and team leaders who did not adopt the Toyota approach.

By observing and imitating GM's interaction with local and state government officials and the community in general, Toyota managers learned the fine art of public relations in an American context. This experience was later transferred to Toyota's manufacturing site in Tennessee. Also, for Toyota, dealing with the labor unions brought about new management experience and insight. "At Toyota, open conflict between and labor and management is taboo, and the kind of bare-knuckles bargaining common in America is unheard of did not only realized the dynamics and complexities of collective bargaining and labor management, but also labor politics and community and media influence."[29] Moreover, unlike its labor force at home, Toyota faced a diverse workforce consisting of different races, ethnicity, and gender that required understanding and appreciation of employee diversity.

The NUMMI joint venture demonstrates that both partners needed asymmetrical competencies of each other, which led to a 50-50 partnership. The partners must have been satisfied with the outcomes of the venture, so they decided to extend the period of the partnership. In other words, both GM and Toyota have somewhat met their expectations of the venture. Actually, the NUMMI partnership has led other collaborations between the two partners. Nonetheless, both partners have also engaged in a number of alliances with other automakers.

We must note, however, that all joint ventures between automakers are not necessarily successful. For example, AutoLatina, a joint venture between Volkswagen and Ford, dissolved after so many years. Similarly, the 50-50 joint venture between Chrysler and Mitsubishi established in 1988 did not produce the expected results, and Chrysler sold its shares to Mitsubishi for $99.7 million—although DaimlerChrsyler still has equity investment in Mitsubishi, which we will outline in the next section.

Equity Participation

Not only through joint ventures but also through equity investment by one automaker into another, the companies are building interfirm linkages. From such alliances, the firms anticipate some synergistic benefits. There are a number of examples of equity investments in the auto industry, which we present in Table 6.3. This mode of partnership has become the most dominant form (among others). The companies owning controlling shares of other companies will be capable of shaping strategies of target firms and molding the controlled firms' operations into their strategic directions. We will take a closer look at some of the equity participations.

Table 6.3
Equity Participation in the Automobile Industry

Partners	Equity	Holdings
GM	Isuzu	GM holds 49% equity in Isuzu.
GM	Suzuki	GM holds 20% equity in Suzuki.
GM	Fuji Heavy Industries; maker of Subaru	GM holds 20% equity in Fuji Heavy Industries.
GM	Fiat	GM holds 20% equity in Fiat, which owns a 5% stake in GM.
Ford	Mazda	Ford holds 33.4% equity in Mazda.
Ford	Samcor, South Africa	Ford holds 45% equity.
DaimlerChrysler	Mitsubishi	DaimlerChrysler holds 34% equity in Mitsubishi.
DaimlerChrysler	Hyundai	DaimlerChrysler holds 10% equity in Hyundai.
DaimlerChrysler	Thai Daimler-Chrysler	DaimlerChrysler owns a 30% stake.
Renault	Nissan	Renault holds 36.8% equity in Nissan.
Renault	Swedish Motors Thailand	Renault owns 20% of Swedish Motors.

Partners	Equity	Holdings
Volvo	Swedish Motors Thailand	Volvo owns a 56% stake.
American Honda Motors Co., Inc.	San Yang Industry, Taiwan	American Honda owns 12.5% equity.
Mitsubishi	China Motors Co., Ltd., Taiwan	Mitsubishi owns 19% of China Motors.

GM's links. GM is the most active automaker in building investment links with a number of other companies around the world. Especially, it has intensified its ties with Isuzu and Suzuki of Japan to expand into the Asian and global markets. These two GM links deserve special attention.

The GM-Isuzu alliance. GM has increased its stake in Suzuki Motors, Ltd., to 49 percent from 37.5 percent to strengthen its ties. Under the agreement, Isuzu will take over development of trucks and commercial vehicles for GM. While GM will be capable of taking advantage of Isuzu's advanced technology in commercial vehicles, Isuzu can strengthen its capital base with GM's investment. According to the agreement, Isuzu issued 232.5 million new shares of stock, valued at 52.5 billion Yen ($456.5 million in U.S. dollars), with GM acquiring all of them.[30]

GM expects from Isuzu as a major manufacturer of commercial vehicles to take a lead role in the engineering of GM's next generation of commercial vehicles. The company will use an Isuzu-based platform to create common cab, chassis, and vehicle designs, aiming for economies of scale. On the other hand, Isuzu, in aiming for the world's No. 1 position, is promoting its global standing. To achieve this goal, it needs to secure volume stability while Japan's truck industry is now in a serious slump both at home and overseas, which makes it hard to invest even in necessary infrastructure and development. GM's investment will give Isuzu a great advantage in competing with other truck makers. The agreement seemed more beneficial for Isuzu than for GM. Despite its large investment in the alliance, GM cannot expect to benefit from the agreement at least for some years. Additionally, GM has allowed Isuzu to remain completely independent.

Isuzu and GM have been developing their partnership since 1971. In 1997, GM established Isuzu as its center of expertise for diesel engines, which led them to set up a joint venture to build diesel engines. Isuzu is also producing low-cab trucks jointly with GM in the United States. Their latest partnership aims to expand the alliance to the global level.

Moreover, GM and Isuzu are planning on sharing the underpinnings for a new generation of SUVs in North America and engines in Europe, further integrating the U.S. auto giant's Japanese operations into its global empire.

Under the plan, they will develop a common platform—basic structure underneath a vehicle—for Isuzu's Rodeo and Trooper SUVs and possible future GM vehicles in the U.S. market. In Europe, GM's Adam Opel AG unit will likely receive a new 2.2-liter Isuzu diesel engine for its Omega car in a deal that would replace the similar diesel power plant now used for the vehicle.

Both moves would further GM's strategy of using equity and other alliances with Isuzu and others to make up for GM's product or marketing gaps around the world. GM is counting on Isuzu and other partners to provide a range of new products and technologies that it lacks. As we will describe, GM also has a network of alliances with Japanese automakers (including Fuji Heavy Industries, in which GM purchased a 20 percent stake). In both cases, GM and Isuzu need to work out questions concerning how to deal with potential labor issues, where to manufacture the products, or how to share the burden of investment. Nevertheless, GM and its Japanese partners are seeking more synergies in their operations. The plan for a common SUV platform would help the future designs of Isuzu's Trooper and Rodeo SUVs, which have not undergone a changeover since 1992. GM, meanwhile, is preparing to launch a new version of its mid-size SUVs starting in 2001, and Isuzu might get versions of this vehicle.

GM has already given Isuzu a lead responsibility for developing its new generation of compact pickup trucks, which is due in about 2003. This shared platform would sharply reduce the cost of developing new models. In Europe, Isuzu, the diesel-engine specialist in the GM family, has been urging the diesel engine upon GM and Opel and has put together a team to develop it. Opel, which has scrambled to keep up with the surging demand for diesels in Europe, now buys diesel engines for its Omega model from BMW. But Opel currently buys 1.7 and 1.9-liter diesel engines from Isuzu for its smaller cars.

The GM-Suzuki partnership. GM has increased its investment in Suzuki Motor Corp., to $600 million by doubling its stake in the company to 20 percent. As a result, the GM chairman joined Suzuki's board, becoming the first outsider and GM representative to do so. Primarily issuing new shares by Suzuki has made GM's investment possible. GM's increased stake will support the development of an extended model lineup based on the new Chevrolet YGM-1 passenger car, other new joint vehicle projects, and manufacturing and distribution initiatives.[31]

Strengthening its alliance with Suzuki is a critical part of GM's growth strategy in Asia, and the company is particularly interested in improving its position in the small-size car market. Suzuki is known for designing and building minicars. While not popular with U.S. buyers, they are essential in attracting customers in developing nations. Some 20,000 cars will be produced in Japan and sold under GM's Chevrolet brand. The companies eventually want to take the car into other Asian markets. As a further partnership, Suzuki and GM will manufacture Suzuki's Escudo SUVs at GM's Argentina plant for sale under both the GM and Suzuki brands. Suzuki will take a 1.4 billion Yen, or 2 percent, stake in the GM subsidiary in Argentina that owns the plant, in the city of Rosario, Santa Fe province. The factory would be Suzuki's first production base in Latin America. Escudos sold in Japan are compact models with engines of up to two liters. The Argentina deal would mark the first time that Suzuki has acquired an equity stake in a GM affiliate or subsidiary. The Argentina plant will manufacture 6,000 Escudos in the initial year of operation, of which 4,200 will carry the GM logo, and the remainder will display the Suzuki label. Suzuki believes that the arrangement under which it will invest in the existing GM factory will enable the company to save the cost of investment in a new plant. The company feels that it is an appropriate time to develop a production base in Latin America when the Latin American market offers great opportunities.

This new GM-Suzuki deal is just the latest example of a foreign automaker gaining a foothold in Japan. Likewise, DaimlerChrysler AG has arranged to take a 34 percent stake in troubled Mitsubishi Motors while Ford has a controlling interest in Mazda Motor Corp. Moreover, GM, Isuzu, and Suzuki announced an environment-friendly car, and GM unveiled three new models for the Asian market—built with Isuzu and Suzuki. Isuzu introduced a new diesel model of its Asian utility vehicle, also called the 160 program, which will be built with GM in plants across the world while Suzuki announced a new two-seater, small sports car, the EV-sport, which uses a GM electric engine. GM further unveiled its Triax car, built with Suzuki, which uses an internal combustion engine, a hybrid half-electric, half-traditional engine, and a wholly electric system. All these reflect a crucial part of GM's global strategy—considering the Asia-Pacific region—as the world's fastest-growing automotive market and has the potential to become the largest. GM views both Isuzu and Suzuki partnerships as critical to its growth not only in the Asian region but also around the world.

The GM-Fuji Heavy Industries alliance. In another strategic move for the Japanese market, GM purchased a 20 percent stake in Fuji Heavy Industries, the maker of Subaru cars in Japan. As a result of this deal, GM sent two executives to become vice presidents at Fuji Heavy Industries, and the two car makers exchanged mid-level managers to tighten cooperation. While Fuji Heavy Industries needs a big partner to compete in the consolidating automotive industry, it does not want to surrender management control. Thus, it agreed to give only 20 percent of its equity to GM.

A link with Fuji Heavy Industries would give GM entree to a much broader spectrum of the Japanese auto market than it could reach with its trickle of imported Cadillacs, Saturns, and Opels. Fuji Heavy Industries offers compact and midsize models that fit the mainstream of the Japanese market, and it has all-wheel drive and continuously variable transmission technology that GM might want. Isuzu, meanwhile, already is a strong competitor in commercial vehicles, with advanced diesel-engine technology—

and Suzuki, in which GM holds a 10 percent interest, is a specialist in small cars.

Fuji Heavy Industries expects that additional capacity and cooperation with GM will help increase sales. The car maker also announced plans to spend 60 billion Yen to increase capacity at a plant in the United States, jointly operated with Isuzu, where it will build pickup passenger cars based on its popular Legacy line. There are also plans for Fuji Heavy Industries to start production at a plant owned by Suzuki or Opel—also a GM group company—in Hungary. Fuji Heavy Industries was also planning to develop an SUV with GM (expected to launch in five years). By that time, Fuji Heavy Industries hopes to have lifted sales in Europe by 52 percent to 87,000 vehicles.[32]

The GM-Fiat alliance. In addition to its Japanese investments, GM formed a strategic alliance with Fiat, creating an important partnership for the companies in two of the world's largest automotive markets: Europe and Latin America. The alliance promises significant benefits for both GM and Fiat through synergies in the areas of material cost reductions, the leveraging of each group's powertrain activities, efficiency in financial service operations, the cross-sharing of automotive technologies, and the effective leveraging of each other's platforms. The synergies that both companies have identified amounted to an estimated $1.2 billion annually by the third year and are growing to an estimated $2 billion annually by the fifth year when common components are achieved.[33]

In this alliance, GM acquired a 20 percent stake in Fiat while Fiat bought approximately 5.1 percent of GM. Fiat expects a cost leadership status based on the unique synergies provided by this alliance and the capability to draw upon the great R&D resources of GM to face the increasing technological challenges of this new century. Importantly, GM and Fiat will remain independent from one another and will continue to compete in markets around the world.

To realize its key strategic objective of strengthening its position in Europe and South America, GM is aggressively moving ahead to grow its global automotive business. By creating an alliance with a large and technologically strong company like Fiat in a capital-efficient manner, GM serves its objective. The alliance enables GM to capture significant benefits in the areas of platform and component sharing as well as cost efficiencies, thus providing a more competitive base for GM brands. It is an important illustration of the commitment of GM's approach to grow profitably through the use of alliances. On the other hand, Fiat is aggressively creating key sources of cost advantage based on the combined strengths in Europe and Latin America and on the opportunities that both companies are seeking to capture the growth trends in emerging markets. This situation will enable Fiat to further accelerate with structural measures and ongoing profitability recovery. Fiat believes that such an alliance helps the company focus more clearly on serving the customer with a leaner organization. Both companies try to build upon each other's strengths while continuing to operate autonomously and competing aggressively in the marketplace.

Furthermore, as a part of the definitive agreement, Fiat, at a future point in time, will have the right (if it so chooses, at its discretion) to put its remaining 80 percent equity interest in Fiat into GM at fair market value, and GM will have a right of first offer if Fiat decides to sell its interest. Fiat Group's other sectors, including Ferrari and Maserati, are not involved in this transaction. The key to the alliance will be the establishment of dedicated joint ventures in purchasing and powertrain sharing. In the area of purchasing, Fiat and GM will leverage all their purchasing capabilities, including Fiat Auto's "component platform" inter-functional team and GM's "creativity teams."[34] The combined purchasing volume of the two companies provides significant opportunity for synergy. In addition, Fiat and GM, along with its diesel partner Isuzu, will leverage their resources to improve powertrain offerings, performance, and cost. Finally, in the area of automotive financing, GMAC and Fiat Fidis will pursue operating synergies and growth opportunities in Europe and Latin America. A steering committee co-chaired by the CEOs of Fiat and GM will define the joint ventures' strategies and will identify new possible areas of industrial cooperation, such as the return of the Alfa Romeo brand to the United States as well as e-business opportunities such as in-vehicle communications involving GM's OnStar and Fiat's Viasat—telematic services by two companies, respectively.[35]

Clearly, from this explanation, despite its vast resources and marketing power, GM has heavily pursued various forms of strategic alliances in its Asia-Pacific, European, and Latin America expansions. In fact, while GM's ownership stakes in the Japanese companies helped the company strengthen its position in Japan, they leveraged the links with other multinational companies.

The Ford-Mazda link. Ford and Mazda have established a variety of alliances over the years that encompass equity participation, joint venture, and non-equity partnerships. In this context, Ford owns 33.4 percent of Mazda while the companies formed a joint venture called Auto Alliance in the United States to manufacture cars together. Additionally, both companies will develop at least six common platforms for a range of vehicles, including SUVs, compact cars, trucks, and medium-size sedans over the next three years.[36] All these close ties mean that Mazda is increasingly integrating with Ford.

In many ways, the reason the alliance succeeded is because Mazda had no other choice. When Ford sent a team to Mazda in 1994, an ambitious expansion program had left the car maker on the verge of bankruptcy. The company, once known as Toyo Kogyo, had huge debts and net losses. Mazda took five years to produce a profit. The remarkable turnaround can be attributed to the focus on positive cash flow, reducing the level of debt. Cash flow analysis is still relatively new in Japan, where decades of continuous growth in demand meant that companies could afford to make some investments with little prospect of return.[37] With low interest rates, companies could borrow easily and enable debts to accumulate.

Nevertheless, the Ford-Mazda alliance in Japan has experienced tough times. After the two years of his appointment, Mazda's American president from Ford was replaced with another American executive drafted from Ford. This system really shows the problems and difficulties in the alliance between the partners. Conflicts have emerged in several areas. Mazda, originally a family-owned business with roots in the Hiroshima area, is fiercely protective of its engine technology and manufacturing expertise.[38] There was also latent resentment of the top-down management style employed by Ford (designated president to Mazda). Time will show whether the new president will be able to handle the same pressures of corporate culture and keep his job longer than his predecessors.

Ford is keen to solidify its ties with Mazda. To be a leading global company for automotive services, Ford realizes that it is necessary to have a footprint in the Japanese and Asian markets. For example, as an extension of their alliance, Mazda and Ford jointly operate a pickup truck factory in Thailand called Auto Alliance. In other words, their partnership expands to exploit new opportunities.

Nevertheless, Ford has to deal with some difficult problems. The focus on cash flow management, for example, meant that the Ford team had to face one of the most powerful industrial structures in Japan: the *keiretsu* system. The *keiretsu* system binds groups of companies in what were once profitable relationships. The Mazda group includes machinery manufacturers, components groups, and finance companies. These affiliates needed immediate attention. One of the Ford-appointed presidents at Mazda explained the major problems as follows: "The dealers are financially very weak. We have made considerable progress, and they have improved financially, but it is not where it needs to be, and the debt levels are grossly excessive. There is a lot of work to be done. We have set goals for each company, operational plans to improve profitability."[39] Under Ford-appointed leadership, Mazda has dramatically accelerated its asset sales. These included the sale of its finance company to Ford, a components maker to Visteon, the Ford-affiliated components group, and several parcels of real estate. The company was also restructuring its heavily debted dealership network faster than any other car maker in Japan.

Improving profitability would simply be a matter of lowering costs by laying off workers or closing factories. But in Japan, these are considered an option of last resort—partly because labor policies encourage companies to keep excess workers on staff during a downturn to prevent unemployment. It is also very expensive to pay workers to retire ahead of schedule. Cash flow management at Mazda has therefore meant using existing staff in a different way, rather than shedding workers. Earlier in 1999, the company introduced merit-based incentives to replace its seniority-based promotion system. There are still obstacles in the road ahead, however. As part of its effort to reduce debt, Mazda is trying to pair its suppliers with foreign components makers to improve their international competitiveness. But many suppliers have resisted on the grounds that they do not want to be taken over by a foreign rival. It is believed that Japanese managers wish to get acquainted with their alliance partners gradually, over a period of several years. Hostile takeovers are essentially impossible. This situation is in contrast to the United States and Europe, where bids for a controlling stake in another company are common.

In addition, Mazda has suffered from some scandals recently—hiding some product defects in its vehicles in Japan. Mazda probably needs more strategic directions and restructuring. Mazda and Ford are struggling to put together a number of cooperative arrangements, ranging from parts design and manufacturing and joint consumer finance operations to the first car built on a shared platform.[40]

The DaimlerChrysler, Mitsubishi, and Hyundai equity partnership. Chrysler (before its merger with Daimler-Benz) and Mitsubishi Motors Manufacturing of America (MMMA), a unit of Mitsubishi Motors Corporation (in short, Mitsubishi) agreed to extend their existing vehicle distribution agreement for five more years. In other words, the agreement will now extend until the 2005 model year. Under the agreement, vehicles will be designed jointly, engineered by Mitsubishi, and made by MMMA. At present, Mitsubishi produces two specialty coupes for Chrysler: the Dodge Avenger and the Sebring coupe. MMMA makes about 65,000 models annually for Chrysler, although future production will depend on demand trends.

Now, DaimlerChrysler is preparing a "strategic blueprint"—setting out for the first time the potential product benefits of linking the Mercedes-Benz, Chrysler, Mitsubishi, and Hyundai car brands. The proposals will recommend options for extracting new savings from common purchasing and shared vehicle architecture. The program would define the advantages that DaimlerChrysler could gain from its brand portfolio, which has increased in 2000 following the acquisition of 34 percent of Mitsubishi and a 10 percent holding in South Korea's Hyundai Motors. Costs associated with DaimlerChrysler's new product strategy are likely to be covered by an estimated $35.2 billion budget for R&D and new capital investment over the coming three to four years. The proposal would concentrate on expansion opportunities in small cars, light trucks, and pickups. It would set out the synergies from pooling small car developments at Hyundai and Mitsubishi while also considering new derivatives for the Smart car brand. This mission is about producing cars more efficiently and on a more international basis. Although Chrysler has experienced some financial loss lately,

DaimlerChrysler expects that it would deliver improved contributions, particularly following the launch of a generation of new products. DaimlerChrysler management plans for the products that come out in 2003–2004 to share components and systems with other models and brands.

DaimlerChrysler's other equity partner, Hyundai, is doing well in the small car market in North America. Hyundai has even been considering building a plant when its sales to North America reach 500,000 cars. For larger sales, shipping cars from South Korea would not be more profitable. The car maker expects to sell more than 500,000 cars in North America by 2003. Hyundai and its affiliate, Kia Motor, exported a total of 450,000 cars to the region in 1999. Hyundai's U.S. sales are up 54 percent in 2000 to 170,000 units through August. Therefore, DaimlerChrysler plans to exploit its partnership with Hyundai.

The Renault-Nissan partnership. Renault of France and Nissan of Japan signed an agreement in which Renault bought 36.8 percent of shares of Nissan by paying $5.4 billion. The Renault and Nissan alliance has created the fourth largest automobile manufacturer in the world. Another dimension of the Renault and Nissan agreement is a synergy investment of $3 billion between 2000 and 2002. By this accord, while Renault has expanded its presence worldwide, Nissan found a source for its debt of approximately $20 billion. As a result of this agreement, Carlos Ghosn, vice president of Renault, was appointed to the general director position in charge of operations at Nissan. Additionally, two top executives of Renault will join the top management of Nissan. In return, Yoshikazu Hanawa, chairman of the board of Nissan, will join the board of directors of Renault.

Nissan engaged in this alliance to improve its financial position and to stimulate the growth in cooperation with its partner. The new partnership will produce 4,800,000 motor vehicles in a year. According to the agreement, Renault cars will be sold in Mexico and Nissan trucks will be sold in Latin America. While Nissan will use the Renault facilities in Latin America, Renault will use the Nissan facilities in Asia and Mexico.

As a result, the accord between Renault and Nissan will enhance competitive positions of the partners by reducing costs over the short run and increasing the joint production capacity. This situation means a new era for both companies in their global expansion and competitiveness.

The integration of two different cultures might be a major challenge for this alliance. Renault's No. 2 executive, Carlos Ghosn, will try to reduce its $19.65 billion debt and bring order to a product plan run amok. At the same time, however, he faces a gaping cultural chasm—one that could bog down restructuring at troubled Japanese car maker. Ghosn's task is bridging the cultural gap and making the linkup work. His first task is drawing a plan of action that will achieve the $3.3 billion in savings by 2002 that both companies promised according to the accord. In shaping that plan, Ghosn will consult with employees in as many parts of the company as possible, from the factory floor to Nissan's marketing department and executive suite. He started his mission with the following notion: "I am not going with any preconceived ideas. You need to be sure that you keep an alliance spirit and systematically look for the best solution."[41] Ghosn faced challenges in three key areas: Nissan's purchasing processes, which account for 50 percent of the company's total costs; design, which in the past has been overshadowed by Nissan's powerful engineers; and the company's product lineup, which is based on a costly, crazy quilt of 27 different platforms.

Renault believes that Nissan has failed to retire aging models quickly enough. Those are likely to get the ax. Investment in future models and the tooling to build them are likely to be slashed, too. A recent analysis by Merrill Lynch showed that Nissan has overspent in that area. The company's amortization and depreciation costs are about 50 percent of sales. That figure compares with the industry average of about 27 percent. Because of its dowdy models that are selling poorly, Nissan's factories are operating at a low rate compared with Renault. The French company's assembly plants operated at 42 percent of capacity in 1998, based on Renault's internal yardstick of three factory shifts a day, 365 days a year. Nissan, by comparison, was operating at only about 25 percent of capacity. Because about 50 percent of an assembly plant's costs are fixed, closing some Nissan factories might be the only way to cut costs quickly. Moreover, the company's white-collar ranks are about 20 percent larger than needed because of the company's employment-for-life tradition. The rank of middle managers needs to be trimmed as part of the cost-cutting plan.

The most concrete plans so far are for cutting Nissan's debt overhang. In addition to Renault's $5.4 billion cash infusion, the debt-reduction plan includes $2.7 billion from the sale of non-core assets, $500 million from a reduction in inventory, $1.7 billion in synergies between two companies, and $3.4 billion from the cash flow. Such drastic steps will likely meet strong resistance at Nissan, however. The company has earned a reputation in the past decade as a technology powerhouse and a producer of high-quality cars. The pride in those achievements and know-how that created them might block Ghosn's efforts at reform. Nissan is, despite its financial situation, very arrogant. Renault is virtually nonexistent in the Japanese market and does not command a great deal of respect in that arena. Furthermore, Japan's tradition of consensus decision-making could slow the process, as well. Strategy discussion can go interminably. And sometimes, the compromise decision that is finally agreed upon is not the best one. Japanese consensus building makes the decision-making process longer and more difficult than Ghosn is probably used to.

Despite the announced accord between Renault and Nissan, there remain some fundamental differences. For example, while Louis Schweitzer, chairman and CEO, stated that a full merger of the two companies might be possible in the future, Yoshikazu Hanawa clearly stated that the two companies would remain separate. He said, "It's a different alliance. It's not a merger. It's not a takeover. It'll be like this for a long time, for ever."[42]

Despite everything, so far it seems that Ghosn's turnaround strategy at Nissan is working. Nissan has recorded quarterly profits for the first time in the past six years and is forecasting earnings in the future as a result of his Nissan revival plan. The company is counting on its new models to boost its comeback. Yet, it is soon to draw a conclusion about the future state of Nissan and its partnership with Renault.

All of these equity participations by automakers show a pattern of alliance, as pointed out in Figure 4.3 of the Equity Participation Model. While the investing companies attempt to expand their markets and achieve strategic benefits, the target companies seek resource acquisitions and revitalize themselves. In such endeavors, Ford, DaimlerChrysler, and Renault have been struggling to revitalize their Japanese partners. Now, let's look at some of the non-equity alliances in the global automobile manufacturing industry.

Non-Equity Alliances

Major vehicle manufacturers worldwide also engage in non-equity partnerships, which are considered less risky and more flexible in comparison to equity alliances. They do that primarily to develop new technologies and products by exploiting each other's resources and competencies. As explained in Chapter 3, the resources and competencies of a single company are not sufficient any longer to undertake a breakthrough in the industry. All of the motives cited in Figure 5.1 in reference to international contractual ventures are at force in case of global automobile alliances, including achieving efficiency, reducing risks and costs, accessing markets and resources, securing supply sources, developing technology and products, and transferring knowledge between partners. Nonetheless, the most pressing motives for ICVs in the auto manufacturing industry seem to be the development of new technology and products and securing supply sources while reducing costs and risks. Of several ICVs, technology partnership, co-production, joint marketing agreements, and supplier agreements appear to be the most common forms. Some specific examples of non-equity alliances or ICVs are given next to illustrate their details.

GM has cooperated with the NUMMI partner, Toyota, in development of alternative fuel engines such as fuel cells. Also, Honda could well want to become GM's partner in fuel-cell development too, because the company's sales volume is too small to easily support the enormous costs of fuel-cell development. As a result, GM forged new business links with Honda Motors.[43] In addition to discussions about buying engines from Honda, GM is interested in developing a broader relationship with the automaker.

Technology partnership and co-production are the focus of the GM-Honda collaboration. Although GM already is nearly a year into an advanced-technology partnership with Toyota, now it also wants access for North America and elsewhere to some of Honda's industry-leading technology for producing extremely low-emission gasoline engines. In their accord, GM and Honda have struck an unusual deal that GM wants to buy 100,000 low-emission, six-cylinder gasoline engines a year from Honda for use in vehicles in North America. The deal also involves Honda's possible purchase of a like number of low-emission diesel engines from a factory in Poland operated by GM's 49 percent-owned Japanese affiliate, Isuzu, for use in Honda cars in Europe. Such a deal could help Honda defray the huge costs of developing engines. Rather than making engines for GM, however, the No. 3 Japanese automaker would prefer to license GM's use of Honda technology in one of GM's own factories. Honda wants to avoid the risk of winding up with excess engine-making capacity, although right now it cannot make enough engines in North America. The deal on engines now could lead to a broader GM-Honda relationship in the future. The collaboration would more likely include joint purchasing, joint product development, or joint manufacturing.

Although the deals of one car maker supplying engines to another were not common in the past, we can frequently see them today. GM currently buys vehicles from Japanese partners for sale as Chevrolets but does not purchase engines for use in its mainstream North American models. By allying with Honda, GM is taking another big step away from its historical strategy of self-reliance. Instead, GM is creating a web of alliances, particularly in Asia, to stay ahead of its rivals. On the other hand, for fiercely independent Honda (which has stood aloof from the auto industry's global consolidation), the agreement with GM marks a significant turning point—although GM will not be acquiring stakes in Honda.[44]

A key pointer to the future evolution of supplier-vehicle manufacturer relations in the car industry is provided by the far-sighted Alcoa-Audi R&D alliance for the development of a new lightweight aluminum car body structure, which began in 1982 and persisted in its endeavors even when commercialization was a technically difficult, distant, and risky prospect. Environmental considerations in the form of stricter emission regulations and the need to reduce fuel consumption and thereby weight led Audi to search for a lighter material than steel and to form a partnership with Alcoa. The first commercial result of this long-run collaboration was a quantum leap in weight-reduction technology and automotive structural manufacturing, embodied in the development of the aluminum space frame. The aluminum-intensive vehicle introduced by Audi in 1994 is a significant first step toward a "green" car that is cost-effective, high-performance, low-emission, and recyclable.

A good example of cooperation between automobile makers while they compete is the GM-Toyota partnership. Both companies cooperate with each other on clean-car research and the joint production at the NUMMI plant while competing with each other worldwide. In addition, Ford and Toyota have been discussing a range of possible cooperative ventures, including financial services and low-emission cars. Through such cooperation, one area in which Ford would like to benefit is the development of gasoline-electric hybrid vehicles. "Toyota is a leader in hybrid vehicles, which produce less-harmful emissions than conventional gasoline-powered engines because they use electric motor for propulsion in low speeds. Toyota has already sold tens of thousands of such vehicles."[45] On the other hand, Toyota hopes to benefit from Ford's experience in financial services. Toyota established a financial subsidiary that concentrates on automobile loans and wishes to increase its profits from this venture by learning through a collaboration with Ford.

CONCLUDING REMARKS

In the global automobile industry, companies have employed a variety of alliances to build their competitive positions while averting risks. As Table 6.1 shows, major players such as GM, Ford, DaimlerChrysler, Fiat, Renault, and Volkswagen have engaged in joint ventures with other car manufacturers around the world. Additionally, the four distinct cases of GM, Ford, DaimlerChrysler, and Renault demonstrate that the investor companies seeking leverages in global competition used equity participation as a strategic tool. Their strategic moves reflect the characteristics of the equity participation model introduced in Figure 4.3. Furthermore, the automakers worldwide have struck a number of non-equity deals to accomplish technological and product innovations and marketing accomplishments.

Through its equity alliances, GM wants to expand internationally—especially in the Asia-Pacific market—and strengthen its position in Europe and South America. Additionally, GM hopes to exploit synergies and the combined capabilities of the partnership. To accomplish such goals, the company has already launched and plans to develop many joint projects with its partners consisting of collaboration in the area of new vehicle production and marketing. Unlike its other equity partnership, GM has a controlling stake in Suzuki and can direct its partner the way it desires. Although GM does not hold a controlling stake in other cases, it has still a great influence because of its large economy of scales and vast resources. GM's partners, on the other hand, hope to gain some benefits from their partnership with the world's largest automaker. They expect to exploit GM's resources and network. They sought the GM link not because they needed financial bail out but because of their growth purpose through leveraging GM's huge size and worldwide network.

Likewise, Ford has been trying to strengthen its Mazda link as part of its global expansion strategy. While it wanted to reinforce its position in Japan and other Asian markets, Mazda received the financial resources and strategic leadership it needed. By revitalizing Mazda and solidifying its ties with its partner, Ford would like to respond to the expansion strategies of other major players such as GM, DaimlerChrsyler, and Renault. In accomplishing such goals, in addition to restructuring Mazda, both partners have already developed a number of joint projects.

DaimlerChrysler, however, is trying to catch up with GM and Ford by penetrating the Asian market and by seeking synergistic benefits from its equity participation. While it hopes to strengthen its position in Asia where it has less presence, it intends to develop a number of joint projects with its partners. It sees the cars made by Mitsubishi and Hyundai, especially small ones for the low-end of the market, as complementary to its product line—whereas Mitsubishi and Hyundai view their access to resources of DaimlerChrysler as consolidation in the global auto manufacturing industry (which is rapidly taking place). Yet, Ford still needs to overcome the obstacle stemming from Mazda's corporate and national cultures to further collaboration between the partners.

In the case of the Renault-Nissan alliance, Nissan was hemorrhaging from consecutive financial losses and a heavy debt burden; therefore, it needed a partner to help itself out of this financial trouble. While the alliance provides expansion and synergistic benefits for the French car maker, it has revitalized Nissan with new leadership and restructuring. It seems that Renault has put forth a successful turnaround strategy so far. Nissan recorded quarterly profits for the first time in six years and anticipates doing so in the years ahead. Nevertheless, there seems to be a cultural difference between the partners. While Renault was acting with Western strategic orientation (such as cost cutting, downsizing, and profit maximizing), Nissan—under the influence of corporate and national culture—is less apt to undertake such drastic measures expeditiously.

Overall, these cases reflect that the equity participation model developed previously in Chapter 4 captures the salient characteristics and dynamism of such alliances. In other words, equity participation cases can be examined thoroughly within the framework of the equity participation model, alluding to the motives and forms of such alliances. In general, we can say that companies in the global automotive manufacturing industry have realized the necessity of strategic alliances in gaining and sustaining a competitive advantage. The several cases examined in this chapter illustrate the point that scale and scope economies, market expansion, and organizational learning are vital components of ultimate success in the automobile manufacturing industry. Companies have been engaged and will be seeking consolidations in the industry. Some will accomplish this goal through strategic alliances, which might take various forms ranging from joint ventures and equity partnerships to non-equity participation. Such interfirm collaborations could improve the core competencies of partnering companies.[46]

Alliances in the international automobile manufacturing industry can also be used as a vehicle to expand in new markets. This situation is especially feasible for firms wishing to enter or expand in controlled markets such as Japan, China, India, and some other emerging markets. Increasing global competition will make under-performing companies vulnerable or forced to engage in a partnership. Nissan in Japan and Kia in South Korea are examples of such developments.

Finally, technology collaboration and organizational learning are accountable for the recent popularity of global alliances. No company has all the resources and competencies to become (or stay) innovative. Excelling in one area will not be sufficient to hold a competitive advantage. For example, superiority in design and production should be complemented by excellence in marketing. The cases discussed here illustrate this point well.

Overall, automobile manufacturing companies should view global, strategic alliances as a viable strategic option in their future growth plans. Technological advances coupled with globalization trends will require automobile manufacturers worldwide to consider mergers, joint ventures, and other forms of partnerships. Those firms that can successfully form and manage strategic alliances can develop their own resource and knowledge bases.

NOTES

1. J. Burrows, Automotive industry snapshot, Hoovers Online (October 10, 1998).

2. Anonymous, Not so smart, *The Economist* (September 6, 1997): 63.

3. Anonymous, *Industry Outlook* (Update October 3, 1998).

4. Ibid.

5. E. Levy, Autos & auto parts, *S&P Industry Survey* (June 1, 2000): 5.

6. Ibid.

7. M. Maruka, Foreign carmakers fight for the share of Japan's market, *Japan Times Weekly International Edition*, 37, no. 4 (1997): 14.

8. A. Taylor, III, Danger: Rough road ahead, *Fortune*, 135, no. 5 (1997): 114–118.

9. Hoovers, available at www.hoovers.com/features/industry/nonav/automobile.html (1998).

10. AAMA, available at American Auto Manufacturer Association, industry data, www.aama.com/data/contents.html (August 10, 1998).

11. Taylor, 115.

12. Burrows, 2.

13. Anonymous, *S&P Industry Outlook*, 3.

14. Ibid.
15. Anonymous, U.S. Industry Survey (1998).
16. Hoovers, 1.
17. AMMA, 1.
18. Levy, 3.
19. Anonymous, *S&P Industry Outlook*, 4.
20. R. Dove, Managing core competency knowledge, *Automotive Manufacturing & Production*, 109, no. 12 (1997): 18–19.
21. Anonymous, *Economist*, 63.
22. Anonymous, *Industry Surveys, Autos & Auto Parts* (June 1, 2000): 24.
23. Ibid.
24. R. Culpan (ed.), *Multinational strategic alliances* (New York: International Business Press, 1993).
25. N. Shirouzu, Line managers are blamed for ills at NUMMI plant, *Japan Economic Journal*, 8 (1990): 14.
26. M. N. Keller, The auto industry. *Vital Speeches of the Day*, 63 (1997): 472–475.
27. D. Forbes, The lessons of NUMMI, *Business Month* (June 1987): 34–37.
28. M. Burstiner, *The Business Journal*, 2, no. 44 (January 23, 1995): 12.
29. D. Henne, M. J. Levine, W. J. Usery, Jr., and H. Fishgold, A case study in cross-cultural mediation: The General Motors-Toyota joint venture, *The Arbitration Journal*, 41, no. 3 (1986): 5–15.
30. Japan Economic Newswire (12/18/1998).
31. The Associated Press state and local wire services (September 14, 2000).
32. R. L. Simison and N. Shirouzi, GM pursues new links with Japanese, *The Wall Street Journal* (December 3, 1999): B1.
33. Associated Press (3/13/2000).
34. Ibid.
35. Ibid.
36. AFX News (October 20, 1999).
37. *Financial Times* (October 19, 1999).
38. Ibid.
39. *Financial Times* (December 16, 1999): 4.

40. Ibid.

41. D. Woodruff, Ghosn faces challenges at Nissan, *The Wall Street Journal Europe* (March 31, 1999): 3.

42. Ibid.

43. R. L. Simison and N. Shiruzi, GM pursues new links with Japanese, *The Wall Street Journal* (December 9, 1999): B1.

44. J. White and N. Shirouzu, GM and Honda strike deal for engines, *The Wall Street Journal* (December 21, 1999): A3.

45. T. Zaun, Toyota, Ford map series of new links, *The Wall Street Journal* (March 19, 2001): A12.

46. J. Hagedoorn and J. Schakenraad, The effect of strategic technology alliances on company performance, *Strategic Management Journal,* 15, no. 4 (1994): 291–310.

7

Global Alliances in the Pharmaceutical Industry

Despite the augmenting number of mega-mergers and acquisitions in the pharmaceutical industry worldwide, many companies have chosen strategic alliances such as co-promotion deals with other drug makers, licensing agreements to manufacture and/or distribute drugs developed by other firms, and research collaborations with other firms to develop new biotech products. In analyzing alliances in the pharmaceutical industry, we will first introduce general industry characteristics. Then, we will examine specific cases within the framework of the strategic alliance conceptual model (refer to Figure 3.4).

INDUSTRY CHARACTERISTICS

Worldwide sales of pharmaceutical products, both prescriptions and over-the-counter (OTC) medicines, reached $315 billion in 1998—up from $297 billion in 1997 with prescription drugs accounting for approximately 60 percent of sales.[1] The United States accounts for about 40 percent of the total of retail sales worldwide, with Europe at 32 percent, Japan at 24 percent, and other areas accounting for only 4 percent of total sales.[2] In other words, the most important market is a "triad" consisting of the United States, Europe, and Japan. Then, any pharmaceutical company trying to be internationally competitive must have operations or links in this "triad." Once, Ohmae asserted that the global competitive success of companies depends upon their presence in all markets in the "triad."[3] For global pharmaceutical firms, it is especially important to have a presence in the U.S. market, which represents the majority of the worldwide market. Therefore, it is important for non-U.S. pharmaceutical companies to enter the U.S. market either directly or via an alliance.

In the pharmaceutical industry, the prescription drug sector consists of two segments: brand-name drugs and generic drugs. In the United States, prescription drugs produced six times the revenue of generic drugs, although generic drugs accounted for 43 percent of all prescriptions filled.[4] Companies holding patents for major drugs enjoy a competitive advantage for about 10 years. Actually, drugs are patented for 20 years, typically starting with the discovery of the compound. Ten years might be necessary to bring a successful drug through regulatory approval, which leaves a shelf life of about 10 years before competition from generic drug companies begins. Given the huge cost of drug development, pharmaceutical companies have been trying to minimize the risk of R&D, which is the key factor to success in the pharmaceutical industry.

Competition in the pharmaceutical industry is global. Big drug companies such as Merck (United States), Pfizer (United States), and Warner-Lambert (United States), which are in the merging process; Johnson & Johnson (United States), Pharmacia-Upjohn (United States), Glaxo-Wellcome (United Kingdom), and SmithKline Beecham (United Kingdom), which are in the merging process; Novartis (Switzerland), and Ciba-Geigy (Switzerland) compete worldwide. As the current examples suggest, drug companies rely on scale economies through mergers and acquisitions. Thus, one of the major trends in the pharmaceutical industry has been the increasing number of mergers and acquisitions among big players. To gain economies of scale advantages and market power, numerous companies have merged in recent years. Refer to Table 7.1 for more information. Langert *et al.* claimed that "the drug industry is in the throes of a merger frenzy that is likely to continue. Driving the merger mania: an urgent need for scale in both marketing and research."[5] Such mergers will invite other big players to join this trend. "These deals will create titans with armies of salespeople to swamp smaller competitors and mammoth research budgets to beat others to market with innovative drugs. It seems there will be continued consolidation in the industry. The name of the game is really about productivity in R&D and in sales and marketing."[6] The recent merger trend proves that scale is critical in the industry. Because of their impact on the industry in general and on strategic alliances in particular, some recent mergers are presented in Table 7.1. A number of companies might look for deals in North America, which happens to be the most lucrative market in the industry. "Despite the pressures on big drug makers, the torrid pace of mergers is likely to slow because the obvious deals have been struck. Remaining independent companies may resist mergers and may not make a move until forced."[7]

Table 7.1

Mergers and Acquisitions in the Pharmaceutical Industry

Acquirer (country)	Target (country)	Date	Status	New name	Value $bil*
Pfizer (U.S.)	Warner-Lambert (U.S.)	11/4/1999	Pending		70.00
Zeneca Group (U.K.)	Astra (Sweden)	12/9/1998	Confirmed	Astra Zeneca	34.64
Sandoz (Switzerland)	Ciba-Geigy (Switzerland)	3/7/1996	Confirmed	Novartis	30.09
Monsanto (U.S.)	Pharmacia & Upjohn (U.S.)	12/20/1999	Pending		23.30
GlaxoWellcom (U.K)	SmithKline Beecham (U.K.)	12/27/200	Completed	GlaxoSmithKline	22.20
Glaxo Holdings (U.K.)	Wellcome (U.K.)	1/20/1995	Completed	Glaxo Wellcome	14.28
Bristol-Myers (U.S.)	Squipp (U.S.)	7/27/1989	Completed	Brystol-Myers-Squibb	12.09
Sanofi (France)	Synthelabo (France)	12/2/1998	Completed	Sanofi-Synthelabo	11.12
Roche Holding (Switzerland)	Corange (Bermuda)	5/26/1997	Completed	Roche Holding	10.20
American Home Products (U.S.)	American Cyanamid (U.S.)	8/2/1994	Completed	American Home Products	9.56
Beecham Group (U.K.)	SmithKline Beckman (U.K.)	3/31/1989	Completed	SmithKline Beecham	7.92
Hoechst (Germany)	Marion Merrell Dow (U.S.)	2/28/1995	Completed	Hoechst Marion Roussel[**]	7.26

Table 7.1
Continued.

Acquirer (country)	Target (country)	Date	Status	New name	Value $bil*
Upjohn (U.S.)	Pharmacia (Sweden)	8/21/1995	Completed	Pharmacia Upjohn	6.99
Dow Chemicals	(U.S.) Marion Laboratories (U.S.)	7/17/1989	Completed	Marion Merrell Dow **	6.21
Roche Holding (Switzerland)	Syntex (U.S.)	5/2/1994	Completed	Roche Holding	5.31
Hoetchst (Germany)	Rhone-Poulenc (France)	12/26/1999	Completed	Aventis	12.09
Roche Holding (Switzerland)	Genentech (U.S.)	12/15/1999	Completed	Roche owns 60%	4.82
Investors (unknown)	Sanofi-Synthelabo (France)	9/1/1999	Pending		4.71
Johnson & Johnson (U.S.)	Centocor (U.S.)	7/21/1999	Completed	Johnson & Johnson	4.33

* Debts are excluded

** Now Aventis

Source: Adapted from Thomson Financial Securities but modified and updated.

Despite the popularity of recent mergers, research evidence to date has shown the success of drug industry mergers to be mixed. "Although the elimination of redundant expenses can initially yield meaningful savings, studies have shown that merged firms have not perform better over the long term than drugmakers that go it alone, such as Merck and Pfizer (prior to the latter's recent merger with Warner-Lambert). Some of the combinations consummated over the past five years that have failed to deliver long-term growth targets include that Pharmacia AB of Sweden with Upjohn Co., Glaxo's combination with Wellcome plc, and Ciba Geigy's merger with Sandoz."[8] As a result, many pharmaceutical companies have preferred strategic alliances with other pharmaceutical or biotech companies to costly mergers and acquisitions.

Thus, another popular trend has been the formation of strategic alliances between two pharmaceutical companies or a pharmaceutical and biotech firm. One recent deal that illustrates a partnership between two pharmaceuticals is the collaboration between Merck and Schering-Plough, which involves the joint development of new drugs in the asthma and allergy areas. Pharmaceutical companies also have been linking with biotech companies for the development and production of new drugs. For example, Genome Therapeutics has extended its partnership with Schering-Plough. The alliance calls for the companies to work together to identify and develop novel anti-infectives for drug-resistant bacteria, including *Staphylococcus aureus* (a leading cause of hospital-acquired infections).

A breakthrough development in biotechnology is scientists deciphering the entire sequence of human genetic code, and more practical advances are flowing from other genomic discoveries. Human Genome Sciences (HGS), for example, will begin human tests of a protein that is one of the body's primary natural weapons against infection. The component, known as B-lymphocite simulator (BlyS), is the fourth gene-based drug candidate developed by HGS to advance to human trials, expanding the company's early lead in the race to convert information from the human genome into drugs. Similarly, Johnson & Johnson recently disclosed that it is close to human tests of a gene-based drug that targets a brain receptor associated with memory and attention. It also reflects the impact of new robotic and other technology that is enabling drug companies to rapidly translate genomic data into potential new medicines. Although there is not any assurance that BlyS or any other HGS proteins will pass muster in human trials and make it to the market, the genomic discoveries will continue to advance and make a remarkable contribution to the treatment of many diseases.

In addition, HGS and Celera Genomics focus on genes that produce natural growth factors acting as molecular switches that signal cells when to grow or stop growing, when to mature, when to die, when to move, and when to stay put. Many drug companies including Smith-Kline Beecham, Pfizer, Johnson & Johnson, and Bristol-Myers Squibb are racing to use the emerging DNA sequence data to find such switches. Their goal is to create medicines that attack diseases by acting on these switches. But the strategy of biotechnology companies is to use the newfound genes and proteins they make as drugs themselves.

ALLIANCES IN THE PHARMACEUTICAL INDUSTRY

In our investigation, we looked at international strategic alliances (business collaborations between two or more companies from different countries and a couple cases of domestic alliances but with a global impact) in the pharmaceutical industry. To do so, we screened the pharmaceutical business alliance announcements in major business publications in the past five years as reported in the Dow Jones database and company press releases. We selected only the signed agreements but not alliance negotiations. Of the 981 cases identified, some were irrelevant and others were only domestic alliances. Consequently, the database developed contains 128 international alliance cases. The database included information about dates, partner firms, their nationalities, activities involved in the value chain, and the type of alliance (equity or non-equity alliance). Basically, in this qualitative research, we examined the selected strategic alliance cases in detail in the pharmaceutical industry in the context of the strategic alliance model given in Chapter 3. The content analysis of these selected cases demonstrates salient features of strategic alliances in the pharmaceutical industry.

Basically, this chapter examines international strategic alliances in the pharmaceutical industry by considering such partnerships as a corporate or business strategy. In other words, global strategic alliances in the pharmaceutical industry are linked to competitive advantages of firms. Moreover, it investigates the developments in interfirm cooperation in the pharmaceutical industry and presents the main characteristics and dynamics of alliance cases within the framework of the conceptual model offered previously in Chapter 3. Finally, it draws a conclusion on pharmaceutical alliances and makes an assessment of current alliances between pharmaceutical firms.

By forming strategic alliances, pharmaceutical firms ultimately seek to develop new products yielding competitive advantages over their rivals. That is, a strategic alliance is a way of building competitive advantage. As a result, like any other business strategies, this alliance intends to achieve a competitive advantage by developing or acquiring unique resources and competencies (refer to Table 7.2). In implementing an alliance strategy, however, pharmaceutical firms follow a variety of paths and modes, which were outlined in the introduction of the strategic alliance model in Chapter 3. As the model suggests, a pharmaceutical firm could collaborate either with its competitor or non-competitor through an equity or non-equity partnership. If it collaborates with a competitor, there are basically three modes: (1) cooperate first then compete, (2) cooperate while competing, and (3) cooperate among themselves and compete with others. The first mode means that two firms collaborate initially in developing a new product prior to competing. The following revelations explain the reasons for this kind of engagement. In the pharmaceutical industry, innovation is the key to success. When a single firm's competency is insufficient for product development, the firm tends to seek the collaborations of others. This situation is more common in the pharmaceutical industry because its boundaries overlap with others. Consequently, developing a new drug or technology might require the commitments of companies for collaboration between pharmaceutical and biotechnology firms.[9]

Another situation that might call for prior collaboration is a common defensive or offensive strategy among the members of the industry group. An increasing number of mergers in the pharmaceutical industry presents a good example of building market power and scale advantages between merging partners. By establishing synergies and scale economies through complementary production and marketing advantages, pharmaceutical firms attempt to fence off the rivals—especially big players and emerging challengers in the global marketplace.

Table 7.2

Strategic Alliances in the Pharmaceutical Industry

Year	Partners	Nationality	Value Chain Activity	Type of Alliance
1982	Merck, Astra AB	US, Sweden	Develop and market Astra's products	Licensing
1989	Merck, Johnson & Johnson	U.S., U.S.	Develop and market a broad range of nonprescription medicines in the U.S., Europe (1993), and Canada (1996)	Joint venture
1994	Merck, Pasteur Merieux Connaught	U.S., France	Market vaccines and collaborate with the development of combination vaccines for distribution in Europe	Joint venture
1994	Merck, Astra AB	U.S., Sweden	To develop and market most of Astra's new prescription medicines in the United States	Joint venture
1994	Merck, Chugai Pharmaceutical Co.	U.S., Japan	Develop and market over-the-counter pharmaceuticals in Japan	Joint venture
1997	Merck, Rhone-Poulenc	U.S., France	Discover, manufacture, and market veterinary pharmaceuticals and vaccines	Joint venture

Table 7.2

Continued.

Year	Partners	Nationality	Value Chain Activity	Type of Alliance
2000	SmithKline Beecham, Asahi Chemical Industry Co.	U.S., Japan	Development agreement for AZ40140,the novel Beta-3 receptor agonist and related compounds with potential for the treatment of obesity and diabetes	R&D and licensing
2000	Pfizer, Inc., Warner-Lambert	U.S, U.S.	Create the world's fastest-growing pharmaceutical company with product innovation	Merger
N/A	SmithKline Beecham, Europharm	U.S., Romania	Acquired 65% of Europharm market entry	Acquisition
1998	AMRAD Corporation, Ltd., Becton Dickinson & Co.	Australia, U.S.	Development and distribution of rapid diagnostic tests	Licensing
1996	SYNSORB Biotech, Inc., Takeda Chemical Industries	Canada, Japan	Development and marketing of SYNSORB Pk®	Licensing
1999	Genome Therapeutics, BioMerieux	U.S., France	Develop, manufacture, and sell in vitro diagnostic products for human clinical and industrial applications	R&D, production, marketing
1995	La Jolla Pharmaceutical Co., Leo Pharmaceutical Products, Ltd.	U.S., Denmark	Develop and market the lupus compound	Production, marketing

The general strategic alliance model presented in Chapter 3 mirrors collaborations in the pharmaceutical industry as well. The application of the model to the pharmaceutical firms posits a number of combinations: cooperating with a competitor or non-competitor, building an equity alliance or non-equity alliance, involving any of the three major modes, and engaging in specific value chain activities. We will discuss them in reference to some cases of collaboration. In this vein, we will look at specific cases of international alliances between pharmaceutical companies or pharmaceutical and biotech firms to illustrate the characteristics of such ventures.

Cooperation with a Non-Competitor: a R&D Partnership

Genset (United States) and Algene Biotechnologies Corporation (Canada) entered into a strategic alliance for research on Alzheimer's disease. As a result of internal research activities over the past several years, Algene has compiled an extensive and comprehensively phenotyped collection of clinical samples from Alzheimer's patients within the Quebec founding population. A large number of patient phenotypes were confirmed by the presence of senile plaques and high concentrations of protein bundles (neurofibrillary tangles) in post-mortem diagnosis.[10] By applying its gene mapping and statistical analysis platforms to these samples, Algene has identified several chromosomal regions that are susceptible to contain genes associated with Alzheimer's disease.

Under the strategic alliance, Algene will license its proprietary gene mapping results and provide access to its existing Alzheimer's disease DNA collections exclusively to Genset. In return, Genset will fund a one-year research program at Algene to pursue further sample collection and analysis to provide DNA samples to Genset, which satisfies optimal genetic, epidemiological, and biostatistical criteria for a large case control association study.[11]

Genset will use its integrated genomics technologies to rapidly generate proprietary biallelic markers in the chromosomal regions identified by Algene, perform high-throughput genotyping of the complete sample collection, and apply its advanced biostatistics and bioinformatics tools to analyze the resulting association data.[12] Under the terms of the agreement, all intellectual property rights to the results of the program will belong to Genset. Algene will receive license fees and one-year program funding with possible milestone payments based on the results of Genset's continued research and future revenues from the commercialization of the program's discoveries.

By combining its unique genomics approach using association studies with Algene's clinical expertise and exceptional clinical collection with well-characterized phenotypes, Genset hopes to rapidly discover and patent novel genes that will put it on the path toward better therapeutic options to deal with Alzheimer's disease. On the other hand, this agreement with Genset represents a major milestone for Algene. Its Alzheimer's program had reached a point where rapid progress towards the identification of associated genes required the scientific expertise, proprietary technology base, and critical mass of a major genomics partner. Genset is clearly the ideal ally for Algene to pursue the next phase of research in this program and to eventually commercialize the results. This alliance also reflects the new business strategy at Algene, which aims for early strategic partnering of its gene discovery programs to accelerate research and to generate revenue for the company.

Genset intends to establish targeted collaborative projects in the field of Alzheimer's research with pharmaceutical companies and to license its related gene discoveries for the discovery and development of novel drugs. Although both companies are collaborating on this Alzheimer's research, there was no indication that they would collaborate on the commercialization of the results. Each company would more likely pursue their own paths after the research is completed.

Cooperating while Competing: R&D and Marketing Collaboration

Another content analysis refers to a strategic alliance between NeuroSearch of Denmark and Abbott of the United States. NeuroSearch is a neuropharmaceutical company dedicated to the R&D of new drugs for disorders of the central nervous system (CNS). The company has four compounds in Phase II clinical trials for the treatment of depression, Parkinson's disease, Alzheimer's disease, and anxiety as well as two compounds in Phase I clinical trials for the treatment of brain damage after stroke and cocaine addiction. On the other hand, Abbott, a diversified health care company, also has a strong research program involving the CNS.

Both companies built an alliance to develop and commercialize compounds for the treatment of a number of nervous system disorders.[13] Under the pact, Abbott will finance the R&D done by both partners. In addition, Abbott will pay up to a total of $17 million to NeuroSearch in milestone payments for each successfully developed compound, as well as royalties on sales of compounds resulting from the alliance. Both NeuroSearch and Abbott decided to cooperate in the areas of R&D and marketing of the treatment of a number of nervous system disorders while they compete in other areas.

Another case of cooperating while competing in R&D and marketing is the Soltec and Mipharm cooperation. Soltec Research Pty, Ltd., a wholly owned subsidiary of the health care company F. H. Faulding & Co., Ltd., has entered a strategic agreement with the Italian group Mipharm. The agreement provided Mipharm with exclusive access to certain Soltec drug delivery technology platforms, especially in dermatological and gynecological areas, in Italy and some other Mediterranean countries. The parties will also collaborate on the development of new technologies for the delivery of drugs used in the treatment of diseases in these fields.

The terms of the transaction involve the payment of an up-front fee and research costs and royalty payments in respect to any future licenses granted pursuant to this agreement. Soltec managing director Ross MacDonald stated, "This agreement provides a further facet to the globalization of Soltec's technologies, joining a range of Soltec-developed products that are sold in markets throughout the world. We are looking forward to working with Mipharm, a young and dynamic company with an experienced management, which bases its development on the exploitation of leading edge technologies."[14]

The first product under the arrangement is Soltec's mousse for the treatment of head lice. This product is currently sold in Australia under license to Pfizer and has proven to be a commercial success. The item is also sold in the United States with the approval of the Food and Drug Administration (FDA).[15] Mipharm aims to launch the product in Italy under the trademark Milice, with launches in the other countries in the licensed territory to follow shortly afterward.

Likewise, Millennium Pharmaceuticals, Inc. (United States) announced that three of its pharmaceutical partners have signed extensions on their existing strategic alliances. Millennium's four-year partnership with Pfizer Inc., which expired in 1998, has been extended and expanded for an additional two years. Millennium's partnership with Astra AB (Sweden) will extend for its full term—an additional four years. In the field of oncology, Millennium's partnership with Eli Lilly and Company (United States) will continue for its full term—an additional two years. These extensions reflect the significant progress that Millennium believes has been achieved in all three research programs.

The Astra-Millennium alliance began in December 1995 and focused on drug discovery for inflammatory respiratory diseases, including asthma, allergic rhinitis, chronic bronchitis, emphysema, and other chronic obstructive pulmonary diseases. The four-year extension of the relationship to its full term is based, in part, on Millennium's successful delivery of novel respiratory inflammation drug targets to Astra and the development of Astra's target pipeline during the alliance's first phase. Efforts of the alliance during the extension phase will focus on the application of the targets for drug discovery and the continued discovery and validation of new targets.

Under the terms of the original agreement, Astra funds the research program and pays licensing fees to Millennium. Millennium is eligible to receive milestone payments based on the attainment of certain research and product development achievements and royalties on therapeutic products resulting from the collaboration. The alliance provides Astra with exclusive worldwide rights to develop and commercialize drugs based on Millennium's gene discoveries arising from the collaboration.

Cooperating while Competing: Production and Marketing Collaboration

Despite its market leadership and huge size, Merck has not gone alone all the time but rather formed numerous strategic alliances in the marketplace.

Merck (United States) and ASTRA AB (Sweden) signed a royalty-bearing licensing that aims to develop and market ASTRA's products by Merck. In 1994, both companies advanced their cooperation by creating a joint venture to develop and market most of ASTRA's new prescription medicines in the United States. Also, Merck and Johnson & Johnson (United States) created a joint venture to develop and market a broad range of nonprescription medicines in the United States, Europe, and Canada. Additionally, Merck and the Chuhai Pharmaceutical Company (Japan) formed a joint venture to develop and market OTC pharmaceuticals in Japan. Moreover, Merck and Rhone-Poulenc (France) established a joint venture to discover, manufacture, and market veterinary pharmaceutical pharmaceuticals and vaccines.

Another major firm using strategic alliances heavily is Abbott Laboratories. It is a global, diversified health care company devoted to the discovery, development, manufacturing, and marketing of pharmaceutical, diagnostic, nutritional, and hospital products. Abbott is committed to the R&D of novel treatments for neurological and psychiatric conditions through a number of alliances. It completed about 60 alliances in 1999—as many as it accomplished in the previous two years combined. Some will provide returns in the short term, while others will be realized in the years to come.[16] Above all, these agreements help Abbott build its leadership in key therapeutic areas such as cancer, diabetes, Acquired Immunodeficiency Syndrome (AIDS), urology, and vascular medicine. To minimize the impact of generic competition to Hytrin, Abbott's flagship drug, the company entered into agreement with Boehringer Ingelheim Pharmaceuticals to co-promote Flomax, the market-leading drug for benign hyperplasia.

Cooperating while Competing: Marketing Collaboration

Abbott Laboratories and SuperGen in late 1999 announced the signing of a worldwide sales and marketing agreement for the cancer drug rubitecan. Rubitecan is an oral chemotherapy compound in the camptothecin class and is currently in Phase III studies for the treatment of pancreatic cancer. Pancreatic cancer is associated with high patient mortality, causing more than 75,000 deaths annually in the United States and Europe. This disease is the fourth-leading cause of death by cancer in the United States, with an average survival rate of four to five months following diagnosis at an advanced stage.

Richard A. Gonzalez, senior vice president of hospital products at Abbott Laboratories, stated, "Rubitecan is a potentially valuable addition to our oncology franchise. Clinical data suggest that rubitecan has the potential to become a safe and effective therapy for the treatment for pancreatic cancer, a disease for which there is limited treatment options available. Furthermore, feedback from patients and clinicians worldwide has indicated a great need for an oral chemotherapy alternative."[17] On the other hand, Joseph Rubinfeld, chairman and chief executive officer of SuperGen, defined the benefit of this alliance for his company as follows: "Completing this agreement with Abbott is certainly an historic milestone in our continuing mission to build an independent pre-eminent cancer-fighting company. As one of the world's largest health care companies, Abbott possesses the resources to ensure significant global market penetration of rubitecan upon regulatory approval. This agreement allows SuperGen to maintain its considerable U.S. presence and oncology franchise."[18]

Under the terms of the agreement, Abbott will make an initial equity investment in SuperGen. Additional equity investments, cash milestones, and option exercises are contemplated over the life of the agreement. Abbott will have exclusive distribution and promotion rights for rubitecan outside the United States and co-promotion rights with SuperGen for rubitecan within the United States. In addition, Abbott will become the exclusive U.S. distributor for Nipent, SuperGen's currently marketed product for the treatment of hairy-cell leukemia. SuperGen retains U.S. marketing rights for Nipent. Rubitecan is currently being studied at more than 200 clinical sites for the treatment of pancreatic cancer. SuperGen has previously reported that it expects to initiate clinical trials of rubitecan for additional tumor types. Under the agreement announced, SuperGen will be responsible for funding the clinical development of a pancreatic claim for the drug.

Co-Promotion and R&D Agreement through Equity Participation

Abbott Laboratories and Triangle Pharmaceuticals, Inc., announced a worldwide strategic alliance for six antiviral products. Abbott Laboratories is a global, diversified health care company devoted to the discovery, development, manufacturing, and marketing of pharmaceutical, diagnostic, nutritional, and hospital products. The company employs 56,000 people and markets its products in more than 130 countries. Abbott Laboratories has been a leader in AIDS research since the early years of the epidemic. In 1985, the company developed the first licensed test to detect HIV in the blood and remains the leader in HIV diagnostics. Abbott retroviral and hepatitis tests are used to screen more than half of the world's donated blood supply. In addition, Abbott developed the HIV protease inhibitor Norvir and Advera®, a nutritional supplement to meet the unique dietary needs of people who are living with Human Immunodeficiency Virus (HIV). Abbott continues to conduct aggressive research on new treatments to fight HIV and AIDS.

Triangle Pharmaceuticals, Inc., based in Durham, North Carolina, is engaged in the development of new drug candidates primarily in the antiviral area, with a particular focus on therapies for HIV, including the AIDS and the hepatitis B virus. Prior to their employment with Triangle, members of Triangle's management team played instrumental roles in the identification, clinical development, and commercialization of several leading antiviral therapies.

In the United States, Abbott and Triangle will co-promote the four Triangle products currently in development for HIV and hepatitis B (HBV) and Abbott's two HIV protease inhibitors (PIs). Outside the United States, Abbott will have exclusive sales and marketing rights for the four Triangle antivirals. The agreement significantly expands Abbott's antiviral pharmaceutical product portfolio to include three nucleoside reverse transcriptase inhibitors (NRTIs) and one non-nucleoside reverse transcriptase inhibitor (NNRTI)—medications that are commonly used for the treatment of HIV and HBV. This marketing provides Abbott and Triangle with an unequaled development portfolio of all marketed classes of HIV treatments.

Arthur Higgins, senior vice president of Pharmaceutical Operations at Abbott, asserted, "This alliance is a prime example of Abbott's strategy to partner with top-quality companies, such as Triangle, whose products fit strategically with our worldwide pharmaceutical business. One of our goals is to be the leading healthcare company in the HIV arena, and this agreement strengthens our position worldwide by giving us access to every segment of pharmaceutical intervention in HIV."[19] Abbott's HIV franchise is unique in that it offers a broad portfolio across pharmaceutical, diagnostic, and nutritional products for people who are living with HIV and AIDS. On the other hand, the CEO of Triangle claimed, "Our success in bringing a number of HIV and HBV drug candidates forward in development provided us with a unique situation to make a portfolio deal. Along the way, we resisted licensing away any of our global rights to the drug candidates, thus increasing the opportunity for a deal with a single strong partner rather than having to make numerous country-by-country deals with multiple partners. Our strategic alliance with Abbott introduces a strong international presence, additional strength in the U.S. market, and the financial support to provide added stability to our development and commercialization goals. This alliance positions the two companies to potentially launch at least one new antiviral each year over the next four years."[20]

Among the four Triangle products Abbott will co-promote is Coactinon™ (emivirine), formerly known as MKC-442—an NNRTI that is currently in Phase III clinical trials. Triangle expects to file a New Drug Application (NDA) for Coactinon soon, while Abbott expects to submit a European application. The other two NRTIs included in the agreement are in earlier development stages. DAPD, an NRTI, is in Phase I/II for the treatment of HIV. Triangle plans to begin Phase I/II trials in HBV later this year. Phase I/II trials are underway with L-FMAU, a compound that is under investigation for the treatment of HBV.

Under the terms of the agreement, Abbott will purchase approximately 6.57 million shares of Triangle's common stock at $18 per share. Additionally, the agreement provides for non-contingent research funding of $31.7 million up to $185 million of contingent development milestone payments and the sharing of future commercialization costs. In addition, the partners plan to execute a manufacturing agreement before closing that will enable Abbott to manufacture certain Triangle products worldwide. Triangle and Abbott will share profits and losses for all Triangle drug candidates. Triangle will receive detailing fees and commissions on incremental sales that it generates for Abbott's protease inhibitors. In addition, Abbott will have the right of first discussion to market future Triangle compounds. The closing of the agreement is subject to the satisfaction of several conditions, including Hart-Scott-Rodino antitrust clearance and the negotiation of the manufacturing agreement between the parties.

Equity Participation: Strategic Alliance for Biopharmaceutical Production

Lonza Biologics, a subsidiary of Algroup Lonza Fine Chemicals and Specialties (Switzerland) and Genzyme Transgenics Corporation (United States) entered into a strategic alliance to develop purification and production methods for therapeutic proteins, including monoclonal antibodies. Lonza Biologics is the world's leader in contract development and production of recombinant proteins. The company undertakes highly specialized services for the pharmaceutical and biotechnology industries based on its nearly 20 years of experience in mammalian cell culture and on proprietary technology for the large-scale manufacture of innovative pharmaceutical products. With headquarters in the United Kingdom, Lonza Biologics operates cGMP multi-product manufacturing facilities in Slough, United Kingdom and Portsmouth, New Hampshire.

The Genzyme Transgenics Corporation applies transgenic technology to enable the development and production of recombinant proteins and monoclonal antibodies for medical uses. Primedica Corporation, Genzyme Transgenics' contract organization, provides preclinical development and testing to pharmaceutical, biotechnology, medical device, and other companies. The Genzyme Transgenics Corporation is also developing idiotypic vaccines in collaboration with the National Cancer Institute.

Based upon the achievement of mutually defined goals and objectives, Lonza Biologics' corporate parent, Algroup, has the intention to make a significant equity investment in Genzyme Transgenics' common stock. Formation of the strategic alliance enables Genzyme Transgenics to access Lonza Biologics' extensive existing infrastructure for downstream protein purification, delaying the necessity for substantial capital investments by Genzyme Transgenics at this time. The potential equity investment by

Algroup can enable Genzyme Transgenics to make additional investments in internal R&D programs to further its leadership position in cutting-edge transgenic technology.

The CEO of Genzyme Transgenics said, "The alliance with Lonza Biologics solidifies Genzyme Transgenics' leadership position in the production of therapeutic proteins using transgenic technology. Genzyme Transgenics' expertise in transgenic protein development, combined with Lonza's extensive experience in downstream processing, will facilitate the development of innovative therapies with the potential to treat major human illnesses."[21] Similarly, Ed Robinson, president of Lonza Biologics, claimed, "The remarkable technical strengths of the two companies will strongly position us to continue to meet the expected demand for efficient large-scale purification of therapeutic proteins from a variety of production technologies. This collaboration leverages our leading capabilities in mammalian cell culture and aligns us with the premier transgenics company."[22] The companies anticipate that initial activities will focus on large-scale purification methods for transgenic proteins and monoclonal antibodies under development within Genzyme Transgenics' product pipeline. Technical representatives from both Genzyme Transgenics and Lonza Biologics will explore methods to optimize and enable rapid, efficient, and low-cost production of preclinical and clinical-grade materials as well as downstream processing methods for commercial production.

Cooperating between Them but Competing with Others: Marketing Partnerships

Instrumentation Laboratory S.p.A. (Spain) announced that its majority shareholder, CH Werfen, has entered into a new strategic alliance and cross-distribution agreement with Beckman Coulter, Inc. (United States). The new agreement replaces the former agreement entered in 1992 and continues the strategic relationship between the parties. The agreement has an initial term of 10 years. The parties can extend it for up to 10 additional years.

Beckman Coulter will continue to distribute the company's hemostasis products (including the company's recently acquired Hemoliance product line) in North America. Additional details of the relationship in Asia, Latin America, and Africa will be disclosed as plans develop. The company will continue to distribute Beckman Coulter's hematology, flow cytometry, and particle characterization products in Italy and Austria.

Based on its previous positive experience with Beckman Coulter, Instrumentation Laboratories expects to realize some benefits from using Beckman Coulter's extensive distribution system in North America. This new agreement enables both companies to continue to take mutual advantage of their complementary strengths to serve their existing customers better as well as to gain new customers. Beckman Coulter's strong sales, marketing, service, and distribution capabilities in North America are a good complement to the expanded product offering and customer base and to the aggressive growth strategy of Instrumentation Laboratories.

Furthermore, Beckman Coulter recognizes that its customers would continue to enjoy the Werfen's excellent hemostasis product line in tandem with its own clinical chemistry and hematology systems. This alliance gives Beckman Coulter expanded opportunities to help its customers optimize their laboratory processes and improve productivity. Both companies cooperate on the hemostasis product line but compete with other firms. Because they do not have competitive products in their product lines, they are not in competition with each other.

Although the pharmaceutical cases explained here are limited to make generalizations, they demonstrate interfirm collaborations in different modes and value chain activities. As a resource-based view of the firm suggests, pharmaceutical firms engaged in various partnership to complement each other's resources and capabilities. The examples illustrate that a firm with a potential product usually links with another firm that has extensive marketing and distribution capabilities in different parts of the world.

Equity Participation: R&D and Marketing

Recently, Abbott and American Biogenetic Sciences (ABS) announced an agreement for Abbott to license ABS' novel neurological compound, ABS-103. ABS researches and develops diagnostic tests for cardiac conditions and infectious diseases as well as new treatments for neurological disorders including epilepsy, migraines, mania, Parkinson's disease, and Alzheimer's disease. The company also seeks new technologies and conducts R&D through its Global Scientific Network in the United States, Europe, Israel, Russia, and China.

The agreement gives Abbott exclusive rights to develop and market the compound worldwide. As a result of the agreement, Abbott will make up-front investments, including taking an equity position in ABS as well as making additional milestone payments. Arthur Higgins, senior vice president of Pharmaceutical Operations at Abbott Laboratories, asserted, "We are pleased with this agreement because ABS-103 is an extremely promising compound for central nervous system disorders, and it also demonstrates our strong commitment to our Neuroscience Franchise...Depakote (divalproex sodium), our largest U.S. pharmaceutical product, is used for several neurological and psychiatric conditions. The product has been experiencing double-digit growth in the past few years and we expect that growth to continue in the future. ABS-103 represents one of many strategies we're pursuing to build upon this leadership position in neuroscience."[23] On the other hand, John S. North, president and chief executive officer of ABS, viewed the collaboration with Abbott as follows: "We are pleased to be taking a major step in the development of ABS-103 with the leader in this market. Abbott will build upon the scientific innovation of ABS in the further development of this product. Additionally, Abbott's large and experienced marketing and sales organization gives the greatest opportunity for commercial success."[24] As the CEO of ABS admitted, ABS is counting on Abbott's extensive marketing and sales network while Abbott would have an opportunity to add a needed product line on its list.

Equity Participation and Licensing: Supplying and R&D Agreements

Cambridge Antibody Technology (CAT) in England has entered a multi-disciplinary strategic alliance with Searle, the pharmaceutical business of Monsanto Co. (United States) for the development of fully human, mono-clonal, antibody-based therapeutic drugs across multiple disease areas, focusing particularly on cancer treatment. This alliance is CAT's largest to date. The alliance combines CAT's expertise in high-throughput antibody generation and the development of human antibody drugs with Searle's capabilities in genomics, discovery biology, and drug development. CAT and Searle will both commit technology, intellectual property, and expertise to the alliance. Searle will supply target proteins, including those derived from its own internal discovery programs, and both companies will per-form collaborative research to demonstrate and validate their disease asso-ciation.

As part of the target validation process, CAT will apply its proprietary ProAb technology for high-throughput antibody generation to examine the expres-sion of novel proteins in human tissues.[25] CAT and Searle will jointly develop customized assays. CAT will generate high-potency, human antibody-based drugs directed to potential protein targets. Searle will further develop and mar-ket the drugs.

Under the terms of the agreement, an affiliate of Searle will make an up-front equity investment in 1,870,837 ordinary shares of CAT at a price of $4.15 per share for the sterling equivalent of $12.5 million, giving it an equity stake of approximately 6.9 percent in CAT.[26] Searle will also provide a minimum of $14 million in research funding. In addition, over the potential five-year term of the research collaboration, CAT could receive a further $35 million in license fees, research funding, and technical performance milestones.

According to David Chiswell, CEO of CAT, "CAT has pioneered the devel-opment of fully-human antibody drugs and the high-throughput isolation of antibodies on a scale compatible with the genomics era. It is fantastically excit-ing to combine these skills with Searle's outstanding capabilities in drug devel-opment."[27] Likewise, Philip Needleman, the co-president of Searle, stated that "Searle views CAT as the leader in the field of phage antibodies."[28] Therefore, Searle tries to exploit the competencies of its partner.

Non-Equity Agreement in R&D, Manufacturing, and Marketing

Bio-Technology General Corp. (BTG) of the United States and Teva Pharmaceutical Industries, Ltd., of Israel have entered a strategic alliance that will focus on the development and global commercialization of several generic, recombinant, therapeutic products. BTG's primary role will be to develop and manufacture the products, and Teva will have exclusive marketing rights. The agreement calls for Teva to make payments to BTG of up to $20 million for product rights and milestone payments.[29] Sim Fass, the chair and CEO of BTG, commented, "We consider this alliance highly complementary to our overall mission and challenge of developing and introducing innovative, proprietary pharmaceuticals."[30] Likewise, Eli Hurvitz, Teva's president and CEO, claimed, "Teva views this agreement as an important step, and a broadening of our activities in the continuously developing generic biotechnology area."[31]

Non-Equity R&D Alliances

Wyeth-Ayerst Research of the United States has entered into research agreement with Cambridge Antibody Technology (CAT) Group, PLC of the United Kingdom for the discovery and development of drug candidates based on human antibodies. Under the deal, Wyeth will pay CAT $4 million per year for up to four years. The total value of the agreement—including research funding, potential library license fees, and potential fees and milestones from the product collaboration—is roughly $70 million. Along with other research work, CAT will apply its proprietary functional genomics technologies to potential protein targets based on gene sequence information provided by Wyeth. Wyeth will also use CAT's bioinformatics software and phage library technology.

CAT was also granted a U.S. patent for the "production of anti-self antibodies from antibody segment repertoires and displayed on phage."[32] The significance of the patent is that it covers the isolation of human antibodies against all human proteins, except those that generate natural antibodies in humans.[33] Such human proteins will often be drug targets, particularly as drug targets emerge from human genome initiatives.

AN EVALUATION

From the qualitative analysis conducted, it becomes clear that strategic alliances in the pharmaceutical industry show that the firms engage in collaboration with other pharmaceutical firms in various modes: "First compete and then cooperate," "Cooperate while competing," and "Cooperate among them but compete with others." As a result of the empirical inquiry described here on the pharmaceutical strategic alliances, however, it is noticeable that the mode of "Cooperate while competing" is the most popular. Another mode of alliances, "Cooperate among them and compete with others," seems to be the least attractive of the three modes. Although, this last mode could face legal restrictions such as antitrust regulations in Europe and the United States. Such practices are not so strictly controlled in countries outside Europe and the United States. An investigation of alliances in other industries or in particular countries such as Japan and South Korea, where such alliances are allowed, might show a different picture from those of Europe and the United States. In other words, the legal environment influences the strategic alliance mode. A cross-national comparison would reveal different practices in this area.

Given the critical role of R&D in the pharmaceutical business, the firms continuously attempt to build or preserve their innovations through R&D partnerships. Even the long-lasting process of R&D (10 to 15 years to develop a new drug) seems to not be a predicament to such alliances, managing an alliance could be extremely difficult for such a long period of time. Engaging in R&D partnerships between pharmaceutical firms requires a change in their managerial minds and organizational cultures. The traditional attitude exists that the firms might feel that because R&D provides proprietary advantages in this particular industry, they would like to reserve it for themselves rather than sharing it with another firm. Such an attitude reflects internationalization by multinational companies, rather than entering into strategic alliances.[34] This attitude has been changing in the past two decades, however. Consequently, pharmaceutical firms seem to favor equity participation and non-equity participation, including co-development, co-production, and licensing as the forms of alliances. Probably, they find that such alliances provide more control or entice trust while building a competitive advantage.

NOTES

1. Anonymous, Pharmaceuticals, _S&P Industry Report_: (1998): 4.
2. Ibid.
3. K. Ohmae, The global logic of strategic alliances, _Harvard Business Review_ (March–April, 1989): 143–154.
4. Anonymous, Pharmaceuticals, _S&P Industry Report_: (1998): 5.
5. R. Langreth, S. Lipin, and T. M. Burton, After big drug-firm mergers, the prescription calls for more, _The Wall Street Journal_ (February 9, 2000): B1.
6. Ibid.
7. Ibid.

8. Anonymous, *Industry Surveys:* Healthcare: Pharmaceuticals (June 29, 2000): 3.

9. P. M. Swamidass and W. W. McCutchen, Jr., Explaining the differences in domestic and cross-boundary strategic alliances in the pharmaceutical/biotech industry, *International Journal of Technology Management,* 15, no. 3, 4, 5 (1998): 491–506.

10. Genset, Company Release (May 20, 1999).

11. PR Newswire Association, Inc. (May 26, 1999).

12. Ibid.

13. Soltec and Mipharm reached an agreement, *The Wall Street Journal* (2000).

14. *Asian Pulse News* (1999).

15. Ibid.

16. Abbott Laboratories, Press Release (December 20, 1999).

17. Ibid.

18. SuperGen Company Report (1999): 3.

19. PR Newswire Association, Inc. (May 19, 1999).

20. Ibid.

21. PR Newswire (May 19, 1999).

22. Ibid.

23. Abbott Press Release (January 27, 2000): 1.

24. Ibid.

25. Basic Research, *Applied Genetics News,* 20, no. 6 (January 2000).

26. Ibid.

27. Ibid.

28. Ibid.

29. Basic Research, *Applied Genetics News,* 20, no. 3 (October 1999).

30. Ibid.

31. Ibid.

32. Anonymous, Wyeth-Ayerst, CAT in major R&D alliance, *Chemical Market Reporter,* 255, no. 14 (1999): 27.

33. Ibid.

34. P. J. Buckley and M. Casson, *The future of multinational enterprise* (London: Macmillan, 1978).

8

Global Alliances in the Airline Industry

INDUSTRY OUTLOOK

In the past two decades, rising concentrations through mergers, acquisitions, and bankruptcies has marked the airline industry. "The top airlines have gained greater control over markets since the mid-1990s through code-sharing agreements with regional carriers, and more recently, through global marketing alliances."[1] The U.S. deregulation of the airline industry in 1978 has dramatically modified the market, which required the carriers to adopt the use of a hub-and-spoke system of airport networks. Control over hub airports has intensified the competition and contributed to big losses, mergers, and several major bankruptcies in the United States.[2]

Airlines derive most of their revenue from passenger fares; however, they also earn ancillary revenues from transporting mail, shipping freight, selling in-flight services, and from serving alcoholic beverages. The commercial airline industry concentrates its efforts on attracting the business traveler segment because it is the primary revenue for airline companies. Business travelers yield higher margins because they typically book flights that are paid for by their companies. Therefore, business travelers have a tendency to be price inelastic with regard to airfares. Consequently, airlines offer special deals to attract business travelers. These special services can include priority check-in, expedited baggage handling, luxury lounges, and in-flight amenities such as cellular phones, faxes, and outlets for laptop computer usage.

In contrast, leisure travelers are highly price conscious. They usually try to save money by using the Internet for comparisons, looking for discounted airfare, and accepting unusual flight schedules.

Airlines are classified according to their size of operation. There are primarily three kinds of airlines: major airlines, national airlines, and regional airlines. Major airlines encompass the most common types that travelers use because they have the greatest geographical reach. To be considered a major airline, an airline must have at least $1 billion in revenue. They usually operate with 130 to 450 seats per aircraft. Some even have aircraft that can travel 5,000 miles before refueling. In this book, the focus will be on major airlines and their international partnerships.

National airlines are more limited to regional markets. A national airline can have between $100 million and $1 billion in revenue. National airlines usually operate aircraft with 100 to 150 seats. They operate short-haul trips because of their limited geographical reach. They specialize in point-to-point services. Regional airlines (called commuter airlines) serve low-density and short-haul markets. They primarily have point-to-point service up to 400 miles with fewer than 100 seats. Charter airlines usually transport passengers on an "on-call" basis. These are unscheduled services to various destinations.

COMPETITIVE DYNAMICS

Airlines compete for price and service to attract the consumer/vacationer market. But business travelers require flight frequency and reliability when choosing an airline. Airlines usually differentiate themselves from the competition through frequent-flyer programs. These programs enable travelers to accumulate bonus miles to receive discounts on future travel. They are often redeemed for free air tickets or service upgrades. These programs are designed to promote repeat business and to solidify a customer's choice to use one airline carrier.

Airline fares fluctuate frequently. Airlines often reduce fares to attract leisure travelers; however, they rarely discount business fares because the demand for these seats is highly price inelastic. Passengers flying coach might get a variety of quoted fares. Walk-up fares (paid by passengers at departure) are the highest because consumers have less of a chance to compare competitors' fares. Airline seats are perishable inventory. To reduce the revenue loss, the airline industry develops sophisticated computer programs to determine the demand by the hour, day, week, or month. Airlines also attempt to calculate how much a flight should be booked by a given point in time through a practice known as "yield management." Yield management alerts airlines to abnormal booking patterns, an estimated number of passengers, overbooking, the number of seats that can be overbooked, and how many customers will cancel.

Airline Operating Costs

Labor represents 35 percent of an airline's costs. This amount includes costs for flight crews, flight attendants, ground service personnel, dispatchers, maintenance crews, and customer service (booking and boarding). Most airline personnel belong to a union in the United States. Most union negotiations last a year before a settlement is reached. Then, a settlement lasts for about three years. Fuel costs are the second-largest operating cost category, representing approximately 10 percent of costs. Some airlines hedge fuel prices by buying and selling futures on the commodity market. Weather can also affect airline costs and operations. Wind speed and air temperatures influence how much fuel an aircraft needs. Weather is the second-largest cause of airline fatalities. The airline industry must obtain a detailed weather forecast that includes cloud height, horizontal visibility, wind speed, and direction. Aircraft itself represents about 10 percent of total costs. Airlines either buy or lease their fleet of aircraft. Most airlines perform routine maintenance, but many outsource heavier repairs to firms that specialize in such business. Airlines are strictly regulated by government agencies (for example, the Federal Aviation Administration, or FAA, in the United States) for safety, labor, and operating procedures.

As major airlines face the competition of group alliances in the global market, they are subject to competition in domestic markets by other major players and regional players. Regional airlines have gained new ground with the development of newer, smaller jets that are faster than turbo-prop planes and that have greater ranges. The new regional jets have also made operating in previously underserved markets more cost-efficient. Recognizing their potential, major U.S. carriers such as Delta Airlines, which owns regional carriers Delta Express, Atlantic Southeast, and COMAIR, and American Airlines, with its American Eagle, have sought to control all or part of the upstart regional airlines. There is a similar trend in Europe, where regional airlines are seeking partnerships with major airlines to more effectively gain access to certain hubs.

Major carriers merging with each other have not found an easy solution as they consolidate operations and fend off competitors. They have encountered strict scrutiny by regulatory agencies in the United States and Europe, as has been the case with United Airlines' bid for US Airways (still held up in review). Similar efforts have been stymied in Europe, as was the failed merger between KLM and Alitalia. Given this background information on the airline industry, we will turn to strategic alliances between airline companies and examine the salient characteristics of interfirm collaborations in the global airline industry.

STRATEGIC ALLIANCES BETWEEN AIRLINES

Airlines worldwide have been trying to strike a balance between cooperation and competition. They have been seeking alternatives to their conventional merger and acquisition strategies, such as strategic alliances, to expand services rapidly and to buttress market share without undertaking the difficult task of acquiring a rival. Nonetheless, collaboration in the airline industry presents a different picture from other industries we have examined so far. While airlines continue to establish links in the forms of equity participation and contractual alliances with the leadership of major airlines, others engage in networks of constellations of players. As we will explain, STAR and OneWorld as networks of airlines include a number of individual airlines. On the other hand, there are also a number of dyadic relationships reflecting cooperation between two airlines. For example, British Airways and Aer Lingus signed a cooperative agreement while American Airlines and Swiss/Sabena agreed on a code-sharing. A number of European and U.S. airlines have also developed trans-Atlantic alliances, as shown in Table 8.1.

Table 8.1
Trans-Atlantic Airline Alliances

Airline Pairs	Flights per Week	No. of U.S. Cities	No. of European Cities
American Airlines— Sabena (Belgium)	49	5	1
Delta Airlines—Air France	147	9	3
Northwest Airlines— KLM (Netherlands)	126	13	1
United Airlines— Lufthansa (Germany)	268	11	3
United Airlines—SAS (Denmark, Sweden, and Norway)	82	4	3

Source: The airlines' annual reports

Many airlines are still partially owned by their respective nations, and treaties between them determine which airlines can land in which locations. To get around national laws and regulatory problems and to compete effectively, airlines have formed global networks and individual alliances.

Basically, major airlines from the United States, Europe, and Asia-Pacific have forged their own alliance groups to offer better services internationally. It is estimated that international travel will grow faster than domestic U.S. travel. Consequently, U.S. domestic carriers find it advantageous to create collaborative ventures with international carriers as an entry point into new markets. Thus, airline alliances can be studied in three primary forms as referred to in the general Strategic Alliance Model (Figure 3.4). First, *equity participation* refers to one airline buying equity into another to build an organic tie and to control a target airline. Second, *bilateral cooperative alliances* mean an agreement between two airlines involving non-equity in dyadic relationships. Third, *network alliances* are a group of airlines collaborating on a number of marketing activities. We will discuss each form; however, network alliances (as a dominant form) will be described extensively.

Equity Participation

A number of airlines have bought equity stakes in other airlines to build a formal link and to mold their collaboration into a formal structure. Principal equity participations by major airlines into others are given in Table 8.2. Through such equity holdings, the investing airline company can influence strategic directions of the target airline and develop complementary activities to its own operations. Of course, building such a formal link between two airlines brings them closer to each other and entices cooperation between them.

Table 8.2
Equity Holdings between Airlines

Investor Airline	Nationality	Target Airline	Nationality	Equity Stake
British Airways	U.K.	Qantas	Australia	25%
British Airways	U.K.	Iberia Airlines	Spain	9%
SAir Group	Switzerland	Sabena	Belgium	49.5%
SAir Group	Switzerland	LTU	France	49.9%
SAir Group	Switzerland	LOT Polish	Poland	37.5%
Singapore Airlines	Singapore	Virgin Atlantic	U.K.	49%
Singapore Airlines	Singapore	Air New Zealand	New Zealand	25%

Table 8.2
Continued.

Investor Airline	Nationality	Target Airline	Nationality	Equity Stake
SAS Scandinavian	Sweden	British Midway	U.K.	20%
SAS Scandinavian	Sweden	Widoroe	Norway	63%
SAS Scandinavian	Sweden	Cimber Air	Denmark	26%
KLM Royal Dutch	Netherlands	Kenyan Airlines	Kenya	25%
KLM Royal Dutch	Netherlands	Air Littoral	France	35%
KLM Royal Dutch	Netherlands	ALM Antillean	U.S.	40%

Bilateral Cooperative Agreements

Commonly, we see two airlines cooperating on code-sharing, frequent-flyer mileage programs, and other expanded passenger services. A major component of many airline alliances, however, is code-sharing, which refers to replicating seamless travel that would be provided by a single airline. This system is called "interline service" in the industry. Interline service offers airline passengers the convenience of single ticketing and check-in. With code-sharing, a passenger carrier can advertise its alliance partner's flights as its own, and without adding new aircraft it can increase the number of destinations and frequency flights it offers.[3] Refer to Table 8.3 for a number of bilateral alliances.

Table 8.3
Bilateral Cooperative Agreements

British Airways	Aer Lingus
American Airlines	Swissair/Sabena
United Airlines	Singapore Airlines
SAS	Singapore Airlines

Air Canada	Singapore Airlines
Lufthansa	Singapore Airlines
Northwest Airlines	KLM Royal Dutch Airlines
Air France	Delta Airlines
Air France	Aeromexico
Air France	Korean Airlines

Alliance Networks

Recently, many airlines around the world have joined in alliance networks to compete effectively by providing superior customer services (refer to Figure 8.1). Principal airline networks include STAR, OneWorld, SkyTeam, and Qualiflyer.

Figure 8.1
Global airline networks

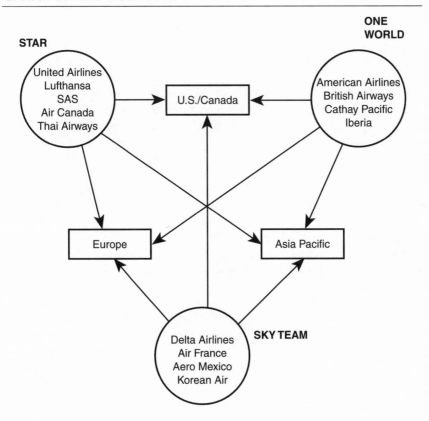

STAR. The first alliance group was STAR, which was established May 14, 1997. The Star Alliance group consists of United Airlines, Lufthansa, SAS, Air Canada, Mexicana, Air New Zealand, British Midland Airways, Austrian Airlines (former Qualiflyer member), Lauda Air Luftfahrt AG (former Qualiflyer member), Tyrolean, Singapore Airlines, Thai Airways, All Nippon Airways, Varig, and Ansett Transport Industries. The STAR group seems to be the most established and the largest alliance network, consisting of 15 airlines. It offers a wide range of flights in many countries.

OneWorld. OneWorld consists of eight full members including American Airlines, British Airways, Cathay Pacific, Finnair, Aer Lingus, Qantas Airways, Iberia, LanChile, and 23 affiliates. Between them, they offer services to 550 destinations in 133 countries, with their 270,000 employees operating fleets of more than 1,850 aircraft, carrying some 210 million passengers in 2000. The alliance is largely restricted to sharing frequent flyer schemes, airport lounges, and some marketing. Because all the members of OneWorld have their own frequent-flyer programs, OneWorld has created a set of symbols: OneWorld Emerald, Sapphire, and Ruby. Regulators refuse to let them make the next steps of selling seats on each other's flights and coordinating schedules and prices.

SkyTeam. SkyTeam consists of Delta Airlines, Air France, Aero Mexico, and Korean Air. The SkyTeam airlines carry a combined 174.3 million passengers per year, trailing the Star Alliance (which is led primarily by United Airlines and Lufthansa). The group sees the Star Alliance as its only real competition, but the alliance still has a long way to go.

In addition, we will discuss two airline network attempts that resulted in failure.

Qualiflyer. The network, which was initiated by SAir Group (Swissair and Sabena), consists of Swissair, Sabena, Crossair, OAM, Air Liberte, Ait Littoral, TAP Air Portugal, PGA Portugalia Airlines, Air Europe, Volare, and LOT Polish Airlines. Swissair, a leader in the group, introduced a symbolic gesture by painting its aircraft with a blue belly as a sign of the Qualiflyer membership. The group focused on only the European market, which limited its geographic scope. Swissair admitted failure in its attempt to build the Qualiflyer alliance around a group of carriers in which it was taking substantial minority stakes, although some frequent-flyer programs still continue among the member airlines.

WINGS. The Wings Group used to include Northwest Airlines, Continental Airlines, KLM, and Alitalia, but after KLM's disengagement with Alitalia, the group dissolved. The original cooperation between KLM and Northwest goes back to 1993. It appears that the two leading partners were KLM, with its affiliate Alitalia, and Northwest, with its affiliate Continental Airlines. Obviously, the group had limited partners, most notably none from the Asia-Pacific region.

Through such networks, airlines seek to exploit each other's resources, which include additional routes and marketing strategies as well as code-sharing agreements, without incurring the high costs of expansion. For customers, airline alliances offer broader frequent-flyer programs, streamlined travel, and simplified systems for purchasing tickets. A review of those airline networks indicates that most airlines feel that to compete effectively with less regulatory hassles and minimum risky investments, they must have connecting flights in three continents: North America, Europe, and Asia-Pacific. All strategic groups have flight connections to North America, Europe, and Asia-Pacific. Thus, the present strategic networks seem to ignore Latin America, but all major U.S. airlines cover Latin America sufficiently. Also, Iberia Airlines in OneWorld and Aeromexico in SkyTeam have numerous flights to South America. Additionally, some airlines have, if not network alliances, dyadic relationships with major Latin American airlines to complement their North American flights.

International airlines naturally follow booming economies, where markets offer great opportunities—especially augmenting business travelers and cargo traffic. Consequently, most networks are particularly interested in Asia-Pacific markets, which are considered the next frontier of economic development (for example, economic explosion in China and India). The coverage of STAR, SkyTeam, and OneWorld reminds us of the "triad" concept of Ohmae, who argued that firms—to stay competitive—must have a presence in three major markets: North America, Europe, and Asia-Pacific.[4]

NETWORK ALLIANCE MODEL

Combining the tenets of resource- and competency-based theory with the case information presented here, a conceptual model is developed to explain the motives and dynamics of airline networks. Although this model is constructed for airline alliances, with minor modifications it can be used for other types of networks in explaining group versus group competition and intra-group relationships. The essential elements of the model are depicted in Figure 8.2. Partners are members who are motivated by a number of factors that contribute to the formation of a network. These networks are also influenced by government regulations and by a competitive landscape that consists of both national and international markets. Networks present a dynamic structure because of intra-network relations and relational interactions among its members, as well as inter-network relations and relational interactions among networks.

Figure 8.2

Conceptual model for networks

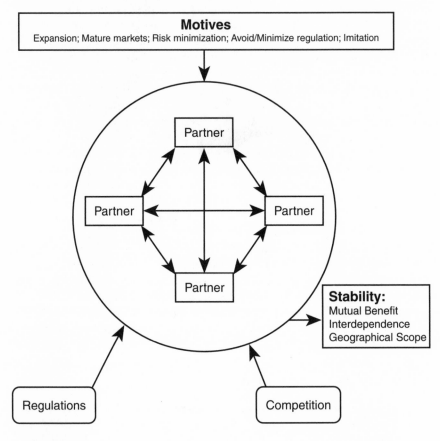

Motives

What are the principal reasons for such alliances? An analysis of the current constellation of airlines shows that five major factors contribute to global networks in the airline industry.

Expansion motive. Airlines want to expand their operations to new overseas markets by collaborating with domestic players that are already established in their respective markets. For this reason, each of the major U.S. airlines has established links with another major European airline: United Airlines with Lufthansa and SAS; American Airlines with British Airways; Delta Airlines with Air France, and Continental-Northwest Airlines with KLM and Italia. Such collaborations between airlines make it easier for both U.S. and European partners to penetrate each other's market or to offer extended services.

Domestic market maturity. Actually, this motive is closely related to the first one. Most domestic markets have reached the maturity stage; therefore, domestic carriers are seeking new horizons and markets. U.S. and European airlines again exploit their markets to an almost full extent so that there is no longer any room for growth. Under such pressure, major airlines look for opportunities in international markets.

Risk minimization. Global alliances present less risk than expensive takeovers. Through global alliances, airlines attempt to capture market opportunities without investing in aircraft, labor, support equipment, and expanded facilities. For example, U.S. airlines had a bad experience with expensive mergers and acquisitions in the past. Consequently, they are determined to not replicate the competitive race that cost the domestic industry $13 billion between 1990 and 1994.[5] "During those years, one-third total U.S. airline capacity filed bankruptcy and 100,000 employees were downsized."[6]

Avoid or minimize extensive regulatory scrutiny. Forming alliances are not subject to the same strict government investigation and review process, which is a lengthy process and often ends up with non-approval in the cases of proposed mergers and acquisitions. The Department of Transportation and Department of Justice in the United States and the counterpart agency in the European Union (EU) closely review the merger and acquisitions proposals to assure competition in the marketplace and consumer interest.

Imitation to rivals. When rival airlines engage in global strategic alliances, others feel that they have to form their own network to avoid not being left out. Imitative behavior explains the emergence of SkyTeam and OneWorld as a reaction to the establishment of the STAR group.

Of these networks, some airlines have developed closer one-to-one relationships, but the most important ones are trans-Atlantic. Table 8.1 shows such trans-Atlantic alliances between airlines.

Partners

The members of each network can be broken down into leaders and followers. The leading airlines, which were instrumental in the formation of the group, include major airlines from the United States and Europe. These leaders contributed to the establishment of the alliance networks, such as United Airlines and Lufthansa for the STAR group, American Airlines and British Airways for OneWorld, Delta Airlines and Air France for SkyTeam, and Swissair and Sebana for Qualiflyer. The list of leading and following airlines in each network is given in Figure 8.1. In general, commenting on group interaction, Cook asserted that centrally located actors are assumed to be important, and peripheral actors are powerless.[7] The centrally located actors are enabled by their position to accomplish their purposes, but the peripheral actors are constrained by their position to powerlessness. In the airline industry, however, we believe that peripheral members are not so much resource dependent on powerful members and are nearly as powerful, if not as powerful, as centrally located members. Both major airlines and peripheral airlines feel that it is necessary to belong to the existing (or soon to be established) networks to compete effectively worldwide. Otherwise, they could be left out with fewer advantages against big and powerful networks. For example, in 2000, Singapore Airlines and Austria Airlines Group (Austria Airlines, Lauda Air, and Trylean) joined STAR while Portugalia and Volare Airlines joined the Qualiflyer group.

Network Stability

Because the present networks are relatively new, it is difficult to make a judgment about the stability of those networks. We can say, however, that the current airline networks are in a state of flux. The more established ones are STAR, OneWorld, and SkyTeam, while Qualiflyer suffered from coordination and management problems. On the other hand, despite its ambitious formation, the Wing Group has resulted in disappointment. Moreover, the members of the existing networks can easily switch from one to another. For example, Austria Group recently switched from Qualiflyer to the STAR group, meaning that membership bonds are not so strong.

Despite extensive studies on alliance stability and survival (particularly involving joint ventures), not much is done on network stability.[8] We believe that network stability is a function of three variables: mutual benefits experienced by members, the degree of interdependence among members, and a wide market scope of the airline network. The network's success can be studied along these three dimensions.

Mutual benefits. As social exchange theory suggests, a member joins the network to gain benefits while other members hold similar expectations. If such expectations are not met, the member could leave the alliance network. Because the alliance is based on a contractual agreement rather than on an equity investment, it is easier for a member to breach the accord. In other words, the governance structure is rather informal.

Interdependency. Members of the network depend upon each other to function appropriately and to provide the coordinated customer services that they try to offer. Unilateral choices are replaced by cooperative choices. Theoretically, a member is continuously motivated to engage in cooperation because of its interest in the network. As a result, the network operation, like a spider web, connects each member by a common tie. In the same network, the members' relations are connected if the exchange in one of them is contingent on the exchange in another. When the members agreed upon code-sharing and connecting flights, an airline passenger flying from the United States to Europe and then continuing to Japan is supposed to have seamless travel in the same network group (for example, STAR or OneWorld).

Nevertheless, it seems that the network ties among airline members are not so strong that one member can easily switch from one network group to another. For example, as mentioned before, Austrian Airlines Group, a former Qualiflyer member, switched to the Star Alliance.

Market scope. A close examination of networks demonstrates that in order to be effective, a network should cover at least two significant markets: the United States and Europe. All the present networks, however (STAR, OneWorld, and SkyTeam), have extensions to the Asia-Pacific markets. A conclusion can be drawn that the larger scope of coverage is better for the network's performance. That is, the larger scope increases the competitive advantage of a network against others.

National and International Competition

Airlines confront a variety of competitors. In some markets, major airlines face competition from other major players as well as from national and regional airlines. Although all airlines compete with other transportation modes, it is not true for very long-distance (for example, more than 500 miles) travel, especially for trans-Atlantic travel. Following the U.S. deregulation in 1978, competition in the airline industry intensified. As regulatory barriers to entry were dismantled and risk capital poured in, established carriers faced an unending parade of aggressive startup airlines that targeted the larger carriers' high-margin businesses. In recent years, however, competitive pressures have eased as risk capital has become scarce for startups, and established carriers have limited their geographic horizons.

Changing conditions such as Internet technology and the introduction of Computer Reservation Systems (CRSs) have intensified competition in the airline industry. The Internet has strengthened the bargaining position of consumers vis-à-vis airlines. Today, both leisure and business travelers make more informed decisions in their selection of airlines. Under the traditional pricing model, the carriers set airfares and the consumer decided whether to accept them or not. Today, airline seats—albeit typically only distressed surplus inventory—are being auctioned off the highest bidder.[9] Online travel agents like Travelocity and Expedia offer a variety of choices and the cheapest fares available to consumers. In response to this booming trend, in late 1999 four airlines—Continental, Northwest, Delta, and United, subsequently joined by American in May 2000—created a travel Web site, Orbitz, by investing about $100 million. Later, 30 airlines signed up for it.[10]

With domestic traffic slowing down, U.S. airlines consider international markets as an avenue for faster growth. Thus, it is not accidental that major U.S. carriers have been leaders in establishing alliance networks by forging with other international carriers. Moreover, international travelers want to deal with one airline to make all their arrangements with a seamless travel itinerary instead of dealing with a number of airlines. To respond to such customer demands, many airlines have sought links with others while competition has shifted from individual-based to network-based competition. In this context, airlines wanted to position themselves into specific groups to enhance their competitiveness by being more responsive to customer needs.

Regulation

An important impediment to airline alliances is government regulation of the industry. In every country, governmental agencies impose stringent control over the operations of airlines because of safety reasons. Moreover, in many countries, particularly in the United States and Europe—two major markets—the governmental agencies act like a watchdog for mergers, acquisitions, and alliances between airlines. Although alliances have been subject to less regulation than mergers and acquisitions, governments still interfere with alliance agreements if they feel that such agreements restrict competition. In the United States, the Department of Transportation (DOT) along with its affiliated agency, the Federal Aviation Administration (FAA), regulates the industry with regard to safety, labor, operating procedures, and aircraft fitness and emission levels. The International Civil Aviation Organization (ICAO), an entity affiliated with the United Nations (UN), proposes noise standards. The standards are not legally binding in a given country, however, unless the country has formally agreed to them. The FAA primarily promotes safe air travel by monitoring the industry's maintenance and operating practices. The FAA certifies aircraft and airlines as well as establishes age and medical requirements for pilots. One of the agency's chief functions is to operate the U.S. air traffic control system at some 288 airports. Another 161 airports are operated under contract from the FAA.

The DOT levies civil penalties against airlines that engage in fraudulent marketing practices or that violate code-sharing rules. It also oversees compliance with denied boarding (bumping) compensation rules and renders decisions on airline ownership and control issues. The DOT also plays an important role in negotiating bilateral aviation treaties with foreign nations.

When U.S. airlines operate in international markets, they are subject to economic regulation by individual foreign governments and collective organizations such as the European Commission. The degree of regulation varies from country to country, and the rules are laid out through formal, bilateral aviation treaties. These accords govern reciprocal landing rights and typically limit the number of carriers that can operate, the level of rates, the types of aircraft, and the frequency of flights. In recent years, the United States has secured "open skies" agreements with more than 30 nations. These agreements provide for reduced economic regulation and unrestricted code-sharing between international carriers, the formation of alliances, and at least partial ownership rights. Nevertheless, other countries (except the European Union) have not been as strict as the United States in regulating the industry.

THE IMPACT, CAVEATS, AND FUTURE OF NETWORKS

The framework provided here helps us understand why alliance networks are formed and how they operate in terms of relationships among members of networks in the airline industry. It signifies that the stability of alliance networks depends upon mutual gains that a network provides for its members and a strong interdependence among its members. For airline alliances in particular, the market coverage of networks seems to be an important factor. The larger the market scope, the stronger the network. In turn, the strong networks provide synergy and some competitive advantages for their members in comparison to those networks that are restricted to limited regions.

It is too early, however, to draw a general conclusion regarding the stability of airline networks, because they are rather a recent phenomenon. The oldest airline network, the STAR group, was established in 1997, and OneWorld originated in 1999. It is, however, obvious that airline networks are in a state of flux; as an old one disbands (such as the Wings group), new ones can be formed. Nonetheless, all the principal carriers acting as leaders in forming networks have already created their own groups (excluding KLM, which is still looking for strategic directions). Another feature of alliance networks is that members move in and out of a given network simply because contractual agreements do not generate strong commitments from members.

We must note that not all alliances are successful, however. Delta Airlines has flopped in its previous Atlantic alliance with Swissair and Sabena. In its second alliance venture in SkyTeam, the airline claims that it has sought out quality partners that can help Delta extend its reach around the world.[11] An airline experiencing dissatisfaction in its current network can easily look for other alternatives. Without a doubt, it damages the stability of the network. Despite their loose governance structures, airline networks will be around for some time as long as they provide mutual benefits for their members and develop interdependence among members. As a result of the pressure from empowered customers by technological advancements and increased customer expectations through greater experience with and knowledge about services, airlines will be increasingly interested in networks. No single airline can fully meet the sophisticated needs of customers, efficient services with reasonable prices in a dynamic and complex environment with stiff competition, and ever-increasing costs (for example, fuel and labor) of operations. Jarillo stated, "A strategic network is an arrangement by which companies set up a web of close relationships that form a veritable system geared to providing product or services in a coordinated way. These networks are becoming dominant in more and more industries, and reason is that they can meet the current competitive requirements better than old ways of organizing economic activity."[12]

We believe that there will be important benefits gained from alliance networks in the airline industry. To understand the need for and benefits of alliance networks, we can first make a theoretical analysis from the perspectives of a resource-based view (RBV) and social exchange theory. The resource-based model suggests that each airline is a collection of unique resources and capabilities that provides a basis for its strategy and is the primary sources of its returns.[13] Over time, an airline acquires different resources and develops unique capabilities. Thus, not all airlines possess the strategically relevant resources and capabilities (for example, landing permits, the restricted use of specific hubs, geographical coverage, and management know-how). Because such resources and capabilities are not highly mobile across firms, by combining them in the form of alliance networks, the partnering firms enjoy synergies and competitive advantages. RBV will throw lights on tangible and intangible resource needs of partners and how synergies can be achieved by combining similar and different resources of each partner.

On the other hand, social exchange theory helps us understand an ever-changing environment in which firms operate and how they link with each other to deal with uncertainties and complexities for mutual benefits. It provides a conceptual basis on which inter- and intra-network relationships can be investigated.[14] Social exchange theory focusing on relationship interactions is effective for organizations exposed to conditions of instability and complexity. Thus, drawing on social exchange theory, an exchange relationship framework that identifies organizational and relational factors that encourage or constrain network forms can be studied.

Another important implication of alliance networks is that they require managers to pay more attention to the process of managing alliance networks in particular industries (for example, airlines and biotechnology). This need arises from the fact that so far, previous studies focused on why alliances are formed but overlooked how they operate. Likewise, Child and Faulkner asserted that more attention has been given to the antecedent conditions and desired outcomes of cooperation rather than to the process of making it work and fostering its development.[15] The critical lesson for today's managers is to understand how alliance networks can be managed effectively and how they can contribute to their members' interests while providing value for customers. In this context, some important questions are as follows: whether alliance networks are worthwhile alternative structures, whether certain types of networks are more effective than others, and whether alliance networks work better in some industries than in others. Other critical questions might be, "What would the feasible governance forms contribute to network stability?" "What would be the effect of organizational culture of member firms on formation and stability of networks?"

Additionally, there is a need for managerial guidelines for running networks effectively. Such guidelines should be developed for each alliance network, addressing how emerging network forms can be structured and managed to create value for customers while satisfying the expectations of network members. If and when networks are chosen, then they must decide what kind of mindset, knowledge, and competencies are needed to run these new alternative organizations. Moreover, an alliance commitment requires training managers for such challenges and preparing them with necessary skills to do their jobs properly, which involves interactions beyond their own organizational boundaries.

We hope that these explanations contribute to our understanding of alliances not only in the airline industry but also in other industries. It becomes clear, though, that each industry presents special characteristics so that alliance formation and applications should be viewed in the context of that particular industry. Nonetheless, a general model of alliance networks with some modifications incorporating industry-specific conditions can be used in analyzing the cooperative relationships in other industries.

NOTES

1. S. R. Klein, *Standard and Poor's Industry Profile: Industry Trends* (July 20, 2000)

2. Ibid.

3. T. A. Hemphill, Airline marketing alliances and U.S. competitive policy: Does the consumer benefit, *Business Horizons* (March, 2000): 34.

4. K. Ohmae, The global logic of strategic alliance, *Harvard Business Review* (March–April, 1989): 143–154.

5. Hemphill, 35.

6. Ibid.

7. K. Cook, Exchange and power in networks of interorganizational relations, *Sociological Quarterly,* 18 (1997): 62–82.

8. See the following on joint venture stability. B. Kogut, The stability of joint ventures: Reciprocity and competitive rivalry. *Journal of Industrial Economics,* 38, no. 2 (1989): 183–198. S. Makino and P. W. Beamish,. Performance and survival of joint ventures with non-conventional ownership structures, *Journal of International Business Studies,* 29, no. 4 (1998): 797–818.

9. S. R. Klein, *Standard and Poor's Industry Profile: Industry Trends* (July 20, 2000).

10. Ibid.

11. Hemphill, 36.

12. C. J. Jarillo, *Strategic networks: Creating the borderless organization* (Oxford: Butterworth-Heinemann, Ltd. 1993).

13. For reference on resource-based view, see Chapter 2, Endnote 25.

14. K. S. Kook (ed.), *Social exchange theory* (Beverly Hills, CA: Sage Publications, 1987). P. P. Ekeh, *Social exchange theory: The two traditions* (Harvard Business Press, 1974). C. Young-Ybarra, Stategic flexibility in information systems alliances: The influence of transaction cost economics and social exchange theory, *Organization Science*, 47, no. 7: 439–459.

15. J. Child and D. Faulkner, *Strategies of co-operation: Managing alliances, networks, and joint ventures* (Oxford: Oxford University Press, 1998).

9

Global Alliances in the Telecommunications Industry

INDUSTRY PROFILE

Like other industries, one of the dominant characteristics of the tele-communications industry is the augmenting number of consolidations (mergers and acquisitions) and alliances. Competitive advantage in this industry depends considerably upon economies of scale. Consequently, many firms in the telecommunications industry worldwide have sought economies of scale through numerous mergers, acquisitions, and alliances. Bell Atlantic first merged with Nynex and then merged with GTE and formed Verizon Communications, while SBC Communications and Bell South formed a joint venture called Cingular Wireless. Qwest Communications acquired U.S. West, and SBC Communications acquired the Ameritech Corporation. Table 9.1 shows major telephone mergers in 2000. As the industry continues to consolidate, it seems that the remaining players are shifting their focus away from slow-growth core markets, such as local and long-distance service, to emphasize greater growth areas such as broadband data, wireless, and international markets. These top-tier global players include WorldCom, AT&T, SBC Communications, and Verizon Communications (formerly Bell Atlantic and GTE). The second tier of global competitors includes Global Crossing, Sprint Phone Group, Qwest Communications (with merger partner U.S. West and investor Bell South), British Telecommunications PLC, and Deutsche Telekom AG.

Table 9.1

Top Telephone Company Mergers as of August 2000

Companies	Amount (billion $)
Vodafone-Mannesman	180.0
SBS-Ameritech	109.1
Bell Atlantic-GTE	95.0
Vodafone-AirTouch	66.0
AT&T-Media One	55.0

Source: Companies' annual reports

British Vodafone (now a partner in Verizon), Deutsche Telekom, and France Telecom appear to be aggressive suitors with an appetite for U.S. exposure and the necessary cash to back it up. Deutsche Telekom has already agreed to acquire wireless provider VoiceStream Wireless, which will give a valuable extension of its Global System for Mobile (GSM) communications network.

On the European side, France Telecom acquired Orange plc of Britain from Vodafone AirTouch plc for 25.1 billion pounds ($37.66 billion U.S. dollars) in cash and stock. While the transaction creates the second-largest mobile-phone group in Europe, it also intensifies the battle for wireless customers in Europe. France Telecom will combine its own mobile operations with those of Orange and sell 10 percent to 15 percent of the combined wireless concern in an initial public offering in 2001.[1] In actuality, Vodafone was forced to dispose of Orange to win regulatory approval for its acquisition of Mannesmann AG of Germany. France Telecom already owns the Itineris wireless network in France and controls operators in Belgium, the Netherlands, Denmark, and parts of Eastern Europe. The combined wireless operation has 21 million subscribers now and expects to raise that number to 30 million by adding Orange, which is the third-largest mobile-phone operator in Britain. France Telecom's more immediate plan is to bid for more third-generation wireless licenses in Europe that wouldenable the company to offer Internet and data services on cellular phones. Nevertheless, several ambitious cross-border mergers recently in Europe have collapsed over disagreements about issues ranging from government ownership to management positions to a fight about the location of a company's headquarters. Previous unsuccessful merger attempts include Deutche Telecom-Telecom Italia, Telia-Telenor, British Telecom-Telefonica, and Telefonika-KPN. The most recent resistance to WorldCom's attempt to buy Sprint PCS originated in Europe and resulted in a refusal by the U.S. government.

Principal characteristics of and trends in the telecommunications industry can be outlined as follows:[2] (a) Falling telecommunications costs: Technological advancements such as fiber optics, digital transmissions, and satellite communications have reduced prices and will continue to do so. In the future, quality or bandwidth will determine telecommunications prices rather than distance between users or the duration of a call; (b) Privatization of state-owned telecom monopolies: A number of nations around the world have allowed new entrants into their markets with newer and cheaper services especially in wireless market. A quite number of nations have either privatized or been in the process of privatizing their telecommunications monopolies to attract advanced technologies or raise capital. They have relatively opened their markets to foreign competition in long-distance and wireless markets, although most are reluctant to open their local voice markets; (c) The Internet and related technologies: As the Internet connections augment tremendously every year through a variety of devices (computers, wireless phones, televisions, and automobiles), traditional telecommunications services such as telephony, facsimile, e-mail, and audio and video files are sent over the Internet at a lower cost. Although many of these services do not provide the same quality and reliability yet as standard telecommunications do, the high demand for these services will enhance the current quality by greater R&D and applications. As a result of Internet advancements, there is a transition from voice telecommunications to data telecommunications. It is estimated that there will be a reversal of voice and data transmission in global traffic in the future.[3] Data networks, private networks, network intelligence, and network applications are the high-growth markets of the future.

Telecommunications in information markets represent three major segments: content (creating information), communication (moving information), and application (using information). The communication segment will consist of only one-third of the total market. It was recommended that companies in the telecommunications industry use effective segmentation to exploit the opportunities in the information market. These segments have become blurred in recent years, however. As we will describe, forging alliances between companies is one way to deal with these different or converging segments and services.

Another emerging characteristic of the telecommunications industry is the rapid advancement of wireless communications by adding text and pictures to voice transmissions. Because of wireless communication's significant impact on the industry, we will look at it closely.

Wireless Communications

Wireless communications present the fastest growing segment of the industry. There has been a growing demand for wireless services for both voice and data transmissions. Although voice communication has dominated the telecommunications market from the beginning, as wireless carriers scramble to integrate data applications into their wireless services, this trend has been changing rapidly. "The catalyst driving this trend is the third-generation (3G) of wireless communications, which is making inroads into Japan and Korea and should spread throughout Europe in a few years. This information wave should hit U.S. shores around 2004, giving consumers the opportunity to use one mobile device for all of their communication needs."[4] The potential market of cellular phones is huge. It is estimated that one billion people, or one of every six people on Earth, will own cell phones in three years. Many of the newer digital models will carry software that enables the user to access basic information—sports scores, stock prices, airline schedules, and the weather—from the Web. The most sophisticated "smart" phones will include an operating system, which means that users can retrieve files, manage address books and calendars, and even compose documents with a mini keyboard. But the bulk of the market is likely to be in "feature" phones that lack full operating systems.

Primary competitors in the U.S. wireless industry are broadband personal communication services (PCS) providers and cellular wireless companies, both of which operate networks based on a system of geographic cells. Other players include enhanced specialized mobile radio (ESMR) operators, which concentrate their signals on dispatch channels. Industry wireless revenues topped $40 billion in 1999, up 21 percent from 1998. As of year-end 1999, roamer revenues represented about 10 percent of the revenue base.[5] The industry's cumulative capital investment in wireless rose 18 percent year to year to $71.3 billion in 1999.[6] Based on 1999 wireless revenues, the largest domestic operators were Verizon (a joint venture between Bell Atlantic/GTE and Vodafone AirTouch, with $16 billion, which we will discuss next), SB Communications and Bell South ($10 billion), AT&T Wireless Services ($7.6 billion), Nextel Communications ($3.3), and Sprint PCS ($3.2 billion). In 1999, British wireless provider Vodafone Group acquired AirTouch, forming Vodafone AirTouch. Subsequently, the company formed a strategic U.S. national wireless alliance with Bell Atlantic (and its merger partner, GTE) called Verizon. In April 2000, SBC and Bell South formed a national wireless joint venture called Cingular. Figure 9.1 displays U.S. market shares in the wireless telecommunications industry.

In terms of the population of the U.S. markets (called U.S. POPs) that a firm is licensed to serve, the leading wireless companies as of year-end 1999 were AT&T Wireless Services (314.6 million POPs), Sprint PCS (234 million), Verizon (179.3 million), Nextel (165.3 million), NextWave Personal Communications (152.9 million), and Omnipoint (126.6 million).[7] This listing by POPs differs markedly from market share rankings by revenues or number of subscribers. POPs rank the major wireless players as far as prospective customers are concerned. The list suggests potential market position as the industry enters a phase of accelerated development, expansion, and in all probability, consolidation.

Figure 9.1
U.S. wireless market shares in 2000

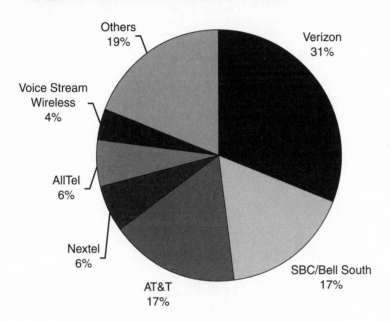

British-based Vodafone is the biggest mobile phone company in the world, with more than 65 million customers in 25 countries on five continents. Vodafone took over Mannesman of Germany and Omnitel of Italy in 2000. These takeovers made continental Vodafone the fastest growing division, with 4.38 million new customers. The company added more than 1.46 million new customers in the Americas and Asia-Pacific region, taking its total to 16.25 million. Its newly formed United Kingdom, Middle East, and Africa division (grouping four countries) added 770,000 customers. The company, however, uses strategic alliances in numerous countries. Another big player is NTT DoCoMo, which holds the highest market share in Japan. Both companies have been pursuing strategies to enter and expand in the U.S. wireless market, as we will describe next.

The mobile-phone sector presents a dynamic, competitive landscape with interesting developments. While major players are competing fiercely, they are cooperating to develop new technologies and services because they want to combine the convenience of cellular phones with the use of the Internet. To accomplish this task, a variety of collaborations are underway.

While alliances are common in the industry, the latest agreements did not preclude further alliances with others in the future. It seems that this situation is really the future of modern telecommunications, because no company can excel in every area.

TELECOMMUNICATIONS ALLIANCES

Although it is futile to try to describe the state of affairs in telecommunications alliances because they change on a regular basis, examining some of the major attempts and events provides insight into this industry's dynamics and future. There had been three primary global alliances—Concert, Global One, and World Partners—of which the first two are already over. These alliances illustrate different approaches to globalization. Concert and Global One were primarily equity relationships. First, in Concert, British Telecom purchased a 20 percent stake in MCI, which was acquired by WorldCom later and became MCI WorldCom. Second, Deutsche-Telekom, France Telecom, and Sprint (United States) formed Global One. According to the agreement, each European partner purchased 10 percent of Sprint. But there was disappointment with Global One, and at the end French Telecom took over the venture. The third global telecommunications business, World Partners, is a combination of equity stakes and agreements on billing, marketing, interconnection, and so on. Operated largely by AT&T and Unisource, a European alliance that has included Telecom Italia (Italy), Telia (Sweden), Swiss Telecom, and KPN (Netherlands), World Partners also includes KDD (the incumbent international carrier for Japan), Telstra (Australia), and Unitel, a Canadian long-distance carrier. World Partners largely relies upon contractual agreements. Because of the large number of companies involved in this partnership, it seems to be the only practical model. It might also be that many of the relationships have grown out of the pre-liberalization contract and settlement arrangements. It is not yet clear whether World Partners' business model will succeed. Two major companies, Telefonica and Telecom Italia, have had inconsistent relationships with the alliance. Telefonica left the alliance while Telecom Italia has made moves to leave World Partners to join Cable & Wireless in multinational ventures.

A close examination of strategic alliances in the telecommunications industry reveals that most of such alliances are "pure play" alliances; that is, ventures in which partners offered unlike (but closely related) products, technologies, and markets. These markets are usually in the same market segments, such as content, communications, and applications. Verizon Wireless is an example of such a pure play alliance between Bell Atlantic/GTE and Vodafone Air Touch, a joint venture established to compete head-on with AT&T in the U.S. wireless market. Another type of alliance is "converging alliances," which means two companies from different industries collaborating because of converging technologies, enabling innovative services.

Microsoft, for example, invested $1 billion for an 11.5 percent share in an alliance with Comcast, the fourth largest U.S. cable operator, to support cable modem entry into telephony and data access to homes. Microsoft also invested $10 million in Teledesic, a low-Earth orbit satellite communications network of which McCaw and Boeing are also partners. Converging alliances are formed when participating technologies or markets are on a converging path. In studying telecommunications alliances, we will again use the typology introduced in Chapter 3 as equity (joint ventures and equity participation) and non-equity alliances.

Joint Ventures

In analyzing joint ventures in the telecommunications industry, the Joint Venture Decision Model given in Chapter 4 will be used in reference to Verizon Wireless, the Ericsson-Microsoft mobile venture, and the Vodafone joint venture in New Zealand. Each case presents different dimensions of the model, but they all are attempts to achieve the objective of market penetration.

Verizon Wireless

In 2000, the Bell Atlantic Corporation/GTE and Vodafone AirTouch formed a joint venture called Verizon Wireless with $16 billion, creating a major player in the industry. As shown in Figure 9.1, Verizon Wireless is the largest wireless communications provider in the United States, with 27.5 million wireless voice and data customers. The new company includes the assets of Bell Atlantic Mobile, AirTouch Cellular, GTE Wireless, PrimeCo Personal Communications, and AirTouch Paging. The company has a footprint covering nearly 90 percent of the U.S. population, 49 of the top 50 and 96 of the top 100 U.S. markets. Verizon Wireless, with its 38,000 employees, is a strong contender in the U.S. wireless phone market. Verizon Wireless will have the national scale and scope to realize revenue enhancements, cost savings, and capital efficiencies. The company will achieve expense savings through reduced roaming costs and increased economies of scale in transport, billing volumes, handset purchases, and advertising. Combining common Code Division Multiple Access (CDMA) technology platforms will also yield capital efficiencies, simplified integration, and superior network quality.

Looking at this alliance within the joint venture framework in Figure 4.1, it becomes clear that two chief players, Bell Atlantic/GTE and Vodafone, although not competing in the U.S. market but competing with major players in different countries, needed each other. Bell Atlantic/GTE needed cash infusion while Vodafone found an easy way of market entry into the U.S. market. The majority of the motives listed in the Joint Venture Model (in

Chapter 4), such as achieving economies of scale, reducing costs and risks, accessing market/resources, and learning from the partner were in play.

At the initial stage, both partners concluded that they needed each other or that they were not self-sufficient, so they preferred a joint venture to internalization or market transactions. At the formulation stage, Bell Atlantic/GTE—despite its experience and capability in traditional telecommunications areas—wanted to deploy asymmetrical competencies of Vodafone, which has been the largest wireless company in the world. Also, it needed a cash infusion for its infrastructure investments. From the standpoint of Vodafone, Bell Atlantic/GTE looked at suitable partners with established market shares and experience in the traditional telecommunications business but with little experience in wireless communications. Vodafone's perception was that by deploying the organizational capabilities of its partners, it could easily expand in the U.S. wireless market rather than struggling for a green-field investment or searching for another qualified partner.

At the operational stage, both partners hold sufficient equity of the joint venture to control operations. After the close of the Bell Atlantic-GTE merger, Bell Atlantic-GTE will own 55 percent and Vodafone AirTouch will own 45 percent of the wireless joint venture. The board has seven members with four designated by Bell Atlantic and three chosen by Vodafone AirTouch. It is too early to draw any conclusions concerning Verizon's financial performance, however. It is apparent, though, that Verizon presently holds the highest market share in the U.S. wireless market. The assessment at the outcome stage is not appropriate at this point because the venture is so recent. Time will decide the satisfaction level of the partners—whether they will continue with this business or exit from the current joint venture.

Ericsson Microsoft Mobile Venture

The software giant Microsoft has been struggling to expand its software, Windows CE, for use in the cellular phone sector. It has not shown the same success of its Windows operating system in personal computers (PCs), however, as in the cellular phone market. As a result, Microsoft has developed Mobile Explorer, which enables browsing the Internet through mobile phones.

Microsoft got its foot in the door in what could be a hot market for cell phones that surf the Internet—a field where big phone makers had shunned the software giant. Sweden's Telefon AB L.M. Ericsson agreed to form a joint venture with Microsoft. Ericsson would use a scaled-down Web browser from Microsoft in some of its phones. We must also note, however, that Ericsson had also been engaged in Epoc, a competing operating system developed by Sambian (which we will discuss later). Ericsson owns 70 percent of the joint venture and also supplies most of the initial staff of 100 engineers. The venture company is based in Stockholm with regional offices around the world. The venture's first product—e-mail for cell phones—has already been launched.

The two companies with different backgrounds combined their resources to establish a viable product/service. This joint venture is a typical example of converging alliances, as we defined previously. The joint venture breathes new life into Microsoft's desire to become a major supplier of software for Internet-based cell phones. Microsoft's attempts to market its Windows CE operating system to cellular handset manufacturers have been a disappointment. Cell-phone makers and service providers have complained that Windows CE requires too much processor power to use in compact phones. As a result, the large mobile-phone manufacturers had ignored Microsoft's efforts.

Microsoft, nevertheless, still hopes that Windows CE will displace Epoc. But in the meantime, it has made an important move in penetrating the mobile-phone market with its new Mobile Explorer, a "microbrowser" that runs on multiple operating systems in addition to Windows CE (including the Epoc system). This concept is a kind of defense on the part of Microsoft, instead of fighting with four major cellular phone manufacturers. Microsoft expects the following benefits from this partnership. Once Microsoft's Mobile Explorer is up and running on Epoc-based phones, Microsoft is likely to persuade Ericsson and others to take the next step— installing Microsoft's Windows CE on newer models that pack more computing power. Microsoft also hopes to gain an advantage by attracting more traffic to its online service, MSN, and it intends to sell software that powers large computers that run the new wireless services. Its whole strategy is to tie the client's handsets to its server. On the other hand, Ericsson expects to benefit from this venture because it could sell more of its handsets to users, especially those who use some form of Windows applications on their personal computers (such as Outlook, an e-mail service). The new venture also plans to develop tools to synchronize software from PCs and mobile phones, which will enable users to carry updated electronic calendars on their mobile phones.

At the initial stage, both companies—Microsoft and Ericsson—expected some synergistic benefits from combining their resources and capabilities (such as Microsoft's Windows CE and Ericsson's widespread market) as an established wireless handset manufacturer and seller. The partners wanted to exploit their core competencies for a competitive advantage.

At the formation stage, Ericsson has chosen Microsoft, which happens to have the Windows CE operating system for wireless units at a risk of damaging its earlier alliance in Symbian, where its major competitors are also partners. The company probably wanted to go alone or to not lose time in incorporating an effective operating system into its wireless handsets. On the other hand, Microsoft needed a lift from a major mobile-phone operator such as Ericsson that would adopt its Windows CE operating system.

Therefore, Microsoft perceived Ericsson as a suitable partner. The joint venture partnership represents the deployment of asymmetrical competencies of both partners.

Ericsson's decision to link with Microsoft threw the old alignment with other manufacturers into confusion. Its Symbian partners might have considered that Ericsson had defected to Microsoft. Ericsson, however, announced that it had no intentions of abandoning Epoc. By this action, Ericsson has developed strategic alliances in both areas to ensure its competitive positions in the future.

As far as the operations and outcome stages are concerned, it is inappropriate to comment on them at this point because it is too soon to say whether the Windows CE operating system will find a wide acceptance as a result of this alliance.

Vodafone's Joint Venture in New Zealand

We can examine Vodafone's joint venture in New Zealand in the context of the joint venture model, as well. At the initial stage, while Vodafone wanted to expand into the New Zealand market, Telstra Saturn, cable TV, landline, and Internet companies in New Zealand decided to diversify themselves with the help of a major mobile-phone player such as Vodafone so that the synergies of two companies would lead to a considerable competitive advantage in the New Zealand market. Consequently, Vodafone of the United Kingdom and Telstra Saturn of New Zealand formed a strategic alliance, creating the biggest "cross network" competition to Telecom, an existing mobile phone operator in New Zealand. In other words, the telecommunications players Vodafone and Telstra Saturn are increasing the pressure on the local company Telecom by teaming up to offer combined services at sharp discounts. The joint venture will mean new services for customers in 2001, such as using the same number for both landline and cell phones, both at home and for business, and a single electronic voice mailbox for both phone services.[8] Also, the companies will offer bundled services, including Telstra Saturn's fixed phone line, TV, and Internet and Vodafone mobile phone services.

Bundling services invariably meant cheaper deals on the standalone costs. It also meant "huge opportunities" to bundle other services for the thousands who presently bought pre-pay phones. The discounts for bundled services would be significant, although they would not be drawn on likely price cuts. Both companies would have the capability to bundle the combined products and send one bill by the company that made the sale. The alliance would not mean any shareholding arrangements between the two companies. In other words, cross-shareholdings had not been subject.

Vodafone has 638,000 mobile phone customers, about 38 percent of the total market, and 50,000 mobile Internet users. Vodafone has spent $300 million since arriving in New Zealand at the end of 1998. Vodafone already has an alliance with Clear in New Zealand, but the new link with Telstra Saturn would not affect that relationship. Interestingly, Vodafone is a competitor with Telstra in Australia.

Telstra Saturn put a fixed-line backbone network through New Zealand and had a range of services. Telstra Saturn has about 33,000 landline phone customers in Wellington and 20,000 pay TV customers, about 5 percent less than Sky TV's market share in Wellington. It is expanding in Christchurch and Auckland.

The joint venture would develop integrated products and services across the combined fixed and mobile networks. It would also strengthen the existing supply agreement where Telstra Saturn and Vodafone use each other's networks. The alliance would not affect either company's individual developments, including the purchase of second and third-generation spectra. Again, although it is early to judge the operations and outcomes of the joint venture, it has been stable so far.

EQUITY PARTICIPATION

The following examples illustrate a different form of alliances: equity participation—one telecommunications company buying some equity stakes into another telecommunications company to establish organic ties so that mutual interests of both companies can be pursued in collaboration. Through equity stakes, telecommunications companies have built an important link to work toward their mutual objectives.

The AT&T-NTT DoCoMo Alliance

NTT DoCoMo, the Japanese telecommunications giant, after achieving a spectacular growth in cellular phones in Japan, used equity participation to expand its mobile Internet services worldwide. The company's objective is to use its stakes in cellular phone carriers to promote 3G services worldwide and to build economies of scale that would motivate Web sites to build interesting applications for 3G phones and to give phone makers a larger market for their wares. To that end, it invested around $17 billion in minority stakes in cellular operations in Asia, Europe, and most recently in the United States. For example, it invested $9.8 billion for a 16 percent stake in AT&T's Wireless unit—one of the largest investments ever by a Japanese company in a foreign company. NTT DoCoMo has an ambitious plan for the U.S. market, such as repeating its Japanese success in the United States. In Japan, "it has signed up 15 million subscribers to its wireless Web service in under two years and has added as many as 50,000 new customers a day. DoCoMo's mobile Internet service, called i-mode, allows people to do such things as download news and cartoons, and check their bank balances on cell phones."⁹ After its first launch in early 1999, i-mode has become popular among young Japanese. DoCoMo combined standard Internet technology and flashy marketing to quickly expand the service beyond its initial projections. The key to its success was getting others—newspapers, restaurants, and video game makers—to format miniature versions of their Internet sites to fit on i-mode's tiny screens. Now, Japanese can order sushi, book plane tickets, or play a video game on their mobile phones. The company already offers a small number of English-language I-mode services in Japan, such as ones from CNN and Bloomberg News, and is helping Japanese content providers set up services for the U.S. market.¹⁰ DoCoMo eventually could increase its stake in AT&T Wireless to 17.2 percent and will acquire five-year warrants to purchase up to an additional 41.7 million shares of AT&T Wireless at $35 each.¹¹ The deal represents an important step toward closing the gap between mobile phone technology in the United States and Japan. Japan has more advanced mobile phone technology, such as 3G telecommunications and i-mode technology.

AT&T, on the other hand, would like to exploit NTT DoCoMo's technology and experience through its partnership with the Japanese company. It plans to license the i-mode technology and brand name from NTT DoCoMo in order to develop multimedia applications.¹² DoCoMo asserted that the U.S. version of i-mode will be available in 2001. Moreover, AT&T Wireless and its parent company will receive much-needed cash infusion from DoCoMo, which agreed to buy 178 million shares of AT&T Wireless from AT&T for $20.50 per share and 228 million new shares of AT&T Wireless for $27 per share. AT&T Wireless will use $6.2 billion of this investment to upgrade its network and to join government-run auctions for wireless spectra. In fact, to make i-mode work in the United States, AT&T will need to rebuild its network by using a faster wireless technology than the one it currently uses. Therefore, AT&T intends to upgrade its network to an interim technology, then eventually boost it to a global standard known as the Universal Telecommunication System.

The AT&T-DoCoMo case illustrates the point that new technology developers, as well as receivers, need each other to promote technology worldwide. Mobile Internet technology has brought together cellular carriers across nations to collaborate in order to offer a variety of new services that consumers demand. In particular, the United States as a large cellular market has been ripe for such services and desperate to catch up with 3G cellular technology. Over the years, DoCoMo has been seeking to acquire minority stakes in strategic partners. Most recently, for example, the company is negotiating a deal with SK Telecom of South Korea in which DoCoMo would take a 15 percent stake in the South Korean mobile phone operator for roughly $5 billion.

The Symbian Venture

The world's leading mobile phone manufacturers, Finland's Nokia and Sweden's Ericsson, Japan's Matsushita, and Motorola of the United States, are usually bitter foes but are cooperating in efforts to link the Internet with the cellular phone. With a tiny British software company, Psion PLC, the phone marketers formed a venture, Symbian, to devise a new operating system called Epoc to run extravagant applications on cellular phones (refer to Figure 9.2).

Figure 9.2
Partnerships in Web cellular phones

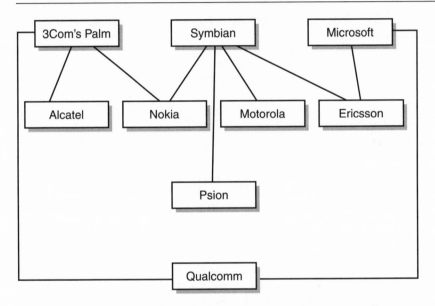

While Ericsson developed a joint venture with Microsoft (as we explained earlier), it had also participated in Symbian's venture. Ericsson's move has caused concerns among other partners of Symbian, like Nokia and Motorola. Nevertheless, separately, Nokia has developed an alliance with Alcatel, 3Com's Palm computer branch, and Qualcomm in using 3Com's operating system.

These complex relationships are a reflection of rapidly changing technologies and competitive landscape in this particular industry. The firms operating in such an environment have tried to reduce uncertainty while strengthening their competitive positions.

Vodafone's Mexican Venture

While Verizon Wireless (Vodafone being its partner) owns a 37 percent controlling stake in Iusacell, Mexico's second-largest mobile phone operator, Vodafone separately is interested in expanding into the fast-growing Mexican telecommunications market. The company plans to buy 34.5 percent stake in Iusacell from its key shareholder, Grupo Peralta. Iusacell had some 1.5 million subscribers and operates primarily in central Mexico.[13] Major global telecommunications players such as Telefonica of Spain, former Mexican state monopoly Telefonos de Mexico, and Verizon are hotly contesting Mexico's market, which already has 11 million cell phone customers. Nevertheless, the Iusacell sale would have to be approved by Mexican competition authorities.

KPN, NTT DoCoMo, and Hutchison Whampoa: A Three-Way Alliance

One of the current trends in the wireless communication arena is that firms form alliances to bid jointly for licenses in many countries. In this fashion, a three-way alliance has been set up among KPN (Dutch), NTT DoCoMo (Japan), and Hutchison Whampoa (Hong Kong) to jointly bid for new wireless licenses in Europe. KNP's KNP Mobile NV unit and DoCoMo will together acquire a 35 percent stake in Hutchison Whampoa's British wireless unit to offer 3G mobile services. Under the terms of the deal, DoCoMo will acquire 20 percent of Hutchison's United Kingdom unit for $1.7 billion (1.2 pounds), while KNP Mobile will get 15 percent for $1.2 billion (900 million pounds). Hutchison and Canadian partner Telesystem International Wireless paid $6.3 billion (4.4 pounds) for a U.K. license.

The coming together of three far-flung wireless operators underscores the large investment that is needed to acquire licenses and build networks to support new services. The United Kingdom recently auctioned its 3G licenses, and the Netherlands is in the midst of a similar process. Other countries—Germany, France, and Italy—also plan to sell licenses, potentially raising billions of dollars. Few companies can afford to bid alone, though. There will be more teams arising in the 3G auctions. KPN and its partners plan to bid for licenses in Germany, France, and Belgium. KPN needed to find partners to help fulfill its goal of becoming one of Europe's three biggest wireless service providers.

The partnership is seen as a good move for Hutchison Whampoa, and in 1999 it sold its controlling stake in the U.K. wireless operator Orange plc for $14.6 billion. In teaming up, Hutchison aims to share costs and spread the risk of developing a new technology.

Vodafone's Stakes in Japan Telecom

In December 2000, Vodafone bought 15 percent of Japan Telecom for about $2.2 billion in cash to gain a foothold in the Japanese telecommunication market before new high-speed mobile phone services are introduced in Japan. Additionally, later in February 2001, it agreed to pay about $1.2

billion for AT&T's 10 percent stake in Japan Telecom as the company seeks to expand its presence in Japan, one of the fastest-growing markets in the world. The deal will lift Vodafone's stake in Japan Telecom to 25 percent while British Telecom, the rival of Vodafone, owns 20 percent of Japan Telecom. Not being happy about Vodafone's increased stake in Japan Telecom, British Telecom might be forced to sell its holding because of its high debt level.

The Global One Failure

Finally, by alluding to the Global One case, we would like to mention that not all telecommunications alliances end up as successes. In 1994, Sprint, France Telecom, andDeutsche-Telecom established Global One, an alliance that would sell telecommunications services to companies across the globe. Each European partner purchased 10 percent of Sprint as part of that alliance and as a way to break into the U.S. market and access multinational customers. But Global One did not reach its business objectives and eventually dissolved, with France Telecom taking control. Two of Sprint's largest shareholders, France Telecom and Deutsche-Telecom, are actively exploring ways to sell their stakes in Sprint.[14]

Non-Equity Agreements

Numerous types of non-equity contractual agreements exist between telecommunications companies. We will discuss some selected cases to demonstrate the widespread applications of such cooperation in the industry.

The AT&T and Nortel Agreement

AT&T Wireless Group, armed with a cash infusion from NTT DoCoMo, tapped four telecommunications equipment suppliers to build the wireless operator's next-generation national U.S. network and formed Canada's Nortel. At the same time, Lucent Technologies (United States), Nokia (Finland), and Telefon AB L.M. Ericsson (Sweden) will supply AT&T Wireless with equipment and services for the network's base stations. Nortel was awarded the core networking portion of the contracts, however, despite the fact that Lucent had long provided AT&T's wireless operations with equipment. It is a significant move by Nortel in making inroads by supplying gears in the western United States.

Nortel's agreement with AT&T Corporation's wireless unit is valued at about $600 million over three years. According to the accord, Nortel will supply switches and offer equipment for a wireless network based on the Time Division Multiple Access (TDMA) digital standards. The equipment will be deployed in five western U.S. states. The agreement is aimed at

increasing AT&T's wireless capacity to accommodate expected subscriber-
base growth. Nortel would also help AT&T build an Internet protocol-based
wireless network. This example illustrates how complex technology of
telecommunications is intertwined and requires the cooperation of various
players.

The Vodafone and ChinaUnicom Accord

ChinaUnicom signed an agreement with Vodafone AirTouch to collaborate on mobile telephone technology and services in China. The deal brings
together Vodafone, the leading cellular provider, and ChinaUnicom, the No.
2 player, in what could be the world's largest cellular market. Initially,
ChinaUnicom and Vodafone AirTouch will enable their subscribers to roam
each other's territories. But the agreement could lay the foundation for a
larger investment by Vodafone AirTouch in ChinaUnicom, which is discussing alliances with several foreign phone companies in advance of China's
membership in the World Trade Organization (WTO).

For all the superlatives, ChinaUnicom's debut has been shadowed by a
lingering dispute with two partners and a flip-flop in its technology. After
signing an agreement with Qualcomm's cellular technology—CDMA—
ChinaUnicom shelved the plan in May 2000. ChinaUnicom's reason is
because its parent company, China Unites Telecommunications, would test
the next generation of CDMA technology before licensing it for the pub-
licly listed subsidiary. Until then, ChinaUnicom will use a competing technology.

This case illustrates how Unicom has been a hostage to the decisions of its
state-owned parent and to the Chinese government. Prior to ChinaUnicom's
Vodafone deal, Qualcomm had worked out a framework agreement to
license technology to ChinaUnicom. The government was supposed to provide Qualcomm with a list of manufacturers. But shortly after the agreement, there were signs of a slowdown. Qualcomm is not the only partner to
feel bruised by ChinaUnicom, though. ChinaUnicom is locked in a dispute
with two foreign investors, Singapore Technologies and Lark International of
Hong Kong, which claim that ChinaUnicom breached contracts with them
at the bequest of the Chinese government. The two companies set up paging
joint ventures with ChinaUnicom in the mid 1990s. To circumvent Chinese
laws forbidding the foreign ownership of telecommunications networks,
they created joint ventures that leased operating sites to ChinaUnicom.
Then, in 1998, Beijing called these arrangements illegal and ordered them to
be broken. These cases suggest that foreign companies seeking alliances with
the Chinese should be aware of surprises in the completion of final deals.

ChinaUnicom unraveled more than 40 partnerships with companies such
as Sprint, Bell Canada, and France Telecom. The company returned $1.2 bil-
lion in investments plus $487 million in compensation. ChinaUnicom also

granted the companies warrants to buy shares in the share offering. But none of these compensations satisfied Singapore Technologies or Lark International. They claim that ChinaUnicom has refused to compensate them for the fair-market value of their joint ventures, and they are preparing lawsuits. These practices symbolize the arbitrary nature of contracts in China.

The Motorola/Cisco Alliance with Telsim

The Motorola and Cisco strategic alliance delivers end-to-end wireless solutions to operators worldwide through a powerful combination of Cisco Internet technologies and Motorola systems integration, radio frequency products, and services. In 1999, the alliance introduced an open Internet protocol (IP) network architecture that integrates data, voice, and video services for mobile networks and provides users with a broad range of wireless Internet access solutions. The alliance has also secured a leadership position in the deployment of General Packet Radio Service (GPRS) systems worldwide, and through these commercial deployments the company is providing a critical path to third-generation mobile communications. Motorola and Cisco continue to work together on the joint development of IP network architecture and products, the promotion of open standards, and the creation of joint ventures such as the Invisix™ Centres of Excellence.

This Motorola-Cisco partnership helped Telsim, a Turkish mobile operator. Telsim, an innovative GSM operator, launched the first commercial network in Turkey—making Telsim one of the world's first operators to implement GPRS. The commercial launch is just four months after the successful completion of the technology trials and the first live GPRS call in Turkey, enabled by the core GPRS network solution supplied by Motorola and strategic alliance partner Cisco Systems. The contract for country-wide implementation of the core GPRS network was awarded to Motorola's Network Solutions Sector with an end-to-end solutions contract worth some $100 million, and the implementation will launch with Motorola GPRS handsets. At the beginning of 2000, the Motorola/Cisco core GPRS network solution enabled Telsim to successfully trial mobile Internet access by using a Wireless Application Protocol (WAP) over GPRS solution. Applications included e-mail access, mobile e-commerce, and mobile banking services. GPRS, as the fastest mobile Internet service available today, would enable Telsim to provide a more effective use of WAP browsing and would give users a virtual permanent connection to Internet-based content and services. Telsim's commercial GPRS tariffs will be based on the data transferred, not the connection time.

Telsim believes that the speed of Internet access achieved with GPRS gives users enormous benefits of mobility and flexibility. The company is implementing GPRS now as the key investment and migration tool for the future third-generation network, which will enable an even greater range of services. An established GPRS network will provide a solid platform for the evolution to third-generation communications. On the other hand, Motorola's perspective is that Telsim is taking technology forward in Turkey by leading the way with the first implementation of GPRS wireless data. With their planned network expansion to some five million subscribers, Motorola looks forward to working with Telsim to achieve the full potential of GPRS in one of the world's first nationwide commercial systems. Basically, Motorola will provide infrastructure, handsets, and associated services to expand Telsim's GSM network. As part of that agreement, Telsim has named Motorola as its exclusive regional supplier of GSM 900 equipment over the next three years. Motorola has estimated that revenues from this supplier agreement could be at least $1.5 billion.

The Motorola/Cisco GPRS architecture can be implemented over an existing GSM network, protecting the operator's investment. Motorola's GSM infrastructure systems are GPRS-ready, requiring only a software load and PCU addition with no modifications to existing hardware. Offering controlled evolution to 3G mobile communications, the Motorola/Cisco GPRS data solution enables operators to take advantage of many new revenue opportunities. Cisco and Motorola together are driving market growth, developing applications and value-added services to provide operators with innovative, competitive, and unique offerings for their subscriber base.

Beyond all of this technical jargon, the fact is that Telsim needed infrastructure and technology to launch its ambitious program consisting of the most recent technical features for local customers. The company found such technical support from the Motorola/Cisco alliance, where two U.S.-based companies had an opportunity to apply their most recent technology with a local provider.

Nokia and Cable & Wireless Alliance for Wireless Data Services

Because of augmenting competition in the mobile phone market, firms have been trying to offer complementary and innovative services through collaboration with each other. Nokia, for example, has taken another step toward delivering the content that is supposed to help wireless devices overtake personal computers. Nokia Networks, an infrastructure division of the company, would collaborate with Britain's Cable & Wireless plc to build wireless data centers. The new data centers will host and deliver wireless services and Web-based content in a method similar to that of traditional application service providers.

Cable & Wireless, one of the largest cable and broadband companies in Britain, will run the centers for information hosting and management operations and provide access to its Internet backbone. On the other hand, Nokia will set up the technology platforms that will deliver software and services to wireless devices. The two companies plan to sell services to large Internet service providers (ISPs) and corporations that want to offer wireless access to company-specific networks and operations. The idea is to give businesses wireless access to applications that those companies can then sell under their own brand without having to build new wireless hosting infrastructure. While European customers would get their services from a U.K.-based data center, U.S. customers will receive services from centers in Santa Clara, California and Reston, Virginia.

The move illustrates the growing race to get in on the wireless services market. Nokia wants to make sure that its devices are the ones that are accessing all the wireless content. The company estimates that more than one billion people will use mobile phones by 2002 and that handsets connected to the Web will outnumber PCs in 2003. The agreement is an excellent example of making Nokia's vision of the mobile information society a reality. For Nokia, the move is the latest in a string of deals to tie its technology to wireless content providers. Meanwhile, C&W is involved in software application-hosting deals in order to branch out from its core cable TV business. Previously, C&W announced a deal with Microsoft and Compaq Computer to team up on hosting software for small and medium-size businesses.

All these alliances—either equity or non-equity—show that in the telecommunications industry it is very common to have some kinds of collaborations, either with other players or companies in converging businesses. As competition and technology in the rapidly evolving telecommunications industry force players to engage in new alliances worldwide, telecommunications companies have been looking for new frontiers and combinations. Such trends have been changing the rules of the game as more cooperation emerges between the major and new players and between the players from developed economies and firms from emerging economies. Consequently, strategic alliances in the forms of pure players or converging partnerships appear as a cornerstone of business strategies of telecommunications companies.

NOTES

1. G. Naik and A. Raghavan, France Telecom to Buy Orange from Vodafone, *The Wall Street Journal* (May 31, 2000): A22.

2. D. Raphael, The future of telecommunications: Connectivity through alliances, at NABE Valley Roundtable (2000).

3. Ibid.

4. P. D. Wohl, Telecommunications: Wireless, *Industry Surveys* (June 22, 2000): 1.

5. Ibid.

6. Ibid.

7. Ibid.

8. *Asia Pulse* (November 1, 2000).

9. Anonymous, A big deal for tiny screens, *The Wall Street Journal* (December 1, 2000): B1.

10. Ibid.

11. Ibid.

12. Ibid.

13. Anonymous, *Financial Times* (January 6, 2001): 14.

14. Anonymous, *The Wall Street Journal* (January 24, 2001): A14.

10

Alliance Management

So far in this book, we have examined global strategic alliances from theoretical and practical perspectives as well as in reference to specific industries —namely, automobile manufacturing, pharmaceuticals, airlines, and telecommunications. You will find it interesting that despite the reported high failure rates of interfirm partnerships, there is a growing interest in such a strategic mode. We can explain this paradox by the fact that strategic alliances, in comparison with alternative corporate strategies such as greenfield investments, mergers, and acquisitions and business strategies such as sole ownership of value chain activities (including R&D, production, and marketing), offer synergistic benefits and flexibility. We discussed this point in Chapter 1, and we presented the rationale for strategic alliances with a comparative analysis. Nonetheless, managing strategic alliances is a challenging task for managers. Reuer noted, "Executives engaged in alliances, as well as those more reluctant to try their hand at collaborative strategy, are keenly aware that success does not come easily."[1] Given cross-cultural differences and geographical distances, managing global business alliances becomes even harder than handling domestic business alliances. Thus, in this concluding chapter, we will address a managerial dimension of global collaborative ventures and offer some insights into effective management of such arrangements in a systematic manner. Rather than summarizing previous chapters, we will describe their implications in a managerial format because managers are mostly eager to learn the practical aspects of interfirm partnerships rather than spending lots of time on theoretical foundations of the alliance phenomenon. Nonetheless, for those managers who are interested in theoretical roots of alliances, Chapters 2 and 3 provide a great deal of information.

THE CIRCULAR MANAGERIAL DECISION MODEL

To provide practical insights into alliance formation and management, we have developed a circular model that consists of the main elements of the decision-making model introduced in Chapter 4 but in a simplified and summary form (refer to Figure 10.1). In other words, from a managerial point of view, it is easier to follow this circular process and dynamics and take the necessary steps corresponding to each component. The circular model is an interactive model, and its principal elements include need assessment, partner selection, structural choice, control and evaluation, and adjustment.

Figure 10.1
Circular model for alliance management

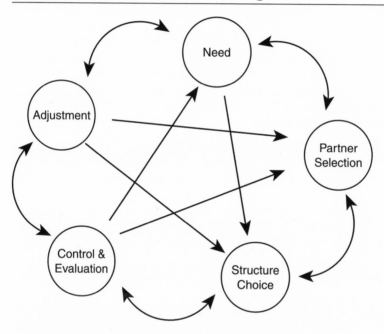

Needs Assessment

Like most things in the marketplace, a partnership emerges as result of a need. To meet its need, the firm makes a choice from its alternative courses of action—internalization, market transaction, and alliance (refer to Figure 4.1). That is, as we explained in Chapter 4, a formation of an alliance is a product of the strategic decision process, which involves phases such as initial, formation, operations, and outcome. A need impact is felt at the initiation stage. An analogy can be drawn between a marriage and an interfirm alliance. In the typical marriage groundwork, a candidate prepares himself or herself by evaluating whether he or she is self-sufficient or ready for a partnership. From a business firm standpoint, a need for a partner emerges under the influence of motives mentioned in Chapter 4, which include achieving economies of scale, reducing costs/risks, accessing markets/resources, developing new technology or products, and learning from the partner. In such evaluations, the most critical aspect is the firm's stock of resources and capabilities, which are supposed to determine the competitive advantage. When and if the firm feels that its resources and capabilities are not sufficient to pursue its strategic path, it looks for an alliance alternative after exhausting other alternatives of internalization and market transactions. Furthermore, the concept of the value chain highlights the nature of needs, whether the firm needs to acquire resources and competencies in R&D, production, or marketing. Depending upon its weakness in any value chain activity(ies), the firm would more likely attempt to complement its value chain activity(ies) where it feels additional resources and capabilities from an ally would help improve its competitive position.

Partner Selection

Drawing from the resource-based view of the firm, we can conclude that when the firm is in need of complementing its resources and competencies with those of another firm, it seeks a partner, provided that an alliance emerges as the most attractive choice. Those resources and competencies cannot be acquired or imitated because they are not mobile across organizations. In selection of a partner, however, managers need to pay attention to two major characteristics. One is the strategic intent of the candidate firm and the other is the cooperation experience of the candidate. Although at the outset, it is rather difficult to find out the strategic intent of the candidate firm, there are signs such as strategic direction, resource repertoires, and leadership characteristics that might give some clues about the intent of the candidate. Additionally, the cooperative experience of the candidate is a good indicator of its future behavior in cooperative ventures. The successful or poor record of the candidate in cooperation with other firms would tell about its stance early on and its handling of alliance arrangements. This dimension, however, is only helpful for established firms with previous alliance records. It is not possible to make a judgment for those firms without any alliance experiences (such as new ventures). In such situations, the strategic intent becomes the only determining factor besides the managers' gut feelings.

In addition, depending upon its need(s), the firm seeks an ally—either a competitor or a complementor (firms operating in adjacent stages of a value chain). In other words, different forms of alliances, horizontal or vertical, would have an impact on the firm's choice of partners. If there is a trend of teaming up with another competitor in an industry (for example, automobile manufacturing) or building a network of alliances (such as the airline industry), it would be wise to select a suitable candidate or a group quickly to establish links. Once other competing firms make engagements with capable and potential partners, the firm might be late to choose a good partner. Acting early in choosing a potential partner(s) would provide more and better choices. In the case of developing complementary alliances, the firm might have to work hard to convince its partner of the mutual benefits of the alliance by changing its attitudes and behavior and enhancing its capabilities.

Another important consideration is performance of the potential partner. A common view is that good performers should be preferred for alliance partnership because of the contributions they can make to the joint cause. It has been argued that firms can gain access to the requisite strategic capabilities by entering into alliances with firms that already possess such capabilities. Therefore, by enabling the firm to quickly gain access to key strategic capabilities, strategic alliances help firms build their own capabilities. Such examples include General Motors' partnership with Honda and Toyota, AT&T's alliance with NTT DoCoMo, and Millennium Pharmaceutical's cooperation with Astra. Of course, this situation is an ideal one—finding a partner with superior performance so that it could provide the requisite capabilities for the other party. Alliances can also be developed under performing firms, however, as long as the candidate firm has potentials and capabilities but is momentarily suffering from mismanagement. Renault's partnership with Nissan and Ford's alliance with Mazda illustrate this point.

Partner selection varies from one industry to another, as well. For example, as explained in Chapter 7, an established pharmaceutical firm could form cooperation with a startup biotech firm while, as discussed in Chapter 6, such alliances do not exist in the automobile manufacturing industry. That is, the industry-specific conditions dictate the kinds of alliance partners available and the common forms of partnerships. As pointed out in Chapter 8, it is common to see network alliances in the airline industry, whereas such networks are not seen in the pharmaceutical industry. In the airline industry, it has become almost a necessity to join a network alliance or at least a dyad relationship.

Structure Choice

For structure choice, managers have primarily two types of alliance formats: equity or non-equity alliances (as discussed in Chapters 4 and 5). An equity alliance can take either joint venture or equity participation forms.

With joint ventures, there is extensive literature explaining their formation, evolution, and stability.[2] International joint ventures (IJVs), as the most common form of alliance, have received the most attention. Although IJVs provide a number of advantages, such as sharing resources and risks and being a flexible arrangement in comparison to internalization, they pose a host of managerial issues. Managing and controlling the operations of IJVs presents a special challenge due to multiple ownerships. Equity participation, on the other hand, depending on the amount of investment, enables the investing firm to intervene with the management of the target firm. The investing firm can assign directors to the boards of the target firm so that they become influential in shaping the policies of the target firm. For non-equity alliances, along the norms of contractual agreements, mutual trust and understanding play a role in achieving consensus.

Moreover, the structural choice is related to the partner selection. Alliances between competitors are referred to as horizontal alliances, while alliances between the firm and its complementors are vertical alliances. Each type might require a different configuration with different emphases. That is, cooperation between two automotive manufacturers or pharmaceutical firms will be designed and managed differently from an alliance between a manufacturer and a supplier. In the case of cooperation between rival firms, managers need to establish more safeguards against opportunistic behavior of the partners than those of complementors.

One of the key issues concerning interfirm partnerships is alliance scope, which is the choice of activities to be included within an alliance.[3] Khanna asserted, "...the choice of scope affects the nature and timing of the benefits that accrue to alliance participants, [he] argues that alliance scope can play a key role in understanding a range of issues related to alliances."[4] Such issues include the initiation, evolution, and termination of alliances. Thus, it is extremely important to clearly define the scope of alliance, which can be done by specifying expected benefits and defining types of activities in the value chain to be included. The former refers to direct and indirect benefits to be gained from an alliance. The starting point is that the firm enters into the alliance with an ultimate objective of building or sustaining its competitive advantage through achieving economies of scale, reducing costs/risks, accessing markets/resources, developing technology or products, and learning from its partner. For all these general motives, by spelling out the specific expected benefits, the firm could formulate a relationship with its partner and charge its managers to seek those ends in order to achieve a certain goal. Additionally, the firm not only defines its expectations but also needs to identify its commitment as expected by its partner. Furthermore, it should define what specific value chain activities of supply chain, R&D, manufacturing, and marketing will be the focus of cooperation and in what form. By specifying the value chain activities, the firm would know its position and responsibilities in the alliance relationship.

Control and Evaluation

To control alliance operations and evaluate the outcomes, there is a need for control policies and standards. Toward this end, we developed a conceptual framework that consists of two major dimensions. The first dimension is resource commitment of the firm, meaning whether the firm allocates equity or not to the alliance (refer to Table 10.1). This concept means the greater the resource commitment by the firm, the more extensive the control exerted by the firm. That is, an equity alliance involves greater control than non-equity alliances. The second dimension of the model is control configuration, which refers to extent, focus, and mechanism of control.[5] The extent of control means the degree to which control is exerted on inter-partner relations. For example, the extent of control is greater in equity participation than in joint ventures. As shown in Table 10.1, the extent of control is high in equity alliances while it is low in non-equity alliances.

The company might also change its extent of the control depending upon its trust on its partners. If the company has a positive experience with its partner as a result of its prior partnership, it could limit its extent of control. The extent of control also depends upon the context of the partnership. A Western company might feel more comfortable working with other Western companies but could be more cautious with its partnerships with the governments and local partners in uncertain markets (such as with China and India).

Focus refers to what end results, operations, and activities, on which control should be intensified. In this respect, two considerations become important: the first one concerns end results with an emphasis on preserving equity investment and return on equity, as well as building core competencies. Like any investor, the alliance partner would be interested in maximizing its returns financially. But it is also keen on building capabilities and core competencies as a result of its strategic investment into the collaborative venture. The second consideration refers to the value chain activities, logistics, R&D, production, and marketing, where core activities in the alliance get close attention. In this respect, the firm would concentrate on the type of value chain activities that are critical for the success of the alliance and for the attainment of its strategic objectives. Nevertheless, in all cases, the firm is concerned with building capabilities and core competencies through a variety of value chain activities. But this specific focus of control might switch depending upon the type of alliance. In an equity alliance, the focus would be on activities yielding financial results such as preserving equity investment and return on investment, whereas in non-equity investments, a variety of end results (such as securing supplies, entering a new market, and gaining knowledge) are sought.

Control mechanism refers to the way in which control is exerted over the partner or collaborative venture. In this regard, control can be achieved in a

Table 10.1
Control Framework for Strategic Alliances

		Resource Commitment	
		Equity Alliances	**Non-Equity Alliances**
D i m e n s i o n o f C o n t r o l	**Extent**	High	Low
	Focus	Core Competence, Preserving Equity and ROI Value Chain Activity	Core Competence Variety of Results
	Mechanism	Equity and Managerial Control	Contractual and Managerial Control

number of ways: contractual control, equity control, and managerial control.[6] Das and Teng explained these three types of controls as follows:

> Contractual control means specifying the details of the usage of properties in the alliance agreement. There should be explicit specifications of when, where, and how money, plants, distribution channels, and patents are to be used. Equity control is about ensuring desirable behavior and outcome in an alliance through equity ownership. While contractual control is useful in virtually all alliances, equity control is relevant only if an alliance involves equity creation, such as joint ventures, or other equity arrangements, such as minority equity alliances. Equity control can be exercised by having majority equity ownership, which implies more authority and bargaining power, or by inviting the partner on board, and asking the partner to take some equity position in the alliance. Shared ownership aligns the interests of partners and deters the opportunistic behavior. As a result, some collegial behavior may be expected...The third type of control for a partner firm is managerial, which ensures tight monitoring of alliance operations.[7]

Managerial controls can be exercised by assigning expatriate managers to key posts at the collaborative venture, having frequent site visits, and holding regular meetings to prevent unexpected developments. Continuous interactions and communications between the managers of partners develop a mutual understanding and reduce the conflicts between the partners that might arise. Managerial exchanges between two partners take place through both formal and informal (in other words, unplanned) face-to-face meetings. Although behavioral in nature, such managerial control requires subjective judgments and might involve intuitive evaluation criteria, and cognitive and cultural diversity among managers helps improve the quality of control. Managers use such controls to find out whether operational objectives are realized by enhancing understanding between themselves within the alliance. Most often, the large manufacturing firm has a bargaining power over its suppliers; therefore, it can incorporate terms into the alliance agreement to exert control over its partners.

Depending on the resource commitment of the firm, an emphasis is placed on equity and managerial controls in equity alliances and on contractual and managerial controls in non-equity alliances, as pointed out in Table 10.1. From another perspective, the firm could emphasize processes (for example, how production and marketing activities are carried out), outcomes (such as checking product quality and volume and profitability or both). An emphasis on end results means giving greater discretion to the venture or partner so that the firm is only interested in outcomes, whereas the firm's checking on the processes of the venture requires its close observation over and scrutiny in the operations and activities.

As a result of all these controls, the firm assesses the performance of the cooperative venture. Although the evaluation of alliance performance is controversial, mainly because there is no generally agreed measure for performance appraisal, the most common measure is the extent to which the alliance meets the original expectations of the partners.[8] In order to use this kind of criteria, the partners should develop clear and measurable objectives at the beginning and then compare their objectives with the results achieved. Vague and general objectives do not help much in the measurement of alliance performances. Thus, it is important to define clear-cut objectives such as increasing productivity or reducing costs in quantifiable terms, entering a given market by certain time, securing quality supplies over a period of time, increasing market share by certain date, and gaining knowledge on specific processes. In outcome assessment, depending on the alliance type, a variety of indicators can be used. Most often financial and market-based indicators such as return profitability, return on investment, new product introduction, and market segmentation are favored. They often represent short-term benefits, however, whereas the focus must be on long-term gains such as building competencies in certain areas, thereby improving the competitive advantage of the firm. Because the thrust of this book is strategic alliances, it is recommended that managers place more emphasis on long-term gains (for example, building competencies). Then, the critical question is how to measure gains in building competencies. As Hamel and Prahalad defined, core competencies of a company refer to distinctive capabilities fundamental to the firm's superior performance and successful strategy.[9] According to Hamel and Prahalad, core competencies are those that make significant contributions to the efficiency and ultimate customer value, and provide a basis entering new markets.[10] In terms of core competencies, the firm's capabilities are those that provide superior advantage to the firm over its competitors. Building and sustaining competitive advantage calls for superior performances of the firm over its competitors by focusing on the value chain activities where the firm excels. Thus, managers of the firm partnering with others should ensure that their firms build links with firms that excel with distinct capabilities for which their firm needs and could exploit. They also need to check whether the alliance serves the purpose of development of core competencies by benchmarking with others, comparing the outcomes of alliance with competitors' and the industry standards, and innovative products and services.

Another performance measure for strategic alliances is whether synergistic gains are achieved as a result of the collaborative venture. As shown in Figure 2.1, the integrative model of the firm, the firms exist to create value for stakeholders. Following the same logic, alliances should also be established to create value for their stakeholders. An alliance can only be justified when the value created by the alliance exceeds the value that can be created by the firms alone. Otherwise, there is no need for an alliance. That is, in an alliance context, synergy exists when the alliance partners produce greater value together for their given constituents (for example, shareholders) than those partners produce individually. From a synergistic point view, strategic alliances create joint economies of scope between two or more firms. By creating synergy across multiple functions or multiple businesses between partner firms, strategic alliances are supposed to facilitate competitive advantage.

Managers can evaluate what economies of scope advantages are achieved from an alliance (for example, joint R&D or joint manufacturing facility) by comparing the joint outcomes with those individual ones.

Adjustment

In the circular process, alliance managers might need to make some adjustments simultaneously and continuously in strategies, behaviors, structures, and processes of the partnership as the alliance unfolds. This statement is a natural consequence of the belief that the positions of partners as well the market conditions change rapidly, which was spelled out in Chapter 1. The core management challenge in strategic alliances, therefore, is to make timely adjustments as the assumptions, the firm's and partner's resource profiles and capabilities, and the competitive forces are altered. Because the circular decision process implies that the facets of decision-making are interactive and interdependent, it is quite normal to revisit other components of the alliance process, the need assessment, partner selection, structure choice, and control and evaluation. Nevertheless, all these facets can be best considered and captured by a review of the strategies, behaviors, structure, and processes of the alliance. In this review, each dimension warrants a close attention.

First, the strategies of the alliance should be compared with those of the firm's and the firm's partner. In other words, the managers need to look at the compatibility of the alliance strategy with the firm's objectives and expectations. For example, Volvo's equity participation in Nissan's truck division has lost its importance after Renault bought a significant equity ownership in Nissan while GM acquired Volvo. GM wishes to reappraise its indirect equity ownership in Nissan's truck division. Similarly, the insatiability among the airline networks caused some partners to rethink their alliance plans. Swissair, after breaking its tie with Alitalia and its disappointment with the Qualiflyer group, is considering new options. In other words, a number of rationales support participation in strategic alliances. When those rationales do not hold any more, the participating firm needs to make some adjustments by either getting out of an existing alliance or joining new alliances.

Second, the behavior of a partner sends important messages for the future of the alliance. Some important questions could help to understand and assess the behavior of the partner. To what extent does the partner meet its commitments? Does it deliver what it promises? Does it act untrustworthy? Are there inconsistencies in its cooperative behavior? Does it cooperate with rivals well? How much does it value the cooperation? Of all, trust between partners has received a great deal of attention. Trust in interfirm partnership includes a set of expectations between partners about the behavior of each and about the anticipation that each will fulfill its perceived obligation.[11] From a behavioral point of view, trust has to do with confidence. In this regard, Moorman et al. define trust as "a willingness to rely on an exchange partner in whom one has confidence."[12] A corollary to this definition is that trust is a significant deterrent to opportunistic behavior in the alliance relationship. Hence, by asking the critical questions posed earlier, a partner could tell how trustworthy the other partner is in a collaborative relationship. For example, Swissair ended its relationship with Alitalia because Altalia (with the Italian government as the owner) could not deliver what Swissair expected.

Third, the structure of partnership here means the configurations of governance form in an alliance. After deciding on the general structure, the type of cooperative venture and scope of alliance as explained earlier, it is important to determine on a governance form. We mean that the relationships between the partners are used to determine strategic direction and performance of the alliance. Governance can be viewed as a means to establish order, coordination, and consensus between the partners, whose interests might conflict. In the case of equity alliances, governance form is rather straightforward: in a joint venture, the board consists of members assigned by the parents according to their equity ownership, while in an equity participation, the investing partner appoints a number of director(s), depending on its equity shares, to the target firm's board. In the NUMMI venture, both GM and Toyota have equal members on the company's board of directors of the company. On the other hand, Renault, based on its 36.8 percent ownership in Nissan, assigned Ghosn to Nissan as the general director in addition its other two appointments as top managers to restructure Nissan. It is more uncertain and complex in non-equity alliances, however, where contractual agreements specify all the necessary conditions. Nonetheless, in all governance forms, the managers should ask the following questions: Does the current alliance governance work effectively and serve the purpose? Does the alliance governance ensure that the interests of partners are aligned? Are there an increasing number of complaints and concerns about the way the alliance is run? Are there adequate safeguards established and used by the alliance governance to protect the interests of the partners? Does the alliance stick to the scope of the alliance or diverge from its original mission? The answers to these questions reflect the efficacy of the governance form in an alliance. Of course, depending upon a particular type of alliance, we can raise many more specific questions.

Fourth, the processes refer to the way in which an alliance is set up, managed, and assessed. Again, the processes require considerations regarding formation and implementation issues. In this regard, a partnering firm should handle three core processes that would underline its approach to alliances. They consist of the *pre-alliance process*, the *integrative process*, and the *re-evaluation process*.[13] We would like to elaborate on each process and link them to the managerial behaviors needed to carry them.

The *pre-alliance process* entails need assessment, search for a suitable partner, and alliance negotiations. Because we explained the first two earlier, we would like to elaborate on the last one. An alliance negotiation is a means by which a firm can initiate, form, or terminate a collaborative venture. Comprehensive bargaining, which is a part the negotiation process, results with an agreement only if there is consensus on the terms of cooperation. But it must be remembered that behavioral factors in addition to economic ones determine the final agreement terms. Cross-cultural and language differences between the parties influence the outcome of negotiations. Therefore, cultural empathy for a foreign partner and the presence of competent translators during negotiations are recommended. An alliance negotiation might take a long time during which numerous proposals are exchanged with modified provisions. "The proposals undoubtedly include provisions that one side or the other is willing either to give up entirely, or to compromise. These provisions are used as bargaining tokens, permitting each side to claim that it is reluctantly giving in on some point in exchange for compromise on another point. They also serve as face-saving devices, allowing either side to report to interested parties that it managed to extract concessions. On some points, however, it is unlikely that any compromise can be reached."[14] It took McDonald's about 10 years to finalize its joint venture and franchising agreements with the Chinese after tough negotiations and exchanges of proposals.

The *integrative process* is necessary for building and maintaining strong links between the parent companies and the venture in case of joint ventures or just between partners in other forms of alliances. A strong integration process helps link the partner's diverse assets and resources into core competencies and leverage these competencies in the pursuit of new opportunities. Without such an integration process, despite some short-term accomplishments by the cooperative venture, long-term development of new capabilities and knowledge will be seriously impeded. Such an integrative process can be accomplished by establishing an effective communication and coordination mechanism (for example, creating joint teams and committees; visiting each partner's facilities; exchanging employees; and developing a bond). For example, in the case of the NUMMI joint venture between Toyota and GM, the company has developed teams and sent 450 employees to Japan for three weeks of classroom and on-the-job training.

The *re-evaluation process* requires an assessment of current affairs of the alliance with respect to its performance and the behavior of the partner in light of changes in the market environment. The firm would like to know what changes have occurred along the way of cooperation and whether it is worth it to continue with the alliance or terminate the venture. Although the firm might be satisfied with the alliance, some drastic factors (such as moves by rivals, government regulations, and unanticipated developments like economic recession) impose changes on the cooperative venture. Then, the firm should be willing to revise its objectives and commitments and those of the alliance.

An alliance must be seen as a strategic vehicle for building and sustaining core competencies; therefore, it must be given not only resources and opportunities but also discretion to come up with new momentum to help the partners in achieving their objectives. Because organizational learning and knowledge have become an emerging impetus for competitiveness, it has been an important consideration for knowledge-based cooperative ventures (such as R&D and technology development partnerships) to create knowledge and disperse that knowledge to the partners. The partners can encourage entrepreneurial spirit and practice creativity by allowing creative thinking, tolerating risks, facilitating resources, and giving discretion.

In addition to the core processes described above, three behavioral qualifications are required to succeed with those processes. Table 10.2 represents the interactions of three core processes with three behaviors needed to follow those procedures. The behaviors are rated as low, medium, or high depending on the degree of their requirements under each process.

Table 10.2
Behaviors and Processes for Alliance Effectiveness

Behaviors	Processes		
	Pre-alliance (search and negotiation)	Integrative	Re-evaluation
Adaptability	Low	High	High
Flexibility	Medium	High	Medium
Agility	High	Medium	High

NECESSARY BEHAVIORS FOR ALLIANCE EFFECTIVENESS

The following paragraphs discuss the behaviors that are needed for alliance effectiveness.

Adaptability

The traditional managerial assumption has been that environmental changes will be relatively linear and incremental.[15] As explained in Chapter 1, however, the pace of changes in political, social, economic, and technological environments has been so fast that any organization—or for that matter, a strategic alliance—needs to update, improve, and modify itself endlessly. The age of certainty is over. This statement might not be true for alliances formed temporarily, but such alliances should not be considered strategic (as defined in the opening chapter). Building core competencies and achieving competitive advantage through alliances require long-term commitments and processes. Then, during this long process, the partners should be willing to adapt to changes in the marketplace by making necessary modifications in the three processes defined earlier. After a re-evaluation, for example, Xerox—because of its slowing sales in the home market and increasing competition worldwide—has decided to end its long-lasting joint venture in Fuji-Xerox while continuing with its joint venture of Rank-Xerox in Britain.

Flexibility

Flexibility means the development of contingency plans by the partnering firm, which entail changes when the alliance is not favorable anymore. It is similar to adaptability, but flexibility is more internal orientation. The firm could be adaptive but not necessarily flexible enough to absorb to changes that it intends to incorporate. GM has demonstrated an adaptability in accepting the lean production of its partner Toyota in the NUMMI interface, but it was not so flexible enough to apply the method to its own manufacturing system. Flexibility also implies that the partner should keep its options open in terms of switching from internalization and market transactions to alliances, or vice versa. The degree of flexibility varies from one business mode to another, however, as well as from one form of alliance to another. While a strategic alliance gives the firm more flexibility than internalization, among alliances non-equity alliances provide the firm with more flexibility than equity alliances. For example, Austrian Airlines easily switched to the STAR group after realizing that its alliance with Qualiflyer group would not be fruitful.

In the case of mutual interdependence between partners, strategic competitiveness results only when the companies recognize that their strategies are not implemented in isolation from their partner's actions and responses. This kind of interdependence is especially true in cases of manufacturer-supplier collaboration, outsourcing arrangements, and co-production. When changes occur in relationships, the partnering firms would be able to make necessary switches to not upset its operations. Nike, for example, outsources its sportswear internationally with a few companies and is not dependent on a single company.

Agility

Another important managerial behavior required for carrying out all three processes described here is agility, meaning acting quickly to form, manage, and even terminate an alliance. Although alliances are built with different purposes (such as introducing new products, services, and technologies, reducing risks or costs, and accessing market and resources), acting timely and quickly more likely puts the alliance ahead of competitiors. Because an alliance is more often a strategic response to market opportunities or a competitive action, quickness is very important. In today's rapidly changing marketplace, agility is one of the determinants of competitive success. Although the role of agility in the pre-alliance, integrative, and re-evaluation processes varies, it is important in all of them (as shown in Table 10.1).

We must note, however, that sometimes obtaining the fruits of an alliance might take many years (for example, R&D partnership between two pharmaceutical firms for developing a new drug). Agility here does not mean getting fast results but rather taking quick actions to start the process that would yield long-term gains. By doing so, the firm can preempt its competitors. AT&T's partnership with NTT DoCoMo would put AT&T in an advantageous position in introducing mobile Internet technology (i-mode) to the U.S. market. The deal is an important step toward launching 3G technology to cellular phones with multimedia applications in the United States. Similarly, Morgan Stanley Dean Witter entered China via a joint venture with the China Construction Bank, China's most important investment bank, to form the China International Capital Corporation. This venture has given Morgan Stanley Dean Witter a first mover advantage. As the given examples illustrate, agility is more effective in certain alliance types such as market entry or technology development, but it is necessary in all.

MANAGERIAL GUIDELINES

Finally, in light of these discussions and the information given throughout this book, we would like to offer some managerial guidelines that would help in effective formulation and management of global strategic alliances. Managers who need to know insights in global alliances can benefit from the previous chapters, but those who want to can get some quick tips by following the steps described in this chapter and also the suggestions given next. Recommendations for successful management of strategic alliances can be summarized as follows:

- Consider a collaborative venture as a viable strategic alternative to internalization and market transactions (short-term contractual arrangements). Compare costs and benefits of each alternative to choose the most feasible alternative.

- Select your partner either from your competitors or complementors by paying attention to its resources and capabilities so that a synergy can be built as a result of the partnership.

- Pay attention to the national environment of partners by considering political, economic, legal, and cultural characteristics. Cultural attributes affect the attitudes and behavior of partners.

- Try to learn the organizational culture of the candidate firm and decide whether your firm's culture matches with those of the candidate. Watch leadership behavior, underlying values of its business strategies (e.g., aggressiveness, opportunism, short-term orientation, and customer-orientation), characteristics of its organizational structure (for example, the use of teams, empowerment of employees, attitudes toward decentralization) to have a sense about the candidate firm. Visit the candidate's facilities and talk to its employees, customers, and partners to get a feeling about the prospective partner.

- Decide on the most feasible pattern of alliance by choosing an equity alliance (joint venture or equity participation) or non-equity alliance (contractual collaboration). Sometimes it is determined by the corporate strategy (for example, franchising).

- Negotiate and reach an agreement on contract terms explicitly by defining the commitments by each party, the timetable for principal events and resource commitments, the responsibilities and rights, the conflict resolution mechanism, and the termination conditions. Be aware of cultural differences between the parties during negotiations. Develop informal mechanisms for communication and arbitration (for example, the CEOs of both parties, an internal or external arbitration team) in addition to legal apparatus.

- Determine on the mode of alliance by choosing among first cooperate then compete, cooperate while competing, and cooperate between themselves but compete with others.

- Clearly define the scope of alliance by specifying type of mode of co-opetition (cooperation and competition) and value chain activities. The scope would affect the nature and timing of benefits to be gained from the alliance and help to deal with initiation, evolution, and termination of the alliance.

- Adopt a control mechanism with specific extent and focus in light of the resource commitment and the form of alliance.

- Review of and adapt to changes in the environment and alliance structure by being flexible to make necessary adjustments. Act quickly to modify or replace outdated or impossible conditions imposed on the alliance.

- Train your employees for cooperative ventures and prepare them to collaborate with and learn form the partners. If necessary, you must change attitudes and behaviors of the employees for interfirm collaboration by demonstrating fruitful outcomes that can be achieved from the partnership.

- Evaluate the performance of the alliance, such as whether the partnership is meeting the expectation of the firm as originally intended, creating synergies out of the parties, and serving to the company's ultimate goal of gaining competitive advantage. Accordingly decide to continue with or exit the alliance timely.

These guidelines would help the managers of the companies in forming and managing strategic alliances and thereby help them access resources and capabilities of their partners in terms of gaining competitive advantages in the long run. We hope that this chapter provided the essentials of global strategic alliance management so that the managers of firms plan to get involved in cooperative ventures would use the framework given here, thereby learning from these explanations. Alliances are more dynamic than the alternative modes of business arrangements; therefore, they need continuous attention and care (especially global ones involving cross-national encounters).

This book started with basic theoretical foundations of the firm and then continued with explanations on strategic alliances between firms. In doing so, it gave essential information on theory and practice of global strategic alliances by providing conceptual models and practical examples from the corporate world. Moreover, it highlighted current trends and strategic alliance patterns in four industries, auto manufacturing, pharmaceuticals, airlines, and telecommunications. These four industries witness lots of alliance activities. Although each one presents its unique characteristics in terms of alliance formation and practices, there is communality among them as well. While they all experience consolidations of companies, international alliances have emerged as common strategic vehicle. Global alliances in these four industries are viewed as strategic means to develop or acquire core competencies needed for competitive advantage. In these four industries it is noticeable that interfirm partnerships have been accepted as a viable strategic alternative. Hence, managers of firms in these industries have welcomed cooperative ventures and have been trying to master formation and management of these kinds of hybrid arrangements. In the future, those managers whom possess and demonstrate skills in construction and management of cooperative ventures will be in high demand and be great assets for their companies. And those companies with such skillful managers will definitely make great progress in developing core competencies and building and sustaining competitive advantages against their rivals.

NOTES

1. J. J. Reuer, Collaborative strategy: the logic of alliances, *Financial Times: Mastering Strategy* (London, Great Britain: 2000): 345.

2. See K. R. Harrigan, *Managing for joint venture success* (Lexington: Lexington Books, 1986). K. J. Hladik, *International joint ventures* (Lexington, MA: Lexington Books, 1985). W. H. Newman, Launching a viable joint venture, *California Mangement Review,* 35, no. 1 (1992): 68–80.

3. T. Khanna, The scope of alliance, *Organization Science* 9, no. 3 (1998): 340–355.

4. Ibid., 352.

5. J. M. Geringer and L. Herbert, Control and performance of international joint ventures, *Journal of International Business Studies,* 20, no. 2 (1989): 235–254.

6. T. K. Das and B-S. Teng, Managing risk in strategic alliances, *The Academy of Management Executive,* 13, no. 4 (1999): 50–62.

7. Ibid., 54.

8. Geringer and Herbert, 235–254.

9. C. K. Prahalad and G. Hamel, The core competence of the corporation, *Harvard Business Review* (May–June 1990): 79–91.

10. Ibid.

11. A. Madhok, Revisiting multinational firms' tolerance for joint ventures: A trust-based approach, *Journal of International Business Studies,* 26, no. 1 (1995): 117–137.

12. C. Moorman, R. Deshpande, and G. Zaltman, Factors affecting trust in market research relationships, *Journal of Marketing,* 57 (January 1993): 82.

13. C. A. Bartlett and S. Ghoshal, *Transnational management: Text, cases, and readings in cross-border management.* Third edition. (Boston: Irwin McGraw-Hill, 2000).

14. J. D. Daniels and L. H. Radebaugh, *International business: Environments and operations.* Ninth edition. (Upper Saddle River, N.J.: Prentice-Hall, 2001): 415.

15. Ibid., 793.

Index

subcontracting, 94-95
supply chain, 95-97

technology dispersion, 9-11
Teng, B-S., 210
theories
    game theory, 22-24
    industrial organization, 20-22
    integrative view, 30-33
    knowledge building, 26-28
    networks, 28-30
    resource-based view, 25-26
    transaction cost, 18-20

Toyota, 6, 106-108, 115-118, 122-126, 136-138

value chain, 61-62
Verizon, 183-184, 186-190, 195
Vodafone, 184, 186-190, 192-193, 195-199

Williamson, O., 18

Yoshino, M.Y., 65

Zander, U., 27

ABOUT THE AUTHOR

REFIK CULPAN is Professor of Management and International Business in the School of Business Administration, Pennsylvania State University. He holds a doctorate degree from New York University and has had extensive experience not only in the academic community but as a consultant to various businesses. Dr. Culpan is a regular contributor to the journals of his fields, and coeditor of a previous book for Quorum, *Transformation Management in Postcommunist Countries* (1995, with Brij Nino Kumar).